HISTORY

OF

THE MISSIONS

OF THE

AMERICAN BOARD OF COMMISSIONERS
FOR FOREIGN MISSIONS

IN

INDIA.

BY
RUFUS ANDERSON, D. D., LL. D.,
LATELY FOREIGN SECRETARY OF THE BOARD.

BOSTON:
CONGREGATIONAL PUBLISHING SOCIETY.
1874.

RIVERSIDE, CAMBRIDGE:
STEREOTYPED AND PRINTED BY
H. O. HOUGHTON AND COMPANY.

PREFACE.

THE first mission of the Board was in India, and the history of its missions naturally commences there. Other considerations led the writer to begin with the Sandwich Islands,[1] and then to go through with the history of the Missions to the Oriental Churches. The volumes stand properly in the following order: The INDIA MISSIONS, the SANDWICH ISLANDS MISSION, and the MISSIONS TO THE ORIENTAL CHURCHES. It may be hoped that others, in due time, will add the history of MISSIONS TO THE NORTH AMERICAN INDIANS, and to AFRICA, CHINA, and JAPAN.

While advancing years deter the present writer from undertaking the history of other missions, he is thankful to the Giver of all good that he has been thus far sustained in a labor so delightful. And he gratefully acknowledges the kind reception which the

[1] See Preface to the *History of the Missions of the American Board to the Sandwich Islands*, p. viii.

churches have given to the volumes already issued.

When it was said at the outset,[1] that the missions of the Board might be embraced in three volumes, the number and importance of the facts to be recorded were greatly under-estimated. Though they have been much condensed thus far, the history of several missions remains unwritten.

A tabular view of Missionaries to India is added, showing the date and duration of their connection with their respective fields; and also a list of the Publications in the several missions, and a copious Index.

The author gladly acknowledges his obligations to several friends, conversant with the working of these missions, for suggestions that have added materially to the value of the history.

Should the facts recorded in this volume in any measure strengthen the faith of others in the future of the missionary work, as they have that of the writer, he will feel that he has not labored in vain.

August, 1874.

[1] Preface to the *Sandwich Islands Mission*, p. xiii.

NOTE EXPLANATORY OF THE MAPS.

THE Maps, illustrative of the three principal missions, were drawn by missionaries for this work. The one for the Madura Mission was drawn in India, with great care to make it perfect; the others in this country, and necessarily with a less amount of labor. The following statement by Mr. Capron, of the Madura Mission, is believed to be applicable to the three maps.

In deference to usage, the spelling of certain well known names is left unchanged. The spelling of the other names is a transliteration of the native names, with the aim to give a nearly accurate representation of the sound. For this purpose it should be mentioned, that the vowels are limited to two sounds each, one long sound, and one short sound, as follows: —

a short, as *a* in Cub*a*, Cub*a*n; or *u* in f*u*n.
ā long, as *a* in f*a*ther, f*a*r.
e short, as *e* in *e*clat, f*e*ll.
ē long, as *e* in caf*e*, f*e*te; or *a* in f*a*te.
i short, as *i* in happ*i*ness, p*i*n.
ī long, as *i* in mosqu*i*to, p*i*que; or *ee* in f*ee*l.
o short, as *o* in p*o*lite, wh*o*lly.
ō long, as *o* in p*o*et, p*o*st.
u short, as *u* in congr*u*ous, f*u*ll.
ū or û long, as *u* in r*u*in, r*u*le; or *oo* in f*oo*l.
ai, as *ai* in *ai*sle; but *ai* final, as *ay* in Mond*ay*.
au, as in the German H*au*s; or *ou* in f*ou*nd.

This is substantially the vowel system of Sir William Jones and of later Orientalists, which has been adopted, also, by some Missionary Societies, and is increasingly followed by the Missionaries. It is less important to indicate the pronunciation of the consonants, except to say, that they have in general the same sound as in the English alphabet.

CONTENTS.

MISSIONS TO INDIA.

PREFACE 1

CHAPTER I.

THE AMERICAN BOARD AND ITS FIRST MISSIONARIES. 1810–1815.

Formation of the Board. — Its Ecclesiastical Connections. — Events leading to its Formation. — Rise of its First Mission. — The Practical Question. — The Passages engaged. — Ordination of the Missionaries and their Instructions. — Their Departure. — Experiences at Calcutta. — Hostile Attitude of the Government. — Escape from Calcutta. — Sickness and Death of Mrs. Newell. — Brief Reunion at Port Lewis. — The Mission becomes Two Bands. — Mission to the Karens. — Struggles for a Missionary Residence at Bombay. — Flight from Bombay and Return. — Commissioners appointed on their Behalf. — Successful Appeal to the Governor. — Favoring Events in England 1

CHAPTER II.

OPENING OF INDIA TO THE GOSPEL. — 1758–1812.

Early Disposition of the East India Company. — A Remarkable Change. — Triumph of the Opposition. — Charles Grant. — A Counter Influence in England. — A less Promising but more Effective Agency. — William Carey. — His Efforts and Influence. — Backwardness of his Ministerial Brethren. — Formation of a Missionary Society. — The Antagonist Forces. —

Carey designated to a Mission in Bengal. — Unpropitious Outset. — A Kind Providence. — Proposed Mission of Mr. Haldane. — Mr. Grant's Appeal for India. — Messrs. Marshman and Ward. — The Missionary Refuge at Serampore. — An Efficient Protector. — The Governor-general pacificated. — College of Fort William. — Mutiny at Vellore, and its Consequences. — Missionary Development in England. — The Great Battle of Missions. — Importance of the Controversy. — Toleration secured. — Further Agency of Charles Grant. — The Victory assured by the Governor-general. — Subsequent Protection from the East India Company. — Grateful Recognition of Carey, Grant, and Wilberforce 22

CHAPTER III.

MISSION TO THE MAHRATTAS. — 1815–1826.

Bombay. — The Mahrattas and their Subjugation. — Missionary Importance of these Events. — Incipient Measures. — Mr. Nott's Return Home. — The Obstacles to be overcome. — Why employ Married Missionaries. — Early Preaching. — Marriage of Mr. Hall. — Use of the Press. — Comparative Estimate of Schools. — New Missionaries. — Interest in Schools. — The First Hopeful Convert. — A New Governor, and his Favorable Disposition. — Return of Mr. Bardwell. — Death of Mr. Newell. — Arrival of a Printer. — First Native Protestant Place of Worship. — Interference on the Continent. — Reception of a New Missionary. — Death of Mr. Nichols. — School for Jewish Girls. — A Comparison. — Association of Missionaries. — Mr. Hall's Excursion on the Continent. — Improvement in Worship. — Publishing the Scriptures. — Death of Mr. Frost. — Visit of Mrs. Hall to the United States. — Death and Character of Mr. Hall. — Death of Mrs. Hall 47

CHAPTER IV.

MISSION TO THE MAHRATTAS. — 1826–1834.

State of the Mission. — Hopeful Converts. — New Missionaries. — A Revised New Testament. — Mission Chapel Congregation. —

Babajee a Brahmin Convert. — Roman Catholics. — The Missionary Union. — Legacy and Church Building. — Preaching by the Wayside. — Additions to the Mission. — Popularity of Girls' Schools. — Schools for Brahmin Boys. — Signs of Progress. — Interesting Cases. — Death of Mr. Garrett. — Death of Mr. and Mrs. Hervey. — New Station at Ahmednuggur, and its Advantages. — Babajee's Marriage. — Dajiba another Helper. — New Church and Native Officers. — Remarkable Christian Woman. — Labors on the Continent. — Public Discussions with Brahmins and others. — Rev. D. O. Allen. — A New Missionary. — Extensive Preaching Tours. — Death and Character of Babajee. — Death of Mrs. Stone. — Change in the Service of Song. — More Extensive Tours. — New Missionaries. — Death of Mrs. Ramsey, and her Husband's Return. — Missionary Devotedness of Mr. Graves. — Death of Mr. Sampson. — Return of Mr. and Mrs. Read. — Mr. Allen at Jalna. — Discovery of a Native Christian Society. — Interesting Sacramental Commemoration. — The Excavations at Ellora . . . 74

CHAPTER V.

MISSION TO THE MAHRATTAS. — 1835–1847.

Temporary Station at Jalna. — Seasonable Liberality. — Baptism of Two Brahmins. — New Missionaries. — The Mahars. — Mahar Gûrûs. — Additions to the Church. — Social Position of the Mahars. — Deaths of Mrs. Allen, Mrs. Burgess, and Mr. Graves. — Increased Toleration. — Conversion of Ramkrishnapunt. — Case of Vishnû. — Union of the Seminary and English Schools. — A Mahar Gûrû converted. — Conversion in the Mang Caste. — Singular Intolerance. — Salutary Discipline. — Death of Mrs. Munger. — New Missionaries. — Return Home of Mr. French. — Native Magazine. — Publication of the Bible in Mahratta. — The Printing Establishment. — Increased Efficiency of the Native Press 97

CHAPTER VI.

MISSION TO THE MAHRATTAS. — 1847–1854.

Results of Boarding-schools. — The Mission Compound. — Licensed Preachers. — An Interesting Convert. — New Station at Satara. — The Law Christianized. — Changes in the Mission. — Lesson in Missionary Policy. — Retirement and Death of Dr. Allen. — Deaths of Mrs. Wood, Mrs. Fairbank, and Mrs. Burgess. — New Station at Kolapûr. — A Vast System of Railways. — Government Patronage of Education. — Increasing Interest in Schools. — Native Periodical Press. — Retirement of Mr. Burgess. — Voyage and Decease of Mr. Hume. — His Character. — A Native Memorial of him 113

CHAPTER VII.

TAMIL PEOPLE. THE CEYLON MISSION. — 1815–1822.

Origin of the Mission. — The Embarkation. — The Arrival. — The Field to be occupied. — Previous Occupation by the Portuguese, by the Dutch, and by the English. — Sudden Relapse to Idolatry. — Jaffna described. — Favor from the Government. — Opening of Boarding-schools. — Preaching in Tamil. — Failure of Health. — Visit to Cape Town. — Death of Mr. Warren. — Return of Mr. Richards. — The Mission reinforced. — The Mission Stations. — Difficulties in remitting Funds. — A Printing Establishment not allowed, and the Printer banished. — Action of the Government at Home. — Excellent Spirit of the Danish Missionaries 129

CHAPTER VIII.

TAMIL PEOPLE. THE CEYLON MISSION. — 1820–1832.

Development of Schools. — Proposal for a College. — Adverse Position of the Government. — Central Boarding-school for Boys. — English Schools. — Central Boarding-school for Girls. — The Schools as Converting Institutions. — Revivals of Religion, and the Results. — Ordination of Dr. Scudder. — Native Preachers. — Gabriel Tissera, Francis Malleappa, and Nicholas

Permander. — An Influential Marriage. — Death and Character of Mr. Richards. — Marriage of Mr. Poor. — Slavery in Jaffna. — Flourishing Condition of the Schools. — Bearing of Education on the Brahminic Philosophy. — Perplexity of an Old Brahmin. — The Result. — Popularity of the Higher Schools. — A Destructive Fire. — A Large-hearted Bishop. — Sir Robert Wilmot Horton removes the Injunction from the Mission. — Its Reinforcement 146

CHAPTER IX.

TAMIL PEOPLE. THE CEYLON MISSION. — 1832–1853.

Batticotta Seminary. — Death of Mrs. Winslow. — Children of Missionaries. — Death of Mr. Woodward. — Resolve of Mrs. Woodward. — Gospel Benevolence illustrated. — New Missionaries. — A Destructive Fire. — Consequences of Teaching the English Language. — Mr. Poor's Removal to Madura. — Succeeded by Mr. Hoisington. — Disastrous Reduction in the Schools. — An Affecting Scene. — Deaths of Mr. and Mrs. Perry. — Seasonable Aid from the Government. — New Missionaries. — Admissions to the Church. — Necessary Abbreviations. — Tamil Dictionaries. — Painful Developments in the Seminary. — Reconstruction of the Institution. — Death of Mr. Apthorp. — Consultation with Returned Missionaries. — Value of the Schools. — Value of the Native Helpers. — The Oodooville Seminary. — Amount of Printing. — New Missionaries. — Death of Mr. Whittelsey. — Roman Catholic Persecution. — New Missionaries. — Death of Mrs. Scudder. — A Good Omen. — The Change. — Death of Mrs. Apthorp. — Testimony of the Governor. — Return of Mr. Minor. — Medical Department. — Accessions and Changes 172

CHAPTER X.

TAMIL PEOPLE ON THE CONTINENT.

THE MADURA MISSION. — 1834–1853.

Southern India delineated. — Why made the Site of a Mission. — The Preliminary Measure. — Commencement of the Mission. —

Mr. Poor's Removal to Madura. — Schools and Helpers. — Enlargement of the Mission. — Deaths. — Absurd Reports. — Seasonable Aid from Government. — Death of Dr. Steele. — The Native Helpers. — Government Connection with Idolatry dissolved. — Native Estimate of the Brahmins. — Death of Mr. Dwight and others. — The Tranquebar Mission. — Extraordinary Length of Missionary Services. — Era of Modern Missions. — The Leipsic Mission. — Consequences of a Higher Evangelical Policy. — Leading Object of the Mission. — Christian Congregations instituted. — Additions to the Mission. — Death of Mr. Lawrence. — Death of Mrs. Muzzy. — New Location of the Seminary. — Why Government Patronage was declined. — A Pagan Missionary. — Opposition to Caste. — Transfer of a Station to the Mission. — Medical Treatment. — Revival in the Seminary. — Preparandi. — A New Station. — Itinerant Preaching. — Extent of the Field. — Admissions to the Church. — Students for the Ministry. — Other Schools. — The Medical Dispensary. — The Jesuit Mission from 1606 to 1776 194

CHAPTER XI.

TAMIL PEOPLE ON THE CONTINENT.

THE MADRAS MISSION. — 1837–1864.

Origin of the Mission. — Death of Mrs. Winslow. — Early Proceedings. — Purchase of a Printing Establishment. — Amount of Printing. — Preaching Tours. — Labors at Vellore. — Perils in the Wilderness. — Visit to America. — Admissions to the Church. — Literary and other Labors. — The First Missionary Son. — Productions of the Press. — Conflict with Caste. — Heathen Opposition. — Enlightened Policy of the Government. — The Mission reinforced. — Death of Mrs. Scudder. — The Father and Son. — Mr. Winslow's Labors. — New Version of the Tamil Bible. — New Station at Arcot. — Summary. — Death of Dr. Scudder. — Mr. Winslow visits the United States. — Reduction of the Printing Establishment. — The Tamil Bible. — Completion of a Tamil and English Dictionary. —

Pocket Edition of the Bible. — Death of Dr. Winslow. — His Character. — Sale of the Establishment. — Discontinuance of the Mission. — Summary View. — Mr. Hunt's Change of Designation 220

CHAPTER XII.

Tamil People. The Arcot Mission. — 1851–1857.

Its Origin. — The Field occupied. — Working of the Mission. — Its Transfer to the Reformed Dutch Church 226

CHAPTER XIII.

The Mahratta and Tamil Missions.

Missionary Conferences. — 1854, 1855.

Necessity of a more Varied Knowledge of the India Missions. — Advantages of Central Positions. — When Visits to Missions are Desirable. — The Deputation. — Intercourse with the Missions. — Proceedings of the Conferences, and Printing of the Same. — The *Mahratta Conference*. — Members. — Ordination of the First Native Pastor in the Mission. — Reasons for the Delay. — On Evangelists. — Development of Village Churches. — Why a Distrust of Native Piety. — Difficulty in Forming Village Stations. — Change in the High School at Ahmednuggur. — On Native Piety. — Self-sustaining Churches. — Education of Native Pastors, and their Salaries. — Ecclesiastical Relations. — Native Preaching Talent. — Results in the Mahratta Mission. — The *Ceylon Conference*. — Subjects discussed. — Native Congregations and Churches. — The High Schools. — Ordination of the First Native Pastor in the Mission. — Proposed Multiplication of Churches. — Native Preaching Houses. — Modifications in the Batticotta Seminary and Oodooville Boarding-school. — The Conference misapprehended at Home. — Special Meeting of the Board. — A Committee of Thirteen, and their Investigations. — The Result. — The *Madura Conference*. — Christian Congregations. — Village Schools. — Modifications in the Seminary. — English High School at Madura. — First Native Pastor in the Mission. — Conference at *Madras* and *Arcot.* — Othei Missionary Conferences. — Baptist Missionary Conferences. — General Missionary Conferences . . . 241

CHAPTER XIV.

MISSION TO THE MAHRATTAS. — 1854–1862.

Tour in the Godavari Valley. — Reception by Christian Villagers. — Preaching. — Location of Missionaries. — Case of Mr. Bowen. — Accession to the Mission. — Government Schools. — Itinerant Preaching. — Interesting Events. — A Converted Gosâvi. — Encouraging Facts. — Mr. Wilder at Kolapûr. — Influence of the Mutiny. — Successful Efforts at Ahmednuggur. — Yesûba as a Devotee and as a Preacher. — Yesûba Salava. — Pastor Modak's Removal to Bombay. — Pastor Haripunt at Satara. — Kolapûr. — As a Station discontinued. — Death of Mrs. Wood. — Death of a Moslem Convert. — A Pastor ordained for Ahmednuggur. — Generous Aid from an English Friend. — Visit from the Governor of Bombay. — Theological Class. — Important Step in Religious Toleration. — Jubilee Meeting. — Erection of Chapels. — Persecution, and Government Protection. — Encouraging Retrospect. — Increase in Church Membership. — Cause of the Sudden Increase of Converts, and their Character. — Who are the Converts. — Interesting Facts. — Government Protection. — Increasing Hopefulness from the Higher Castes. — Solapûr as a Station. — Unexpected Development of Benevolence. — Generous Pecuniary Aid 266

CHAPTER XV.

MISSION TO THE MAHRATTAS. — 1862–1868.

The Native Churches. — Native Pastor Ordained. — The Kirttan. — Death of Miss Farrar. — New Missionaries. — Official Kindness. — Death of Mrs. Barker, and of Mr. Chapin. — Death and Character of Haripunt. — An Ecclesiastical Union formed. — Death and Character of Mr. Ballantine, and of Mrs. Ballantine. — Movement for Native Pastorates. — Plea of Pastor Modak. — Ordination of Seven such Pastors. — Death of Mrs. Harding, and of Mr. Munger 293

CHAPTER XVI.

MISSION TO THE MAHRATTAS. — 1868–1873.

Persecution. — New Missionaries. — Native Laborers. — Bible Women. — Efforts of Mrs. Bissell. — Evidences of Progress. — A New Responsibility. — A Native Christian Alliance. — Labors of an Evangelist. — The Mussulmans. — Accessions to the Church. — The First Self-supporting Church. — A Native Pastor. — A Summary View. — Great Breach of Missionary Courtesy. — Visit and Labors of Dr. J. H. Seelye. — Other English Lecturing. — The Estimated Result of the India Missions 307

CHAPTER XVII.

THE TAMIL PEOPLE. CEYLON MISSION. — 1855–1867.

The Changes in the Batticotta Seminary. — The Movement not Retrograde. — English Schools. — Native English High School. — Position of the Prudential Committee. — Results of a Liberal Education. — The Theological Seminary. — Death of an Old Native Christian. — New Missionaries. — A Native College projected. — Advance in the Mission. — A Desirable Change. — Ordination of Native Pastors. — Death of Mr. Meigs. — Interesting Pastorate at Batticotta. — Letter from the Church. — A Pleasing Retrospect 327

CHAPTER XVIII.

THE TAMIL PEOPLE. CEYLON MISSION. — 1867–1873.

Missionary Printing. — Medical Department. — Deaths from Cholera. — Death of Mrs. Sanders. — Interesting View of the Mission. — Change of Native Sentiment as to Native Pastorates. — Children instead of the Fathers. — Death of Mr. Sanders. — A Pleasing Incident. — Death and Character of Dr. Spaulding. — Mrs. Spaulding. — Native Evangelical Society. — Board of Education. — The Jaffna College 345

CHAPTER XIX.

TAMIL PEOPLE ON THE CONTINENT.

THE MADURA MISSION. — 1855–1862.

Effect of the Conference. — The Seminary Studies. — Higher Village Schools. — The Native Pastorate. — Still Further Advances. — Accession of Native Pastors. — Disturbing Influences. — Native Churches. — Village Congregations. — Native Fondness for Poetry. — Girls' Boarding-school at Madura. — Reinforcements — Encouraging Indications. — An Eccentric Native Helper. — An Extended Revival. — Revival at the Seminary, and in the Madura Boarding-school, and in the Western District. — Sudden Death of Mr. Scudder 364

CHAPTER XX.

TAMIL PEOPLE ON THE CONTINENT.

THE MADURA MISSION. — 1862–1873.

Evidences of the Decline of Idolatry. — One of the Chief Supports of Idolatry. — An Itinerant Ministry. — Accessions to the Mission. — Amount of Evangelical Influence. — Interesting Schools. — The Medical Department. — Death of Mrs. Rendall, and of Dr. Lord. — Death and Character of Mr. Taylor. — Prospective Influence of Native Women. — The Seminary and High School. — A Missionary Daughter. — The Field for Women. — Death of Mr. Penfield. — Native Associations. — A Summary View. — Decline of Heathenism. — A Hopeful View 385

MISSIONARIES 407
PUBLICATIONS 415
INDEX 435

MISSIONS TO INDIA.

CHAPTER I.

THE BOARD AND ITS FIRST MISSIONARIES.

1810–1815.

THE American Board of Commissioners for Foreign Missions is the oldest institution in the United States for sending missionaries to foreign unevangelized nations. It was formed at Bradford, Massachusetts, in June, 1810, by the General Association of that State. The immediate cause of its formation was an application from several young men in the Theological Seminary at Andover, desirous of becoming missionaries. The Board, as originally formed, consisted of nine members, belonging to Massachusetts and Connecticut; and the young men were advised to put themselves under its direction, and await the guidance of Providence. The first meeting of the Board, as an incorporated body, was in Connecticut.

Formation of the American Board.

The connection so long maintained with the Presbyterian Church, grew out of a suggestion, at its second meeting, to the Gen-

Its ecclesiastical connections.

eral Assembly of that church, to form a similar body among themselves. The Assembly replied, that the business of foreign missions would be better managed by a single Board; that the Assembly's engagements in domestic missions made it inconvenient, at that time, to attempt the work of foreign missions; and that their churches rejoiced in the missions organized by the American Board, and would aid in their support to the extent of their ability. Upon hearing this, the Board elected eight commissioners from the Presbyterian Church. Others were added at the same time from the Congregational Churches in New Hampshire, Vermont, and Rhode Island, and thus the Board prepared itself to act as a national institution.[1]

Events tending to its formation.

The rise of this Board among a large body of Christian churches as their acknowledged agent, was by no means a fortuitous event. Though it was the first organization of the kind in this country, similar associations had preceded it in England, as the Baptist, London, and Church Missionary Societies. The more interesting facts connected with these institutions had been published in the "Massachusetts Missionary Magazine," commenced in 1803; in the "Panoplist," commenced in

[1] For a particular account of the origin, charter, constitution, membership, ecclesiastical relations, etc., of the Board, see *Memorial Volume of the First Fifty Years of the American Board of Commissioners for Foreign Missions*.

1805; and in the "General Assembly's Missionary Magazine," commenced also in 1805. In that year, Dr. Griffin preached a sermon before the General Assembly of the Presbyterian Church, in which he eloquently pleaded for the heathen world. In 1807 Dr. Carey, of the Serampore Mission, acknowledged the gift of $6,000 to his mission by American Christians, in consequence of losses by fire at Serampore. Dr. Parish, in a sermon before the Massachusetts Domestic Missionary Society in 1807, spoke of a growing conviction of the value of Christianity, making it "a good time to send missionaries to every nation, to extend the Redeemer's kingdom." In May, 1808, the Presbyterian General Assembly recommended a day of fasting and prayer, for this, among other things, "that God would bless the efforts to Christianize the heathen, and extend the blessings of the Gospel." In the same year, Dr. Abiel Holmes, of Cambridge, Massachusetts, in an anniversary discourse in Boston, hailed the approaching day, "when the Pagan idolater shall cast his idols to the moles and to the bats; when the Indian Powows shall be silenced by the songs of Zion; when the Vedas of the Hindoo and the Koran of the Mohammedan shall be exchanged for the Holy Bible; when the religion of Brahma, the Institutes of Menu, the rites of the Lama, the Zend of Zoroaster, and even the laws of Confucius, shall be superseded by the glorious gospel of the blessed God." [1]

With such experiences among the more eminent fathers of the Congregational and Presbyterian churches, what more natural, more inevitable indeed, than that some of the more intelligent and impressible young men should catch the spirit, and propose engaging personally in a foreign mission? The first movement of this sort was among the Congregationalists. It began with Samuel J. Mills, whose self-consecration dates as early as 1802. At Williams College, in 1807, he unbosomed himself to Gordon Hall and others. In 1808, those young men, while members of college, formed a society "to effect, in the persons of its members, a mission or missions to the heathen." This society the young men afterwards carried with them to the Andover Theological Seminary, where it was joined by Adoniram Judson, Samuel Newell, and Samuel Nott, graduates of as many different colleges. The streams were there united in one, and flowed out thence into the heathen world.

Rise of the mission.

It should be remembered, however, that only on the high places of Zion had the evangelical light then fallen. Only a few among the ministers or candidates for the ministry, and still fewer among the laymen, had intelligently taken hold of the work. The young men kept their society a secret,

[1] See *Life of Dr. Samuel Worcester,* vol. ii. chap. 2.

under the apprehension that the idea of a foreign mission would be unpopular in the churches; and the constitution of the society was not made public for a long time afterwards.

The names of the young men appended to the memorial which led to the formation of the Board, were Adoniram Judson, Samuel Nott, Samuel J. Mills, and Samuel Newell. James Richards and Luther Rice had signed the paper, but their names were taken off, lest the association should be alarmed by the number. Gordon Hall, though among the earliest to consecrate himself to the work, did not come to the seminary in time to take a prominent part in these incipient measures, but was soon recognized as among the leaders. Such also was Adoniram Judson, though among the last in the time of his self-consecration.

The practical question.

The practical question for the Board, at that time, was the safety of undertaking the support of these young men as missionaries. It now appeared, as it did in the formation of the Board, how desirable, in great enterprises, is the combination of youthful ardor with the wisdom and caution of age. The Board, while approving the purpose of the young men, had advised them to pursue their studies until the finances of the institution should justify their going forward. But so anxious were they to be on their way, that Mr. Judson, sharing largely in the impatience of his brethren, was permitted to visit England, and there learn whether the Directors of the London Missionary Society would assist them.

It was well that the London Society, while expressing a willingness to take the missionaries under its exclusive direction, declined to connect itself with the American Board in the conduct of missions.

The passages engaged.

Matters were soon brought to a happy issue. Passages to India were offered, both from Salem and from Philadelphia, and the missionaries were pressing for leave to go.

Samuel J. Mills.

Samuel J. Mills, it was thought, would be more useful to the cause by remaining longer at home; and he found his grave in the ocean, off the coast of Western Africa, while on a mission in the interest of the Negro population of this country.

Ordination of the missionaries.

On the 6th of February, 1812, Gordon Hall, Adoniram Judson, Samuel Newell, Samuel Nott, and Luther Rice, received ordination as foreign missionaries at the Tabernacle Church in Salem. The sermon was preached by Dr. Woods, and the scene, as witnessed by the author, was one never to be forgotten. Drs. Woods, Spring, Morse, Griffin, and Worcester, who laid their hands upon the heads of the five missionaries, and the missionaries themselves, have all gone from earth, most of them long since; though Mr. Nott died as late as the year 1868.

This ordination, in connection with the sailing of the missionaries, produced a great effect on the Christian community. It showed that the way to obtain funds is to go boldly forward in the path of duty. Within three weeks after the ordination, the contributions exceeded $6,000.

Their instructions.

The instructions of the Prudential Committee to the missionaries are remarkable for their forecast and wisdom; and, at the same time, for the absence of positive directions as to the field to be occupied. On that point, they did not know what to say. The heathen world was not then open and known as now.

Their departure.

At Philadelphia, where Messrs. Hall and Rice and Mr. and Mrs. Nott embarked in the ship *Harmony*, on the 28th of February, the churches contributed nearly a thousand dollars. Messrs. Judson and Newell, with their wives, sailed from Salem, in the brig *Caravan*, on the 19th of February. These were the only opportunities for a passage to India during many months, as war between the United States and Great Britain commenced in the following June.

Experiences at Calcutta.

The *Caravan* reached Calcutta on the 17th of June, 1812, and Christians of different denominations gave their American brethren a kind and courteous reception. Among those friends, the Rev. Mr. Thomason, an Episcopal clergyman, and the Rev. Dr. Carey, of the Baptist Mission at Serampore, deserve special mention. The Rev. David Brown, of the Episcopal Church, who would have been a cordial friend, died three days before the arrival of the first company.

Twenty years had elapsed since the House of Commons empowered the East India Court of Directors to close India against education and the gospel; and desperate efforts were now being made in Parliament to extend this power through another twenty years. The controversy was at its height in England when the American missionaries arrived at Calcutta, but the power of the reforming influences at that time was scarcely suspected in India. Nor did the India rulers rightly estimate all the forces with which they had themselves to deal. With so great a disparity between the physical force of the governors and governed, and with no sympathy between them, the rulers naturally dreaded whatever tended to the elevation of their subjects. Commercial freedom they dreaded, as endangering the profits of their trade; and Christianity, because of the reforms it would require. Yet the period for a change of policy had come. Many European traders had already forced their way into Bengal, and the manufacturing and commercial interests of England had become too strong to allow of their expulsion. But the India government supposed it could still exclude the gospel.

Hostile attitude of the government.

Accordingly, Messrs. Newell and Judson, immediately on their arrival, were ordered to return by the *Caravan*, and informed that the vessel would not be allowed to sail without them.[1] They were thus thrown into great perplexity and distress. Their Christian friends at Calcutta and Serampore deeply sympathized with them, and earnestly pleaded for them with the government officials. Special prayer was also made in their behalf. The order was at length so far modified, that they were allowed to go to any place not within the jurisdiction of the East India Company, provided they went at once.[2] But where to go, they knew not. Their thoughts had been turned somewhat to Burmah, before leaving home, but information received, after landing, discouraged a movement in that direction. They therefore turned their eyes westward. Just then they received letters from their brethren in the *Harmony*, dated at the Isle of France, stating that the Governor of that Island was desirous of having missionaries there, and on the neighboring island of Madagascar. As the Isle of France was not within the jurisdiction of the Company, Messrs. Newell and Judson resolved to go there by the earliest opportunity. Accordingly, on the 4th of August, Mr. and Mrs. Newell embarked for that island in a vessel that afforded accommodations for only two passen-

[1] The reader will understand, that this was not because they were Americans, but because they were missionaries.

[2] Marshman, vol. i., p. 488.

gers, with the expectation that Mr. and Mrs. Judson would soon follow.

The *Harmony* arrived, with Messrs. Hall, Nott, and Rice, four days after the departure of Mr. Newell; and meeting with the same reception from the government, they came to the same determination. They were detained at Calcutta, however, until the latter part of November. An unfriendly official then reported them as being still in the country, and the government, without seeking explanation as to the cause of the delay, chose to regard them as having forfeited all claim to further indulgence, and decided to send them to England by the fleet then about to sail. Mr. Marshman says that the orders were for them to mess with the gunner. This, to those ladies and their husbands, would have been a sort of "middle passage," and it was right for them to flee from such oppression. The fleet was lying a hundred miles below the city, and they were to be sent down under guard.[1]

Escape from Calcutta.

Messrs. Judson and Rice, hearing of a vessel bound to the Isle of France, went on board at midnight, with Mrs. Judson, having prevailed on the commander to receive them. The police followed them down the river, and forbade the vessel's going to sea with them on board. They accordingly landed, without knowing what to do. But a kind Providence had interposed, and a letter was

[1] Marshman, vol. i., p. 489.

soon put into their hands with permission to embark. Hiring a boat, and rowing day and night, they overtook the vessel just as she was preparing to weigh anchor for the last time. It appears that the Governor-general (Lord Minto) on being informed of their flight, recollected that he had already given them permission to go to the Isle of France.

Messrs. Hall and Nott effected their escape also, not without suspicion of a connivance on the part of the authorities. They had received what was called a general pass, and obtained passage in a vessel bound to Bombay, but to touch at Ceylon, and were regularly reported as passengers. The police made search for them, but not where they must have been known to be. Their voyage was long, and their funds running low, they decided to incur the risk of proceeding to Bombay, where they arrived in February, 1813, after a passage of eleven weeks.

Sickness and death of Mrs. Newell.

Mr. and Mrs. Newell's passage to the Isle of France was long, perilous, and distressing. They were driven about the Bay of Bengal for a month, and at length the vessel sprung a leak, and was obliged to put into Coringa, on the Coromandel coast, for repairs. This was well for Mrs. Newell, as it gave opportunity for her to recover from a dangerous illness. On the 19th of September they reëmbarked, hoping for a short passage to the Isle of France. Three weeks after leaving Coringa, and before reaching the end of the voyage, Mrs. Newell gave birth, prematurely, to a daughter. In a storm both she and her infant took cold, and the babe soon died. The mother was thrown into a consumption, and not long after arriving at Port Louis, the husband found himself compelled to relinquish all hope of her recovery. When informed of the near approach of death, her response was, "Glorious intelligence." She said she had never repented leaving her native country, and that the consideration of having left it for the cause of Christ, now afforded her great consolation.[1] She died on the 30th of November, 1812, and an iron railing — lately renewed — marks the place of her burial. The letter of Mr. Newell to Mrs. Atwood, the mother of his wife, was read at the time with deep interest by thousands; and there are thousands now, after the lapse of sixty years, who would be interested in its perusal.

Mrs. Newell probably accomplished more by what seemed her untimely death, than she could have done by a long life. The memorial of her cultivated mind and unwavering devotion to the missionary cause, soon afterwards published by Dr. Woods, secured for her a high place in the affection of the Christian community, which she still retains.[2]

Messrs. Judson and Rice were detained at Calcutta

[1] *Memoir of Mrs. Harriet Newell*, p. 92.

[2] The eighth edition of this Memoir now lies before me.

till the 30th of November, the day of Mrs. Newell's death, and arrived at Port Louis on the 17th of January, finding their bereaved brother of course in great affliction. They were together about a month, when Mr. Newell embarked for Ceylon, and they never met again on earth.

Brief reunion at Port Louis.

The missionaries now formed two bands. Indeed they had become such very soon after arriving at Calcutta. On the 27th of August, Mr. Judson wrote to the Baptist missionaries at Serampore, that he and Mrs. Judson had changed their sentiments on the subject of baptism, and desired to be baptized by immersion. Mr. Rice, not long after, made the same request. We now see how these trials, so inscrutable at the time, contributed to the furtherance of the cause in that part of the world. It was the divine purpose that the mission should have a far more extended influence for good than had been originally contemplated. The two brethren withdrew from their connection with the Board; and, at the Isle of France, decided that Mr. Rice return to the United States to enlist the Baptist churches in foreign missions, in which he happily succeeded. Mr. Judson's attention was now turned to Pulo Penang; and as there was no opportunity to sail thither from Port Louis, he went with his wife to Madras, where they were once more under the jurisdiction of the East India Company. Their only resort was a vessel bound to Rangoon.

The mission two bands.

In this, after a tempestuous and dangerous voyage, they arrived at that city on the 13th of July.

Such was the providential arrangement for an American Baptist mission to Burmah and the Karens. The unpleasant feeling among the supporters of the American Board occasioned by the unexpected division of the mission, gave place at length to gratitude on seeing the beneficent designs of the Head of the Church.

The mission to the Karens.

The situation of Messrs. Hall and Nott, at Bombay, was seriously embarrassed by the arrival of intelligence, that the United States had declared war against Great Britain. The declaration was made about the time of their arrival at Calcutta; but, happily for them, there was then no ocean telegraph with its rapid transmission of intelligence. It was probably in consequence of this outbreak of war that the Supreme Government wrote to Sir Evan Nepean, Governor of Bombay, — a man of liberal views, and a friend of Mr. Charles Grant, — directing him to send the American missionaries to England. The Governor was exceedingly reluctant to carry out these orders, and suspended the execution of them, in consideration of the illness of Mrs. Nott and of Mr. Hall; but when informed of their convalescence, he engaged a passage for them at an expense of £400. William T. Money, Esq., was in the confidence of Sir Evan, and proved a very valuable friend to the missionaries,

Struggles for a missionary residence at Bombay.

both in India, and afterwards in England. He advised them to explain their case to the Governor. They did so; and their memorial was so satisfactory, that he wrote in their behalf to the Governor-general. A new difficulty now arose. A schooner, called the *Alligator*, had arrived at Calcutta, from Salem, bringing books, letters, and funds for the missionaries, with a letter from Sir John Borlase Warren, Admiral of the British fleet on the Halifax station, describing the *Alligator* as a missionary vessel, sent out to communicate with American missionaries in India, and, as such, granting her protection. Mention is made of this vessel in the Report of the Board for 1813, and there is evidence of interest having been used by the Prudential Committee with the Admiral, to procure protection for her; but we have no copy of the precise terms used by the Admiral in speaking of the vessel. She was seized, condemned, and her crew were sent to England as prisoners of war, in the belief that she had forfeited her neutral character by cruising off the Cape of Good Hope to apprise American vessels of the declaration of war. The government allowed the letters and supplies to be forwarded to Bombay, but took occasion to suspect some political plot in the mission, under the pretense of religion, and renewed the order for sending the missionaries to England. Their passages were accordingly engaged in a vessel then about to sail. In another memorial they showed to the Governor, that they had no connection with the war.

They flee from Bombay.

Receiving a letter from Mr. Newell, then in Ceylon, favoring their coming to that island, which was under the government of the Crown, they asked permission to go thither. Not obtaining this permission, they saw no way of remaining in the East, but by departing secretly for that island. Lieut. John Wade, an Aide to the Commander-in-chief of the Bombay Station, regarded them as the means of his conversion, and informed them of a vessel to sail in a few hours for Colombo, in Ceylon. He made all needful arrangements, and saw them safely on board the vessel at the mouth of the harbor. Mrs. Nott and her child remained behind. After they had gone, Mr. Wade prepared and circulated a defense of their conduct, though at a personal sacrifice.[1]

"In reflecting on our present situation," Mr. Hall wrote, during the voyage to Cochin, "I have fears lest we have sinned in leaving Bombay as we have. Perhaps we ought to have waited and trusted in the Lord to deliver us in his own way. Yet, after all, I know not why it was not as right for us to escape from Bombay, as it was for Paul to escape from Damascus."

An interesting event is noted by Mr. Hall in his journal, showing the care of a kind Providence. As

[1] Bardwell's *Life of Gordon Hall,* p. 53.

they were leaving the small boat to go on board the native vessel, their young friend, Lieutenant Wade, suddenly thought of the possibility of their landing on the coast, and wrote with his pencil to an officer, to whom he had formerly named the missionaries, "Take good care of my friends Hall and Nott," which soon proved of essential service; for they had not been long at sea before they learned that the destination of their vessel was Quilon, on the coast, and not Ceylon, so that they were without funds and without friends. Having persuaded the captain to land them for a few hours at Cananore, they were kindly received by Colonel Lockhart, the officer above named, who assisted them in negotiating a draft on Bombay, and gave them a favorable introduction to Cochin. They landed at Cochin on the 30th of October, and were received by Mr. Pearson, the magistrate of the place, with great kindness, and provided with gratuitous accommodations; and, while waiting for a passage to Ceylon, they visited the Jews and Syrian Christians in that neighborhood.

But new troubles awaited them. They were expecting, on the 5th of November, to leave the next morning, when their kind host informed them that he had received orders from Bombay to see that they were returned to that place by the first opportunity. "Thanks unto God," writes Mr. Hall, "none of these things move me! I find pleasure in the reflection, that God has ordered this for some wise and good end. He breaks up our plans only that He may accomplish his own, which are infinitely better." [1]

Sir Evan Nepean was not well pleased with their private departure from Bombay, as it might subject him to censure from the General Government for imputed connivance, or delinquency. After reaching Bombay they were confined ten days to the vessel, and then were brought to the police office, and required to sign a bond, in the sum of four thousand rupees, not to leave the place without permission. This they declined to do. They also refused to give their parole to the same effect, or even to promise that they would remain till Monday.[2] Being remanded to the ship, they sent to the Governor a respectful and very able memorial, with which he was so far satisfied as to allow them to occupy a house in the city.

Are brought back to Bombay.

Meanwhile the Prudential Committee at home were doing everything in their power for the relief of the mission. The Hon. John H. Harington, and Drs. Carey and Brown, were requested to act as their committee at Calcutta ; but before the arrival of their communication, Dr. Brown was dead, and Judge Harington was away. On hearing of the death of Dr. Brown, they appointed

Commissioners on their behalf appointed.

[1] *Memoir of Gordon Hall*, p. 57.

[2] Tracy's *History of the American Board*, p. 42.

the Rev. Thomas Thomason to supply the vacancy, and he with Dr. Carey requested the Hon. George Udny, for many years a member of the Supreme Council at Calcutta, to act in the place of Judge Harington. The services rendered by these commissioners are gratefully remembered.

On the 16th of December their friend, Mr. Money, informed the two brethren that he had just been with the Governor, who stated that no orders had been received from Calcutta concerning their stay, and being still under positive orders of the Supreme Government to send them away, he must now send them. On the 20th, the senior magistrate of police officially notified them, that a passage was to be provided for them to England on board a vessel which was to sail after two days. At this critical moment Messrs. Hall and Nott made an appeal to his Excellency, not only as Governor, but as a man and a Christian, which has always been admired for its ability. The closing paragraph should have a place in history. "It is our ardent wish," they say, "that your Excellency would compare, most seriously, such an exercise of civil authority upon us with the general spirit and tenor of our Saviour's commands. We most earnestly entreat you not to send us away from these heathen. We entreat you by the high probability that an official permission from the Supreme Government for us to remain here will shortly be received. We entreat

Successful appeal to the governor.

you by the time and money already expended on our mission, and by the prayers and hopes attending it, not utterly to defeat its pious object by sending us from the country. We entreat you by the spiritual miseries of the heathen, daily perishing before your eyes, and under your Excellency's government, not to prevent us from preaching Christ to them. We entreat you by the blood of Jesus, which He shed to redeem them. As ministers of Him, who has all power in Heaven and on earth, and who with his ascending voice commanded his ministers to *go and teach all nations*, we entreat you not to prohibit us from teaching these heathen. By that holy religion through which you hope to be saved, we entreat you not to hinder us from preaching it to these perishing idolaters. By all the solemnities of the judgment day, when your Excellency must meet your subjects before God's tribunal, we entreat you not to hinder us from preaching to them that Gospel, which is able to prepare them, as well as you, for that awful day. . . . . We entreat your Excellency not to oppose the prayers and efforts of the Church, by sending back those, whom it has sent forth in the name of the Lord, to preach his gospel among the heathen; and we earnestly beseech Almighty God to prevent such an act, and now and ever to guide your Excellency in that way which shall be most pleasing in his sight."

The appeal was so far successful that the brethren

received official notice, next morning, that the Governor would await further instructions from Calcutta. This note was dated December 21, 1813.

The occasion for this, humanly speaking, we must seek in events then transpiring in England, of which vague rumors must have already reached India. As these events involved the opening of India to the gospel, they should have an explicit, though concise, statement in this history, which will be given in the next chapter. It will be seen that the opening of India and the entrance of the American Mission were contemporaneous events.

CHAPTER II.

THE OPENING OF INDIA TO THE GOSPEL.

1758–1812.

THE East India Company received a charter from Queen Elizabeth in the year 1600. It was formed for purposes of trade, and while only a commercial body it seems to have taken considerable interest in the religious instruction of the natives. A few missionaries were allowed to proceed to India in its ships, and were encouraged in their labors. A similar spirit was evinced by the English Parliament.

Its early disposition.

This favorable disposition continued until the celebrated battle of Plassey, in 1758. But as soon as the military genius of Clive had transformed the company of merchants into sovereigns of a great empire, all desire to impart knowledge to the people of India ceased, and repugnance to efforts for the conversion of the heathen seemed to increase, as British influence extended and the facilities for doing good were multiplied. Whether this was owing to ignorance of the Gospel,

A remarkable change.

or aversion to it, — though most probably to both, — the great body of the "old Indians," as those who had resided long in India were called after returning home, came at length to regard its introduction into India with even morbid apprehension. There were intelligent men who did not share in these views, and some who attained to distinction.

Hostility to missions.

The charter of the East India Company had to be renewed by Parliament once in twenty years, and a clause had been inserted in the proposed charter for the year 1792, favoring the sending of missionaries and schoolmasters to India. The Court of Directors in England had then become crowded with "old Indians," and the British empire in the East seemed to them likely to melt away as soon as the ministers of religion touched its shores. Their opposition had its parallel only in that put forth by the same class, on a similar occasion, twenty years later.

Triumph of the opposition.

The clause was omitted, and India was left, for another long period, to the mercies of Leadenhall Street.

Charles Grant.

The chief originator of the movement for opening India to the Christian religion, had been Mr. Charles Grant. Going thither at an early age, he was appointed in 1773 a writer in the Bengal establishment, and rose to be a member of the Board of Trade in Calcutta. He early devoted himself to the moral and religious improvement of the natives, and was himself a living recommendation of the gospel. In 1786 he drew up a plan for a "Mission to Bengal," and after a vain endeavor to gain the approval of Lord Cornwallis, the Governor-general, he sought, through Romaine, Newton, Foster, Cecil, and Simeon, to secure the aid of Christians in England. These gentlemen addressed a letter to William Wilberforce, soliciting his coöperation in Parliament. The letter was drawn up by Mr. Grant, and appears to have been the first occasion on which Wilberforce's attention was specially drawn to the subject of missions to India. The project languished, however, till the return of Mr. Grant to England in 1790. He then succeeded, with the aid of Wilberforce, in bringing the question distinctly before the English Government; but with the result already indicated.

A counter influence in England.

Yet God was preparing an agency, at that time, in a most unpromising quarter, which was to lead the way to victory and triumph.

A less promising but more effective agency.

William Carey was born in a village of Northamptonshire, on the 17th of August, 1761. His father was schoolmaster of the village, and he received what was then regarded in country villages as a good education. His scientific tastes were exhibited at an early age. His room was crowded with insects collected to mark their development, and he never walked abroad without scrutinizing the hedges, and minutely examining the

William Carey.

structure of every plant he gathered. Though rustic in his manners, his appearance was prepossessing, and his more intelligent friends thought they discerned in him the seeds of future promise. At the age of twelve, having obtained a Latin vocabulary, he committed nearly the whole of it to memory, and carefully studied the brief sketch of a grammar in the introduction.[1]

As his parents were poor, he was bound apprentice, at the age of fourteen, to a shoemaker. In a small collection of books in the shoemaker's shop, was a commentary on the New Testament, interspersed with Greek words, which he copied, and took for translation to an educated man in the neighborhood, and this was the commencement of those linguistic studies which so distinguished his after life. His master died after he had served as an apprentice two years, and he engaged himself as a journeyman shoemaker to one of the flock of the Rev. Thomas Scott, the commentator. His pastor was impressed by his intelligence and modesty, and used to remark that the young man would prove no ordinary character. He attended Mr. Scott's ministry at Ravenstone, and regarded his conversion as the result of God's blessing on those ministrations. Up to this time his connection had been with the Church of England. At the age of eighteen he joined a small independent church at Hackleton,

[1] Marshman's *Life of Carey*, vol. i. p. 1.

and soon after commenced preaching at that village, which he continued for three years and a half, going once a month to preach at his native village, ten miles distant. During this time a change in his views led him to join the Baptists. Dr. John Ryland makes this statement of his baptism: "On the 5th of October, 1783, I baptized a poor journeyman shoemaker in the river Nen, a little beyond Dr. Doddridge's chapel in Northampton."

Carey's efforts and influence.

Mr. Carey's acquaintance with the Rev. Andrew Fuller of Kittering, his future associate in the cause of missions, commenced in 1787, and continued to the close of Mr. Fuller's career in 1815. The perusal of "Cook's Voyage round the World" led him to contemplate the moral degradation of the heathen, and to form the design of carrying to them the gospel. The project engrossed his mind and heart. He prepared a large map, composed of several sheets pasted together, on which he entered what he was able to glean concerning the population, religion, and natural characteristics of every country then known; and this he suspended on the wall of his little workshop. While at work his eye was often raised to the map, and he was musing on the condition of the various heathen tribes, and devising the means of evangelizing them.

Backwardness of his ministerial brethren.

Mr. Marshman states, that Carey had little encouragement from his ministerial brethren. "At a meeting of ministers in Northampton, Mr. Ryland, senior, called on the young men around him to propose some topic for discussion, on which Mr. Carey arose and proposed, 'The duty of Christians to attempt the spread of the gospel among heathen nations.' The venerable divine received the proposal with astonishment, and, springing to his feet, denounced the proposition with a frown, and thundered out, 'Young man, sit down. When God pleases to convert the heathen, He will do it without your aid or mine.'" Even Mr. Fuller was startled by the boldness and novelty of the proposal.[1]

Formation of a Missionary Society.

In 1789 Mr. Carey published an address on missions, hoping thus to rouse his denomination. This was followed, in 1791, by the publication of an "Inquiry on Missions." The celebrated sermon, which may be regarded as the foundation of the Baptist Mission in India, was not preached until May, 1792. In this he explained and enforced, that we are (1.) to expect great things from God, and (2.) to attempt great things for God. In October following, a Missionary Society was formed at Kittering, with Andrew Fuller for its Secretary, and Mr. Carey offered to embark for any country which the Society might select. The first subscription amounted to thirteen pounds two shillings and sixpence. It was the harbinger of the millions since laid on the altar of this sacred cause.

[1] Marshman, vol. i. p. 10.

The London ministers of the Baptist denomination stood aloof. The only minister in the great metropolis from whom Mr. Carey received any sympathy, was the venerable John Newton, of the Established Church. Indeed, comparatively few of his brethren in the country really sympathized with him. Among these were Fuller, Sutcliff, Ryland, and Pearce, all men near his own age. Some of the speeches made in the General Assembly of the Church of Scotland in 1796, when a proposal was made to establish a foreign mission, strongly remind one of the anti-missionary speeches, four years earlier, in the Board of Proprietors of the East India Company.[1]

Lukewarmness of ministers.

The Baptist Missionary Society was formed in 1792, the year preceding the action of Parliament on the Charter of the East India Company. The antagonist but apparently very unequal forces were now organized and in the field, — the one to carry the Gospel to India, the other to exclude it. The opposition was never more decided than near the close of this period; but we can notice only the leading facts, until we come to the arrival of the American missionaries at Calcutta in 1812.

The antagonist forces.

Mr. John Thomas, an eccentric member of the Baptist Church, who had gone to Calcutta in 1786, was employed by Mr. Grant, for three years, in mis-

[1] See Marshman, vol. i. p. 18.

sionary labors among the natives, at an expense of a thousand pounds. Returning to England in 1792, Mr. Thomas opened a correspondence with Mr. Carey, and was associated with him, by the newly formed Society, in a mission to be sent to Bengal.

Carey designated to a mission in Bengal.

The question then arose, how they were to reach India. The storm raised by the proposed modification of the Charter was then raging, and left no hope of their obtaining leave to go in one of the Company's vessels, or to go at all. A passage was at length obtained in a Danish vessel, and the party landed at Calcutta on the 11th of November, 1793. Having come in a foreign vessel, cleared at a foreign port, they passed unobserved. Want of thrift on the part of Mr. Thomas subjected Mr. Carey and his family to very great embarrassments. They had no letter of credit, and the committee at Kittering had neither the knowledge of business, nor the funds necessary for such a provision. Mr. Thomas was hunted by former creditors, and induced to resume his medical practice at Calcutta, and Mr. Carey, for a time, was dependent for shelter for his family of seven on the generosity of an opulent native. Twenty years after, when the good missionary had attained an influential position in Calcutta, he placed this native, who had meanwhile lost his property, in a situation of ease and comfort.

How to reach the field.

Unpropitious outset.

Without money or friends, Mr. Carey removed into the Soonderbunds, as a vast tract of jungle south of Calcutta is called, and began to build huts for his family in a neighborhood where persons were often carried off by tigers. From this dangerous situation he was rescued by Mr. George Udny, of the Company's service, afterwards a friend of the American missionaries, a man of genuine Christian benevolence, who had been associated with Mr. Grant in his missionary efforts. He offered Mr. Carey the management of an indigo factory, where he would have a comfortable support, time for study, and a stated congregation of about ninety natives connected with the factory. Here he passed more than five years preparing himself for the wider sphere of usefulness God had in store for him.[1] Of his income of twelve hundred dollars, he devoted a fourth, and sometimes a third, to missionary objects.

A kind Providence.

The London Missionary Society was formed in 1795. A few months after, Mr. Haldane, owner of a large landed property in Scotland, to which he had retired after a career of honorable service in the royal navy, was so affected by the account of the labors of Mr. Carey in India, that he devoted himself to an India mission, and decided to sell a part of his estates, and employ the proceeds in its support. Three of his friends, Mr. (after-

Mr. Haldane's proposed mission.

[1] Marshman, vol. i. p. 67.

wards Dr.) Bogue, Mr. Innes, and Mr. Greville Ewing,[1] — men who became noted in the church at home, — animated with the same spirit, consented to accompany him to India. They intended to take out a printing establishment, and a staff of schoolmasters and catechists. When their arrangements were completed, application was made to the India authorities for permission to embark. Mr. Dundas, President of the Board of Control, was a family connection of Mr. Haldane, and had known him from his childhood. After four months, Mr. Wilberforce came up to London, and used his influence with the Ministry on Mr. Haldane's behalf, but all to no purpose. Mr. Haldane received a very complimentary reply from the Court of Directors, but a peremptory refusal to his application. One more likely to succeed can hardly be imagined. It afterwards appeared, that Divine Providence had an important service for Mr. Haldane at Geneva in Switzerland.

Mr. Grant's appeal for India.

In the year 1797 Mr. Grant was elected one of the Directors of the East India Company; and, three years later, hoping to secure the attention of the Directors, he printed a few copies of "Observations on the state of society among the Asiatic subjects of Great Britain, particularly with respect to morals and the means of improving them." But he found that the idea of sending the

[1] Mr. Ewing's Memoir is before me in an 8vo volume of 672 pages, published in London by John Snow in 1843.

Gospel to India still excited such angry resistance, that his treatise was not published, and remained unknown till it was disinterred at the India House in 1813, by order of Parliament, and printed among other documents. It then contributed not a little to the auspicious resolution, which unlocked the gates of India to the gospel.

Messrs. Marshman and Ward.

In 1799, Messrs. Marshman and Ward, who soon acquired a good name in the missionary world, and two others who lived but a short time, embarked for India in the American ship *Criterion*, Captain Wickes; there being no Danish ship at hand, and the ships of the Company being closed against them. Mr. Grant advised them not to expose themselves to banishment by landing at Calcutta, but to go direct to Serampore, which was under the Danish flag; and they were furnished with a letter of introduction from the Danish Consulate in London to the Governor of that settlement. They arrived at Calcutta on the 5th of October, and the captain, at their request, boldly reported them as Christian missionaries, on their way to Serampore. He procured boats for their baggage, in which they embarked, and, on the 13th of October, found themselves safe at their destination.

The missionary refuge at Serampore.

This little Danish town has, at present, no other interest than as a former refuge of the church in a time of persecution. It is pleasantly situated on the right bank of the river Hooghly, sixteen miles above Calcutta. It was purchased by Danish traders of the Nabob of Moorshedabad, and the Danish flag was hoisted over it in 1758, just before the battle of Plassey. The town, when Messrs. Marshman and Ward landed there, had reached the zenith of its prosperity, and the only trade of the Presidency in the hands of foreigners was concentrated there; the Dutch and French settlements, farther up the river, having been captured by the English during the war of the French Revolution.[1] During the rupture between England and Denmark, at the close of 1800, the Danish settlements in India were all sequestered, but only for fourteen months, and during the administration of Lord Wellesley, who no longer regarded the missionary enterprise with alarm. The place was again occupied by the English in 1808, and was held by them until the termination of the European war, in 1815. Happily Lord Minto, in 1808, had recovered from the panic of the Vellore mutiny, and become better acquainted with the character and views of the missionaries. Had the capture taken place in the previous year, the Serampore mission might have been broken up.

An efficient protector.

Colonel Bie, the Governor of the place, received the missionaries cordially, and offered them all the assistance in his power. But the

[1] Marshman, vol. i. p. 113.

police of Calcutta lost no time in notifying the Governor-general of the arrival of four missionaries without permission from the Court of Directors; and it was resolved, that they be required to leave the country forthwith. Captain Wickes applied, on Monday, for permission to enter his vessel, but was informed that he could not receive it, unless the four missionaries came under engagements to return immediately to England. The captain brought this information to Serampore that evening, and it occasioned some dismay. They determined, however, to remain, unless the Governor declined to protect them. Colonel Bie had been nearly forty years in the service of the Danish Company, part of the time as an officer at Tranquebar, where he was favored with the ministry of Schwartz, but mostly as Governor of Serampore. He was small in stature, but bold, and his independence had given no little umbrage to Warren Hastings. He had resisted the demands of subsequent Governor-generals for the surrender of those to whom he had given protection; and he was now prepared to do the same in behalf of the missionaries, but he advised them to present an explanatory memorial to Lord Wellesley. Explanations were accordingly made, and the Governor-general, one of the most enlightened of the rulers of India, being assured of their Protestant character and pacific designs, and that he had no legal right to refuse an entry to a

The Governor-general pacificated.

foreign vessel simply because she had brought out passengers to a foreign settlement, removed the interdict from the *Criterion.*

It soon became apparent, that although the missionaries were safe at Serampore, they would not be allowed to settle elsewhere, and that the Governor-general would not allow a press in the Company's territories out of Calcutta. But there was reason to believe he was willing the missionaries should establish themselves under Colonel Bie's protection, where he would be relieved from the necessity of disturbing them. If Lord Wellesley was a despot, he was too enlightened to sympathize with the contracted views which then prevailed in Leadenhall Street. He did not consider the missionaries a dangerous class, and saw no reason to persecute them. On the contrary, he looked upon religion as the safeguard of social order, and the most effectual promoter of happiness, and determined to favor it. He forbade horse-racing and gambling on the Sabbath, and the publication of Sunday newspapers, and never failed to appear in his place at church. He even assured Mr. Brown, the worthy chaplain, that he was resolved to recognize the Christian religion as the religion of the State. He appointed the 6th of February, 1800, as a day of general thanksgiving for the success of the British arms in Mysore, and the day was observed at Calcutta with much pomp and ceremony; Mr. Buchanan, another of the chaplains, preaching a sermon appropriate to the occasion. These things were a great step forwards. After the Governor-general became assured that the Serampore missionaries avoided political questions, and restricted themselves to the instruction of the heathen, he showed every disposition to foster their work, though nearly all the influential members of his government were known to be violently opposed.[1]

College of Fort William.

The College of Fort William, established by the Marquis of Wellesley in 1801, for the better education of the young men connected with the civil service, was an important step towards that toleration of missionaries which was coming with a slow but sure progress. Mr. Brown, the chaplain, an avowed friend of missions, was made Provost of the College, the well-known Claudius Buchanan was made Vice-Provost, and William Carey became one of the most noted of the Professors. Translating the Holy Scriptures into the languages of the country, was a favorite pursuit in the college, and it became well known that the eminent statesman at the head of the government did not look with apprehension upon the work of Christian missions. The College was indeed soon very much reduced in its funds by the Directors at home, but not until it had strengthened the hold of Christian missions on India; and it soon gave rise to the College

[1] Marshman, vol. i. p. 134.

at Haileybury, in England, for the same class of young men.

The mutiny and massacre at Vellore, in July, 1806, occasioned great alarm, both in India and England, and was most absurdly attributed, by the enemies of missions, to missionary influence; and they took occasion from it to redouble their efforts to close the door against the Gospel. In the following month, while the excitement was at its height, Captain Wickes brought two additional missionaries from England in his ship *Criterion* for the Serampore mission. Lord Minto, the new Governor-general, had just arrived, and, misled by unfriendly misrepresentations, sanctioned an order for their immediate banishment from the country. At the same time, the preaching and all the other missionary labors of the brethren at Serampore were prohibited, and they were required to remove their printing establishment to Calcutta. But these orders, after some time, were withdrawn through the judicious measures of the Danish Governor, and personal explanations to Lord Minto.

Mutiny at Vellore.

The consequences.

We have now entered upon the year 1807, and within five years the terms must be settled for the renewal of the Charter to the East India Company. Times had changed since 1792, and were rapidly changing, though the upholders of the old regime were the last to apprehend it.

Missionary development in England.

The Baptist Missionary Society had been formed in 1792, the London Missionary Society in 1795, the Church Missionary Society in 1800, and the British and Foreign Bible Society in 1804. Thousands of people had their interest thus awakened, in place of the very few five or six years before. The struggle between the friends and enemies of missions was once more transferred to England, and the years from 1807 to 1812 are noted for what has been called the great battle of missions.

The great battle of missions.

The campaign was opened by Mr. Twining, who had resided in India from 1792 to 1805, in a printed letter to the Chairman of the Court of Directors. His fears were specially excited by the formation of the Bible Society, with the declared object of the universal diffusion of the Christian faith, and with a membership including Mr. Charles Grant and Mr. Thornton, of the Court of Directors, and Lord Teignmouth, once Governor-general of India and then a member of the Board of Control and of his Majesty's Privy Council. He thought their possessions in the East were in a situation of unprecedented peril. This assault was ably met by Mr. Owen, Secretary of the Bible Society.

Major Scott Waring soon followed on the same side with Mr. Twining. He had gone to India in the year 1765, and was there when the European community was preëminently distinguished by indifference to Christianity and partiality to idolatrous superstitions.

These pamphlets were found to be creating a strong anti-missionary feeling in influential political circles, and Mr. Fuller hastened to London to counteract it. He called on the Marquis of Wellesley, who informed him that he was himself decidedly opposed to the recall of the missionaries, which he considered impolitic and unjust, and he promised to use his efforts to dissuade the Ministry from it, should they ask his opinion. Meanwhile four other pamphlets, equally hostile, appeared in rapid succession. Mr. Fuller now published his "Apology for the late Christian Missions in India," making a volume of more than three hundred pages, and Mr. Owen also published a reply to Major Scott Waring.

The next assailant was a "Bengal Officer," who had notoriously abjured Christianity, and become a worshipper of the Hindoo deities. This pamphlet subserved the cause of Christian missions by the ridicule it brought on their opponents. Among the most important of the contributions to the missionary cause, during this controversy, was one by Lord Teignmouth.

After the lapse of sixty years, it is presumed that but few of these publications are obtainable, and Mr. Marshman has performed a valuable service by embodying the substance of them in his "History of the Serampore Mission." The satirical attacks of Sydney Smith, in the "Edinburgh Review" of 1808 and 1809, still attract attention, but they were founded on misapprehension, and the author is said to have lived to regret them.

The discussion closed with an article in defense of the missions, in the "Quarterly Review" of April, 1809, from the pen of Southey.[1]

Importance of the controversy.

It is not possible to overrate the importance of this controversy in its effect on religious opinions in England, as developed in 1812 during the discussion in Parliament on the India Charter.

The difficulties not overcome.

Occurrences at Calcutta, in 1811, made it evident that the standing orders of the Court for the deportation of Europeans found in India without a license, might be put in force at any time by the malevolence of any officer. The toleration enjoyed was only by sufferance, and it was liable to be interrupted, should a new panic seize the Council Board. The missionaries therefore urged Mr. Fuller, as the period for a new Charter approached, to seize the golden opportunity for securing them a legal toleration in India.

Toleration secured.

The question of renewing the Charter of the East India Company came up again in the House of Commons in the year 1813. Lord Castlereagh, the Prime Minister, suggested, as modifications to suit the necessities of the times, that the trade of India be thrown open to the mercantile community of England, and that Europeans

[1] See Marshman's *History*, vol. i. pp. 333–379.

be allowed to resort to India, under licenses from the Court of Directors, or the Board of Control; but leaving the government in full possession of the power they had always held, of expelling any one whose conduct or opinions might be considered dangerous. He would also provide for a bishop and three archdeacons, to superintend the chaplains of the different settlements. There was no proposed concession to the missionaries, and the bishop and archdeacons were intended solely for the European community in India. Wilberforce then rose and expressed his unwillingness to leave the same power in the hands of the Directors for twenty years to come, which they had employed with so much zeal against missions in the twenty years gone by. The conduct of the Prime Minister, in studiously omitting to make provision in the Charter in favor of missions, produced its natural effect in England and Scotland. It showed the necessity of an expression of public opinion, such as even Parliament would not venture to resist. While the Court of Directors spent six weeks in examining witnesses in support of the mercantile privileges which they had enjoyed for more than two centuries, of which the proposed modified Charter would very properly deprive them, the religious spirit of the country was aroused. Wilberforce and his associates, Grant, Stephen, and Babington, were actively engaged in getting up petitions in their respective communities, until the voice of the country became irresistible. Nine hundred petitions were laid on the table of the House of Commons. Wilberforce, regarding the object as "the greatest which men ever pursued," exhibited all the ardor he had shown in the question of the slave-trade. He felt that nothing short of an unequivocal expression of the feelings of the nation would carry the Parliament, even though the Ministry should be favorable. A large and influential meeting was held at the London Tavern, with Lord Gambier in the chair, at which strong resolutions were adopted in favor of the proposed amendment of the Charter, and a permanent committee of twenty-eight gentlemen, of all sects and parties, was appointed to secure the object. The subject was earnestly debated in Parliament, but the most remarkable of the speeches then made, was doubtless that of Wilberforce, which is said to have equaled the noblest of his efforts in behalf of the slave, and to have been heard with the closest attention by all parties.

The bill, as desired by the friends of missions, passed to its third reading on the 13th of July, 1813, by a vote of fifty-four against twenty-two. There being no "old Indians" in the House of Lords, it there met with a far less decided opposition. The demands of the manufacturers and merchants of England for a participation in the trade of India, caused the ministry to see that they could not consistently refuse the grant also of religious privileges; "and thus commerce became, in some measure, the handmaid of religion, and under their combined influence the gates of India were opened at once to the cottons of England and the truths of the Bible."[1]

The Company had hitherto enjoyed a monopoly of the trade between England and all places east of the Cape of Good Hope. The trade between England and India was now to be open for all; though the trade with China was still to be a monopoly of the Company. Missionary operations, and all proper means for the conversion of the native population to Christianity, were to be tolerated.

The victory assured by Charles Grant.

It afterwards appeared that the East India Directors did not regard the new Charter as opening the door for American missionaries. Indeed, the English missionaries who applied for permission to proceed to India immediately after the passage of the Charter, were at first refused. And when the report of proceedings of the authorities at Calcutta and Bombay came before the Court, a resolution was proposed, censuring those who had favored the missionaries, and requiring the American missionaries to be removed from India. The resolution was about to pass, when the venerable Charles Grant, formerly Chairman of the Court,

1 Marshman, vol. ii. p. 45.

read an argument he had carefully prepared from official documents, defending the conduct of the missionaries in every step of their proceedings, and proving that the officials in India had mistaken the extent of their authority, and assumed powers which neither the laws of the British empire nor the laws of nations would authorize. They were not at liberty to do more than order the missionaries from the country. To send them to England, was to treat them as British subjects, or as prisoners of war; and to prohibit their going to any neutral territory, was a stretch of authority which the missionaries were not bound to obey, and to withdraw from which was no crime. The plea was successful; and the dispatches sent to Bombay admitted the object of the missionaries to be simply the promotion of religion, and authorized Sir Evan Nepean to allow them to remain. The decision was communicated to the missionaries some time in 1815.

Still farther assured by a new Governor-general.

Lord Liverpool succeeded Castlereagh as Prime Minister before the action of Parliament, and decided to supersede Lord Minto as Governor-general by the appointment of the Earl of Moira, better known by his subsequent title of the Marquis of Hastings. He was known in the war of the American Revolution as Lord Rawdon, and commanded the British army at the battle of Eutaw Springs. He must have reached Calcutta early in the autumn, since his predecessor embarked for home on the 20th of October.[1] The Earl had not the morbid dread of missionary efforts which haunted the public functionaries in Calcutta, and he had enough of independence and character to check their movements. When waited on by Messrs. Carey, Thomason, and Udny, the newly appointed committee of the American Board, with a request that he would reverse the order for the deportation of the American missionaries, he expressed his conviction that they meant to do good, and that no considerable injury could arise from their continuance in the country. This declaration was made before the adoption of the new Charter was known in India. As soon as these liberal views of the new Governor-general were reported at Bombay, all further proceedings against the missionaries were stayed. Lord Moira had left England after the sentiments of the various religious communities had been largely developed on the subject of missions, and when the table of the House of Commons was covered, night after night, with petitions.

Although the connection of the East India Com-

[1] Mr. Marshman says: "Nothing could exceed the kindliness of Lord Minto's personal feelings. There is reason to believe, moreover, that his own views were far more liberal than those of his government, but he wanted firmness to resist the influence of the clique of secretaries at Calcutta, who had been nursed up in prejudices and despotism." He reached England in March, 1814, and died a few months after, on his way to his seat in Scotland.

pany with the idolatry of the country continued thirty years longer, yet, from this time, protection was extended to missionaries, and to American missionaries not less than to English, and the government has been increasingly favorable from that day to this. The Company was dissolved soon after the great mutiny in 1857, and, to the joy of all friends of missions, Sir John Lawrence, one of the ablest and best of Christian men in India, was placed on the viceregal throne.

Subsequent tolerance and protection from the East India Company.

One cannot look back through the labors and vicissitudes of this great struggle, without admiring the singular aptitude of Carey, Grant, and Wilberforce for their allotted spheres of action. Verily the hand that made them was divine. Nor should we forget the training which Wilberforce, and the religious portion of the British empire, had received for this work, by the long struggle for the abolition of the slave-trade. These champions of religious liberty all lived to old age, and witnessed the consummation of their hopes; Grant dying in 1824, at the age of seventy-seven, Wilberforce in 1833, at the age of seventy-three, and Carey in 1834, at the age of seventy-two.

Grateful recognition of Carey, Grant, and Wilberforce.

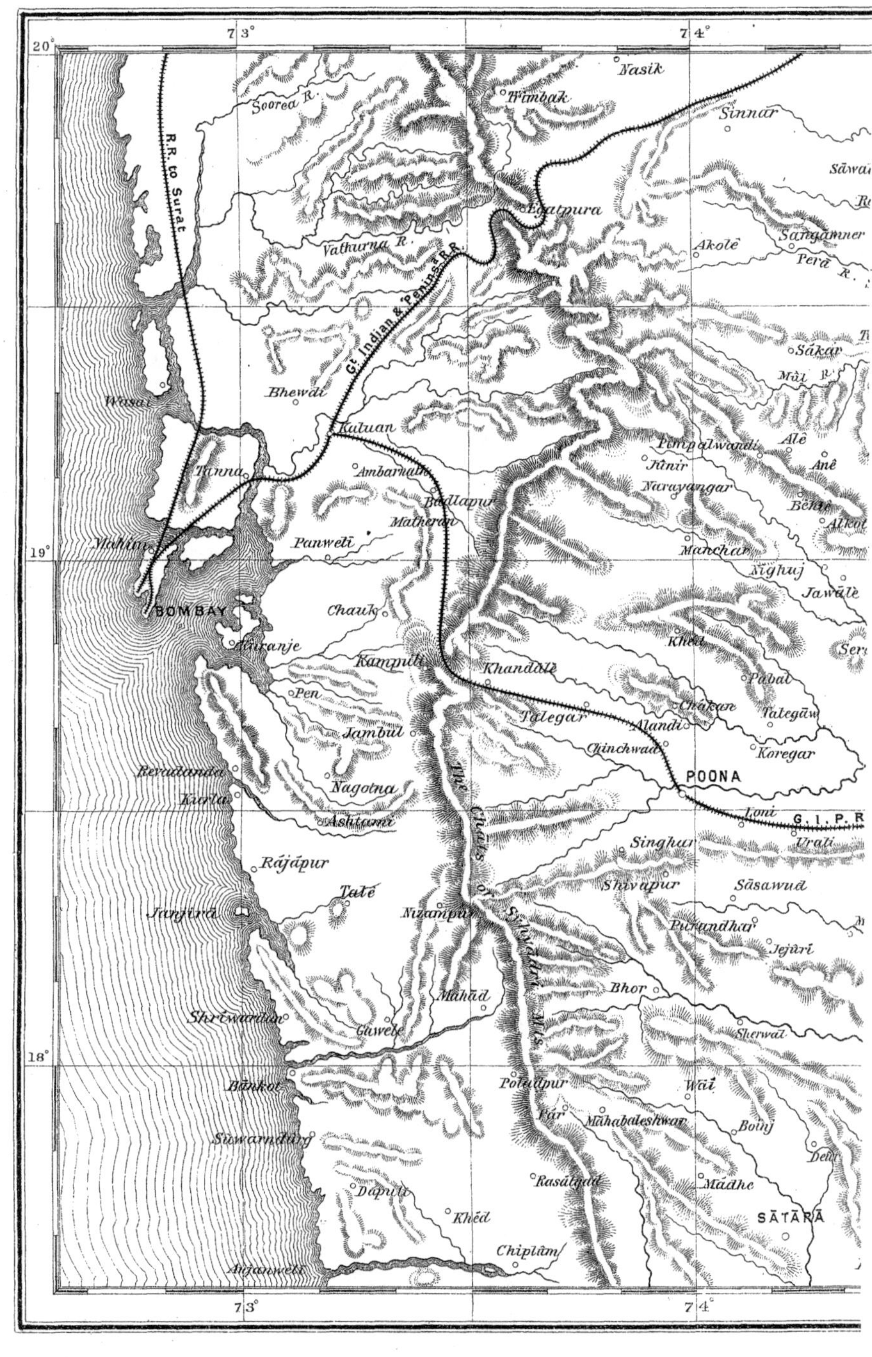

73°
74°
20°
19°
18°
Nasik
Trimbak
Soorea R.
Sinnar
R.R. to Surat
Egatpura
Vathurna R.
Gt Indian & Penins.a R.R.
Akolē
Sangamner
Perā R.
Sákar
Wasai
Bhewdi
Kuluan
Tanna
Ambarnath
Badlapur
Matheran
Mahim
Panweli
BOMBAY
Chauk
Uranje
Kampuli
Khandālē
Pen
Talegar
Jambul
Chinchwad
Alandi
POONA
Koregar
Talegāw
Pabal
Chākan
Khed
Manchar
Narayangar
Pimpalwaadi
Alē
Anē
Jawālē
Revadanda
Kurla
Nagotna
Ashtami
Rájápur
Talē
Janjira
Nizampur
Mahād
The Ghats of Sahyadri Mts
Singhar
Shivapur
Sāsawud
Purandhar
Jejuri
Loni
G.I.P.R
Urali
Bhor
Sherwal
Shriwardhan
Guwele
Bānkot
Poladpur
Par
Mahabaleshwar
Wāi
Mādhe
SĀTĀRĀ
Suwarndurg
Dapuli
Khēd
Rasalgad
Chiplun
Anjanweli

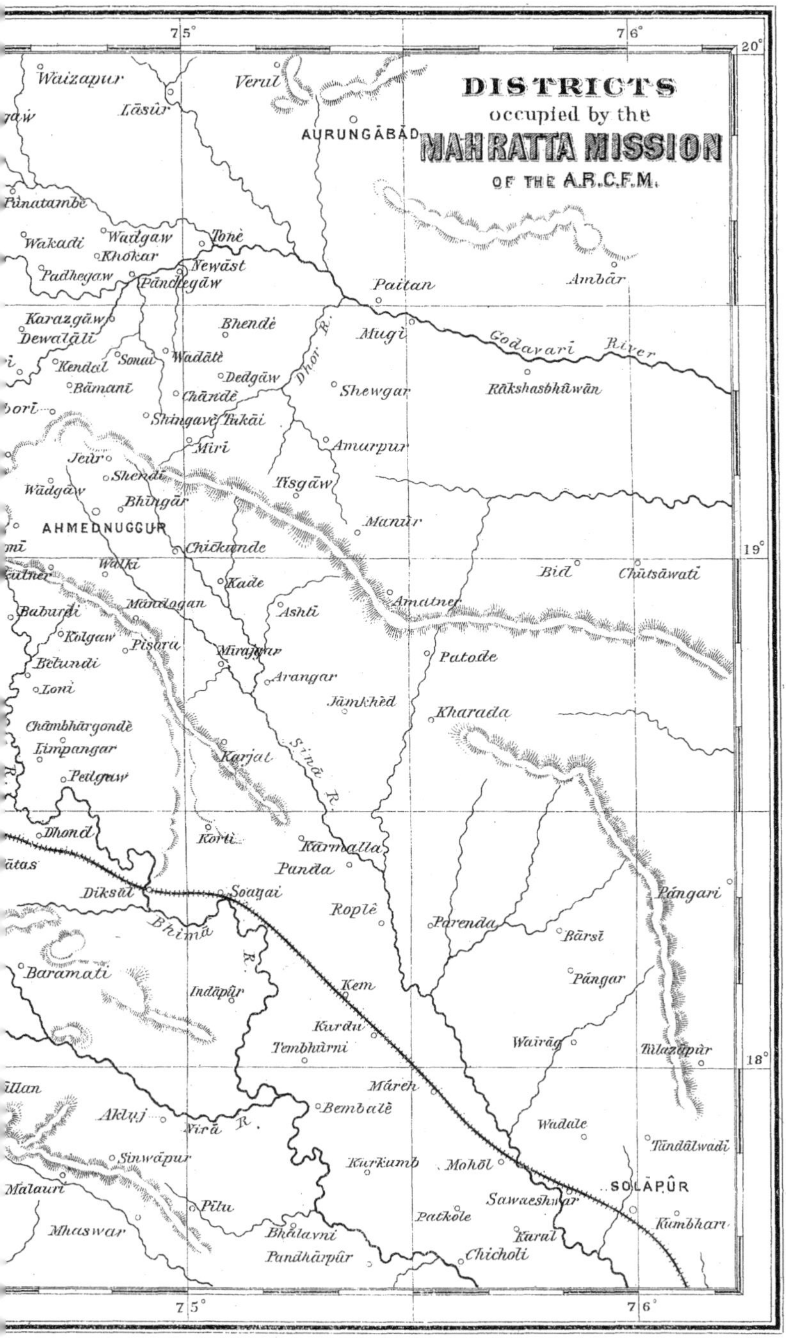

DISTRICTS
occupied by the
MAHRATTA MISSION
OF THE A.B.C.F.M.

75° 76° 20° 19° 18°

Waizapur
Lāsūr
Verul
AURUNGĀBĀD
Pūnatambe
Wakadi
Wadgaw
Khokar
Tone
Padhegaw
Newāst
Pāndegāw
Paitan
Ambār
Karazgāw
Dewalāli
Bhende
Mugi
Godavari River
Kendal
Sonai
Wadāle
Dedgāw
Bāmanī
Chānde
Shewgar
Rākshasbhūwān
Dhor R.
Shingave
Takāi
Miri
Amarpur
Jeūr
Shendi
Wādgaw
Bhingār
Tisgāw
AHMEDNUGGUR
Manūr
Chickunde
Walki
Bid
Chūtsāwati
Kade
Amatner
Baburdi
Māndogan
Ashti
Kolgaw
Pisora
Mirajgar
Patode
Belundi
Arangar
Loni
Jāmkhed
Chāmbhārgonde
Kharada
Limpangar
Karjat
Peilgaw
Sīnā R.
Dhond
Korti
Kārmalla
Panda
Diksal
Soagai
Pāngari
Roplê
Bhīmā
Parenda
Bārsī
Baramati
R.
Kem
Pāngar
Indāpūr
Kurdu
Tembhūrni
Wairāg
Tūlazāpūr
Māreh
Bembale
Aklūj
Nirā R.
Wadale
Tāndālwadi
Sinwāpur
Kurkumb
Mohōl
SOLĀPŪR
Malauri
Pilu
Sawaeshwar
Mhaswar
Bhālavni
Patkole
Kumbhari
Karal
Pandhārpūr
Chicholi

75° 76°

CHAPTER III.

MISSION TO THE MAHRATTAS.

1815–1826.

BOMBAY occupies an island on the western coast of India, and its present population exceeds eight hundred thousand. It is now connected with Christendom by telegraphic lines, and by railways with every important part of India. The Concan is a low, hot country on the adjacent continent, extending two hundred miles along the coast, and from forty to a hundred miles inland, to the Ghâts mountains, which run southward to Cape Comorin, varying in height from two thousand to seven thousand feet. Crossing these mountains to the eastward, the traveller finds no perceptible descent, but comes out among hills, and on table land two thousand feet higher than the sea.[1]

Bombay.

The Concan.

The Deccan.

The Mahrattas inhabit the Concan, the Deccan, and Central India, and number about

The Mahrattas.

[1] Mr. Elphinstone, in his *History of India*, published more than thirty years since, says the Deccan, properly speaking, includes all the country south of the Vindyâ mountains, yet, in modern practice, is often limited to the part lying between that chain and the river Kishna.

twelve millions. In the middle of the last century their formidable irregular cavalry, known as the "Mahratta Horse," overran a great part of Hindostan, and the Mahratta community on the continent partook largely of this marauding character. The victories of Sir Arthur Wellesley, afterwards Duke of Wellington, in 1803, were a check on this evil, but the Mahratta country was in a very disturbed state during the ten years from 1807 to 1817. This arose mainly from the habits of the people. But while they sought plunder, they had a country and a home, and regular occupations which they followed during the intermissions of their predatory raids. The aim of their chiefs was not booty merely, but also political power.

Their subjugation.

The avowed occasion of the war of 1817, which led to their subjugation by the English, was the plundering excursions of the Pindarrees, a low class of mounted freebooters, whose ravages, about the time of Messrs. Hall and Nott's arrival at Bombay, had become a terror to India. They followed different chiefs, in companies varying from two hundred to ten thousand, all mounted and armed, unincumbered by tents or baggage, advancing at the rate of forty or fifty miles a day, and always directly toward their prey. Their aim was not to take possession of a district, but to sweep away what was in it; and being obliged to collect their plunder in haste, they often inflicted merciless torments to enforce its delivery. They trusted to the secrecy and suddenness of their raids for avoiding the military guards, and before a force could be brought against them they were on their return. Their strength lay in making themselves intangible. If pursued, they made extraordinary marches through roads almost impracticable for regular troops. If overtaken, they dispersed, and reassembled at an appointed rendezvous. If followed into their own country, they broke into small parties, and their booty was either safely deposited in their mountain fastnesses, or under the protection of their secret allies among the neighboring chiefs.

The Pindarrees were tolerated and even encouraged by Bajee Row, the Peishwa or Sovereign of the Mahratta confederation, and by Scindia, Holkar, and other subordinate chiefs, in the hope of receiving their aid in wars with the English. Their maraudings became at length insupportable, and the Marquis of Hastings laid his plans for a comprehensive movement to eradicate the whole predatory system from western India. Accordingly, in 1817, he sent a large army to invade the country on three sides. The Peishwa, and his principal subordinates, Scindia and Holkar, took part with the Pindarrees. The last two saved themselves only by timely submission. The Pindarree leaders, Cheetoo and Kurreem, were defeated, and became wanderers in the jungles. The latter surrendered to Sir John Malcolm in February,

1818. Cheetoo refused to surrender, and sought shelter in a dense forest, where he was killed by a tiger.[1]

The hostile intentions of the Peishwa became evident as early as November, 1817, when the residence of Mr. Elphinstone at Poona was suddenly attacked, and all the property either carried off or destroyed; the Resident and his suite having barely time to mount their horses and flee. The Peishwa, being attacked soon after by the British army, commenced a retreat, which he continued for more than six months, ranging over the wide extent of the Deccan, and always distancing his pursuers by the rapidity of his march. Finding himself a hopeless fugitive, he sought to make terms, hoping to retain his rank and office. But the Governor-general, in view of his protracted hostility and treachery, insisted on an absolute surrender. On being assured of a pension of eight lacks of rupees, or about £100,000, he renounced his claims as a sovereign, and agreed to spend the rest of his days at a distance from the seat of his former power. He was conducted to Bithoor, on the Ganges, near Cawnpore;[2] a place memorable, forty years later, as the residence of his adopted son, Nana Sahib, the fiendish murderer of men, women, and children.

This brief statement of the condition of the Mah-

[1] Malcolm's *Central India*, vol. i. p. 445.

[2] Grant Duff's *History of the Mahrattas*, vol. iii. p. 477.

ratta country, in the early years of the mission, will go far toward explaining the embarrassments of such high-minded rulers as Mr. Elphinstone, when asked to sanction the first efforts to extend missionary labors into the Deccan. It will show, also, how time was needed to gain the native confidence. Nor should we fail to notice the interposition of divine Providence, which seasonably suppressed a predatory warfare that threatened to spread anarchy and devastation over western India.[1]

Missionary importance of these facts.

As a preparation for their work, the brethren now adopted "a plan of polity, or social order." They were to form a self-governing mission, in which the majority was to rule, while the minority of the missionaries, in purely missionary matters, had the right of appeal to the Prudential Committee, and ultimately to the Board at home — a right, however, which has been rarely exercised. The principle of common stock was adopted, but with a limit to individual expenditures. No member of the mission was to receive pecuniary compensation for service from any person, without the consent of the mission, and the gain thus acquired was to be placed at the disposal of the mission. This system, derived from the Serampore missionaries, was not found to work economically, and salaries, as private property, at length took the place of

Incipient measures

[1] *India, Ancient and Modern,* by David O. Allen, D. D., pp. 255, 256, note.

the common stock. The extension of the missions made it necessary, about the year 1837, to require from each mission an annual estimate of expenditures, including all important details, to be followed by annual specific appropriations by the Prudential Committee.

Mr. Nott's return home.

The climate of India affected Mr. Nott so unfavorably that, by the advice of physicians, he returned home, with Mrs. Nott, near the close of 1815; but he lived to attend the fiftieth anniversary of the Board, and died at Hartford, Connecticut, July 1, 1869, at the age of eighty-one. His wife survived him.

Obstacles to be overcome.

There was of necessity a varied work of preparation. The Mahratta language was to be acquired, portions of Scripture translated, and school-books prepared. The prejudices of heathen parents against Christian books were to be overcome, even in schools taught by heathen masters; then prejudices against schools taught by native Christian masters; and, more than all, against free boarding-schools in the families of missionaries. They were to find audiences who would hear the Gospel where no one was anxious to hear, or knew well how to behave while hearing; and to gather churches where a public profession of the Christian religion involved the loss of all things, with persecution, which only the civil power prevented from being unto death. In such circumstances, the work might well be accounted hopeless, except as it was ordered by God himself, and had the promise of divine aid.

As this was the first American mission, it seems proper that something should here be said concerning a feature in it, peculiar to modern times; namely, the employment of married missionaries.

Why married missionaries were employed.

The Apostle to the Gentiles was unmarried, though he claimed the right to marry; and so, it would seem, were Timothy and Titus, his missionary associates. So were the Nestorian and Irish missionaries, in the early and middle ages of the Christian Church; and so were those by whose labors Europe was led to adopt the Christian name. This must have arisen, mainly, from the peculiar circumstances and habits of those times. The missionaries were not then in circumstances to support families. It was not deemed wise, nor is it now, for them to look to their heathen converts for support. Were modern evangelists situated as Paul was, they would generally deem it wise to remain unmarried. The feeling was prevalent in the churches, at the outset of American missions, that those who went abroad, especially to barbarous nations, should be single men. This is within the author's distinct recollection; and the biographer of Mrs. Judson, writing in 1829, affirms the general opinion to have been decidedly opposed to the measure of sending married persons. It was deemed wild and romantic in the extreme, and altogether inconsistent with prudence and delicacy.[1] When the mission to the Sandwich Islands was projected, many apprehended, and it was even strongly asserted by some men who had visited the Islands, that women would receive brutal treatment from the islanders; and the belief was not easily shaken, that they would detract from the efficiency of a mission.

Yet the popular opinion was wrong. Those of the Apostles, whose circumstances favored it, appear to have been married men;[2] and the circumstances of modern missionaries are even more in accordance with that condition, than were those of "the brethren of the Lord and Cephas." Missionaries are now sure of support from the churches at home; and those churches probably find it easier to support a mission composed of families, than they would a less interesting mission of unmarried men. We all now see how well it was that the wives of the first missionaries were not left behind, as was proposed by the Prudential Committee. Mrs. Newell and Mrs. Judson awakened a deeper and more general interest in the churches at home than did their husbands, and amply vindicated the right of their sex to engage personally in this work. The former showed how a delicate and cultivated lady could

[1] Knowles's *Memoir of Ann H. Judson*, p. 42.

[2] Gal. ii. 9; 1 Cor. ix. 5.

"endure hardness as a good soldier of Jesus Christ." The latter, having greater opportunity and a different mental constitution, was not only a remarkable illustration of the same truth, but also of heroic courage in the face of extreme danger, and of marvelous resources in the most sudden and formidable emergencies.[1]

The missionary is worth as much more abroad, with a help-meet for him, as the pastor is at home. The wife is endowed with equal courage, and more endurance. With her at his side, he is less likely to flee from danger, and is more safe. Among barbarians the wife, the mother, and children are, under God, a defense. There are grand exceptional men like the Apostle Paul, and grand exceptional cases like his; but marriage should be the general rule, and all missionaries may claim the right with Paul, to "lead about a wife, as the other apostles."[2]

Early use of preaching.

Messrs. Hall and Newell made such progress in the language, that they were able to commence their great work of preaching before the close of the second year, though of course with a stammering tongue. As the people did not come to them, they went to the people; seeking them in the temples, markets, and other places of resort, and often reading brief portions of Scripture,

[1] See *Life of Mrs. Ann H. Judson*, by the Rev. James D. Knowles, 1830.

[2] 1 Cor. ix. 5.

which they had carefully translated. They also established schools for heathen youth, and expected large spiritual results from them.

Marriage of Mr. Hall.

Mr. Hall was married December 16, 1813, to Miss Margaret Lewis, an Egnlish lady familiar with the Hindûstanee language and native character.

Use of the press.

A press was obtained from Calcutta before the close of the year, through the aid of the Rev. Mr. Thomason, and was made available by the arrival of Rev. Horatio Bardwell, who had been sent to Bombay, rather than to Ceylon, because he had learned the art of printing.

A portion of each day was devoted to translating the Scriptures from the Hebrew and Greek, but the main business of the laborers at first was the acquisition of the Mahratta language. In 1817, beside a Harmony of the Gospels, they had translated the Evangelists, the Acts of the Apostles, several of the Epistles, and other select portions of the Bible. The Gospel of Matthew was the first printed. In view of the deficiency of native workmen, the Prudential Committee requested Messrs. Allen Graves and John Nichols, newly appointed missionaries, to acquire a knowledge of type-founding and bookbinding before leaving the country.

Comparative estimate of schools.

At that time, and long after, the Christian public were more ready to appreciate schools as a missionary agency, than the preaching of the Gospel; though probably few well informed Christians would have denied the paramount importance of the latter. In the small number of conversions during the first twelve or fifteen years, missionaries and the churches at home needed the sustaining influence of schools. Every new school, every increase in the number of scholars, every new reader of the sacred oracles, was an omen of success. Indeed it was a success; and the Secretary wrote to the missionaries that the interest of the religious community in the education of heathen children was great and increasing, so that the contributions for this object exceeded the most sanguine expectations. The Annual Report of the Board for 1817 is emphatic on this point.

The interest thus awakened at home was founded, in part, on a misapprehension of facts. The plan involved the reception of heathen children into mission families, and giving them new names, a considerable number of which were sent from this country, with the means of supporting those to whom the names should be given. It appeared, however, that the missionaries had been too confident about obtaining children for a family Christian education, even from the lower castes. The embarrassment at home from this discovery was relieved by information from the mission in Ceylon, that boarding children could there be obtained and named. A portion of the funds was accordingly transferred to that mission, and the residue was used among the different classes of half-caste children at Bombay.

The free day-schools were necessarily taught by heathen masters, as it was impossible then, and for a long time afterwards, to obtain others. Nor could the heathen have been then persuaded to send their children to Christian teachers. Every effort was made by means of school-books, personal supervision, and frequent examinations, to have the instruction Christian as far as possible. The monthly expenses of a school were from seven to twelve dollars, and the teaching was in the vernacular language. There was also a school for teaching the English language to pupils of partially European descent, who were expected to pay a certain amount for tuition.

New missionaries.

The mission was strengthened, in February, 1818, by the arrival of Messrs. Graves and Nichols and their wives. Sir Evan Nepean, the friendly Governor, consented to their remaining. Miss Philomena Thurston arrived with this company affianced to Mr. Newell, and they were married in the month following. Mr. Graves was stationed at Mahim, on the island of Bombay, and Mr. Nichols at Tanna, on Salsette; the one among sixteen thousand people, the other among sixty thousand. The missionaries made tours along the sea-coast, preaching the gospel, and distributing books.

It is interesting to observe the satisfaction which

the brethren then had in their prospects as to the schools. After stating how large a number of heathen youth were instructed in reading, writing, and arithmetic, and in some good degree as to the way of salvation through Jesus Christ, they exclaim; "Here is a measure of success far exceeding our most eager hopes. It animates our hearts, and we cannot but believe it will be highly animating to our Christian friends at home, by whose liberality these schools are supported. In them we seem to see a thousand Hindoo hands at work from year to year, undermining the fabric of Hindoo idolatry."

Interest in schools.

The first hopeful convert was a respectable Mussulman named Kader Yar Khan, from Hyderabad, a city four hundred miles southeasterly from Bombay, who had come to gain instruction in the Christian religion. This was in March, 1819. He had been awakened by reading a tract, while on a visit to Bombay, and came with a train of servants, but sent them back, and lived in retirement. He was eager for instruction, gained constantly on the confidence of the brethren, and was baptized in September, with the strong hope that he was truly born of God. Becoming a Christian laborer in the Hindûstanee, he performed several tours on the continent with books and tracts, as far eastward as his native place. The only other notice that I find of this man was in 1823. In a

The first hopeful convert.

letter then received he stated that, through his labors, five persons in Hyderabad, and the same number in Secundrabad, where he was then residing, had avowed their belief in Christianity. The mission wrote inviting him and his converts to come to Bombay, but there is no record of a response to this invitation.

A new Governor.

Sir Evan Nepean was succeeded, in the autumn of 1819, by the Hon. Mount Stuart Elphinstone, who had held a responsible position in the conduct of the Mahratta war, and was a man of much experience, of fine classical attainments, and liberal views.[1] His impressions of the irascible and warlike temper of the Mahrattas were strong, and the first application of the missionaries for leave to visit their schools on the continent, was refused.

His favorable disposition.

When afterwards visited by a missionary, he made many inquiries, and seemed apprehensive of a too rapid advance against the prejudices of the natives, thus endangering the public peace. At the same time, he approved of the general object, and, in a subsequent conversation with Mr. Hall, requested a statement as to the purpose of the schools, and the manner in which they were conducted. A memorial was therefore addressed to

[1] Among his publications were "*An Account of the Kingdom of Caubul and its Dependencies,* 2 vols., 1819 ; and *The History of India in the Hindû and Mohammedan Periods,* 1 vol., pp. 687.

him, in April, 1820, in which the missionaries stated that their schools were designed to impart useful knowledge to the children of the natives, who would otherwise receive no instruction, or what was very inferior. They expressed an earnest desire that the religion contained in the Scriptures might be made known to the inhabitants of that country, and believed that their schools would promote this end, though the influence would be gradual. Very little success could be hoped for, unless the schools were visited by the missionaries themselves.

To this memorial a favorable answer was returned, with the consent of the Governor to their visiting the schools on the continent; but he expressed the hope, that no reasonable pretext would be given the Brahmins to represent their religion as interfered with.

There were eight schools on the continent in 1822, and seventeen on the islands of Bombay and Salsette, with an average attendance of more than one thousand pupils. We consider our schools, say the brethren, as a very important part of our mission, and are confident that they will be the means of effecting much good. In consequence of an unavoidable delay in remitting funds, it became necessary to suspend ten of them.

Mr. Bardwell suffered from the climate, and having no prospect of continued life in India, he returned to the United States in 1821, Return of Mr. Bardwell.

where, by the advice of able physicians, he spent the residue of a long life. He lived forty-six years after returning from India, and died greatly respected by all who knew him. His widow and companion in the mission still lives.

Death of Mr. Newell.

On the 30th of May, 1821, the mission suffered a great loss in the death of the beloved Mr. Newell, who was a victim to cholera, which had for some time been raging in India. So overpowering was the disease, that he could give no expression of his feelings; but none was needed. Mr. Newell was one of the four young men whose memorial called the American Board into existence, and his devotion to the cause was beyond all question. He generally enjoyed good health, but in his later years his feelings were at times deeply moved by the woeful condition of the heathen, and by a sense of his own responsibilities. Shortly before the sickness, he spent several days with Mr. Nichols at Tannah, and visited a great number of sick and dying. His death was extensively felt as a public loss.

Arrival of a printer.

The Providence which called Mr. Bardwell from the care of the press, kindly brought Mr. Garrett, a professed printer, soon after to Bombay, where his services were more needed than in Ceylon. Sir Edward Barnes, Governor of that island, had refused him permission to remain. He subsequently married Mrs. Newell, who survived him, and died, many years afterwards, in her native land.

A house was erected for public worship at Bombay in 1822, costing, with the land, between four and five thousand dollars, a fourth part of which was contributed in India. It had two stories, the upper for a chapel, the lower for the press, with verandas for schools. This was the first Protestant place of worship, designed for natives, in the vast region from Cape Comorin to the Russian empire, and from India to the Mediterranean.[1]

First native Protestant place of worship.

About this time some difficulties arose at Poona, the former capital of the Mahrattas, in consequence of the circulation of Christian books among the natives. There appears to have been no real cause for apprehension, but the books were seized and sent back to Bombay, with the native agents employed in their circulation, and an order was issued by the government forbidding missionary efforts in the Deccan. Such an order could not pass without a respectful remonstrance, and Mr. Hall prepared one, setting forth the useful nature of the mission and its operations, and requesting a repeal of the order. The Governor replied, that that territory was but newly subjected to British rule, and the request could not be granted with safety to the public peace. The order did not relate

Interference on the Continent.

1 *Missionary Herald*, 1823, p. 314.

solely to the American mission, for Scottish missionaries who afterwards obtained a permanent footing at Poona, were also excluded, nor was the order long in force. As if to take from the apparent harshness of the measure, the government readily granted the request of the mission for a burying-ground, and spontaneously inclosed it at the public expense with a substantial wall, thus showing that the mission was regarded as a permanent institution.

Yet the missionaries had apprehensions, and wrote to their good friend Mr. Money, then in England and a member of Parliament. That gentleman immediately advised the Board to send additional missionaries to Bombay, and promised to use his influence in their behalf. Accordingly the Rev. Edmund Frost and wife sailed for India in September, 1823, accompanied by Mrs. Graves, who had visited the United States for the benefit of her health. The government made no objection to Mr. Frost's joining the mission.

Reception of a new missionary.

Scarcely, however, had it begun to feel the benefit of this reinforcement, before it was called to mourn the death of another beloved member. Late in the autumn of 1824, Mr. Nichols went over to the southern Concan for the purpose of preaching and visiting the schools in that quarter. On reaching Revadanda sixteen miles from Bombay, he became too ill with fever to proceed

Death of Mr. Nichols.

further. Tidings were brought to his brethren, and they succeeded in bringing him to Bombay, but not until ten days after the commencement of his illness, and when he was speechless and nearly insensible. He died in the following night, December 9, 1824. His death was severely felt, as he was of an excellent spirit and firm in the discharge of his duty, a man of prayer and intent on the salvation of the heathen. He was a judicious counselor, a warm and devoted friend, and peculiarly acceptable to several English families residing in and near Tannah, to whom he had been the means of spiritual good. He had successfully studied the character and language of the people, and deserves strong commendation for his economy, diligence, and the conscientious performance of his duty.

School for Jewish girls.

A school for Jewish girls was commenced at Bombay this year, and another of eighty-four Jewish boys and girls at Revadanda. The whole number in the schools at this time, exceeded fifteen hundred. A Mahratta woman named Gunga was employed in a school for girls, and entered upon the business with rare courage and alacrity. But in the midst of great hopes as to her success, she was suddenly cut down by cholera. Among those who had left the schools, the missionaries knew of many boys and young men, who could read with a fluency and propriety far surpassing a great majority of the common brahmins. These, when met in the country, were found among the first to read the Christian Scriptures and tracts.

In the year 1825 the missionaries thus contrasted their condition with what it was ten years before. "There was then no school to catechize, no school-room in which to speak of salvation, no chapel to preach in from morning to night, no portions of God's Word to circulate, no Christian tracts to distribute. Now we see a house built for God, and hear his Word proclaimed in it. There are thirty-five school-rooms to be used, had we the laborers, as so many meeting-houses; thirty-five schools containing two thousand children calling for evangelical instruction, and five times as many districts calling for additional schools. There are the means, had we more help, of printing and distributing annually a hundred thousand tracts and portions of the Bible, and a half million of souls to whom we might have familiar access for preaching the Gospel, while the field for pushing onward all these operations is opening wider every day. Things being thus, is it extravagant to say that a missionary now can in the same period employ five or ten times as many of the appointed means of salvation among these natives, as could possibly have been used here ten years ago?"

Ten years compared.

In November, 1825, an Association was formed by the missionaries of the American Board, the Church Missionary Society at Bombay,

Association of missionaries.

the London Missionary Society at Surat and Belgaum, and the Scottish Missionary Society in the Southern Concan; and the following Rules and Principles of the Union were adopted :—

"1. That an Association be now formed, and called *The Bombay Missionary Union.*

"2. That it be understood that the members of this Union hold the distinguishing doctrines of the Reformation, without compromising any of those tenets on which they may conscientiously differ.

"3. That the object of this Union be to promote Christian fellowship, and to consult on the best means of advancing the kingdom of Christ in this country.

"4. That any other Protestant mission may join this Association.

"5. That an Annual Meeting be held at such place as may from time to time be agreed upon, which shall commence on the first Monday of December, and be open to all Protestant missionaries, ministers, and others, who may be disposed to promote its object.

"6. That at each anniversary the minutes of the preceding meeting be read, two sermons preached relating to missionary concerns, an account of the different missions for the past year laid before the meeting, the missions which are to furnish preachers for the ensuing year designated, and a suitable portion of time spent in special prayer and in religious and moral discussion.

"7. That, according to the seniority of the different missions, a Chairman and Secretary shall come in yearly from them by rotation."

From the sermon preached by Mr. Hall at the meeting of this Union, I extract the following: "If, therefore, we know what were the conversion, love, repentance, faith, hope, and zeal of Paul, we know, in substance, what are the conversion, love, repentance, faith, hope, and zeal of every true disciple of Jesus. Circumstantial diversities there manifestly are among the different members of Christ's body, but the ground-work in every new-born soul is one. The great outlines of the Christian character are everywhere the same. It is but one image, and that — O wonder of wonders! — the image of the God of glory, which is stamped, by the Holy Ghost in regeneration upon the whole assembly of the redeemed, a multitude which no man can number."

Mr. Hall's sermon.

The month preceding the death of Mr. Nichols, Mr. Hall went to the Ghâts, chiefly to look for a health retreat, going by way of Bankote and thence to Mahad at the head of navigation on the Bankote river. From thence he travelled on foot twelve miles to Beladpû. Ten miles further on he rested at Parr, a small village with a market, where the only lodging place for Europeans was a temple open on one side, but with a wall of masonry on the other three occupied by

Mr. Hall's excursion on the Continent.

the idol. Securing a spot most protected from the winds, with the help of his blankets and a fire, he slept tolerably well. The next day he reached Mahabaleshwar, where the mission, thirty years afterwards, had a sanitary station. The place was famed for a spring of excellent water, which was the reputed source of the Krishna river. His return was by the same route, and he reached home on the 29th.

The worship in the mission chapel being defective in the department of song, the mission adapted the most appropriate native tunes to hymns they had themselves prepared.

Improvement in the worship.

The printing establishment was now enriched with new and improved type, and the British and Foreign Bible Society presented a hundred reams of paper for printing the translation of the New Testament, which had been completed and revised by the mission. Our hopes, said Mr. Hall, are often revived by reflecting that we have distributed more than one hundred thousand Christian books.

Publishing the Scriptures.

Mr. Frost died of consumption on the 18th of October, 1825. Though less than a year and a half in the mission, he had shown the genuineness and fervor of his devotion to the cause, and was enabled to meet death with a hope full of immortality. He encouraged his wife to remain a missionary after his decease, which she

Death of Mr. Frost.

did, having seen the need there was in that country for the labors of Christian women.

Visit of Mrs. Hall to the United States.

The two sons of Mr. Hall were much out of health, and the only hope of prolonging the life of the oldest, then four years of age, was in a voyage and change of climate. Mrs. Hall therefore embarked for America in a Salem vessel with her two children, expecting to leave them in this country for education. Toward the close of the voyage the eldest, whose restoration had been the principal object, died of fever. The other, now the Rev. Gordon Hall, D. D., of Northampton, Massachusetts, arrived in good health November 18, 1825.

Death of Mr. Hall.

On the 2d of March, 1826, Mr. Hall entered upon his last tour, taking with him two lads who had been inmates of the mission families, and reached Trimbukeshwar on the 11th, and Nassick on the 15th, both populous and celebrated places, the latter about a hundred miles from Bombay. At both these places he found the people in great consternation on account of the recent appearance of the cholera. It was then making dreadful ravages at Nassik. More than two hundred died on the day of his arrival. He labored among the distressed population till he had nearly exhausted his supply of books and medicines. On the 18th he left for Bombay, and at 10 o'clock P. M. on the 19th arrived at Dûrlee D'hapûr, about thirty miles on his way homeward, and put up at a heathen temple for the night. Spreading his mat in the veranda of the temple he lay down to sleep. As it was cold he sought a warmer place, which he found occupied by two sick men, one of whom soon died. Finding no good accommodations there he returned to his former position in the veranda. At four in the morning of March 20th, he called up the lads and began preparations for the journey, when he was suddenly seized with the cholera. So sudden and violent were the spasms, that he fell helpless to the ground. Being laid upon his mat, he attempted to take a small quantity of medicine which remained in his possession, but it was immediately rejected. He then told his attendants that he should not recover. After giving directions to the lads concerning his watch, clothing, etc., and the manner in which they should dispose of his body, he assured them and the natives who stood around him, that he should soon be with Christ. He exhorted them to repent of their sins and forsake their idols, that they too might go to heaven, and prayed earnestly for his wife and children, for his missionary brethren, and for the heathen around him. Repeating thrice, "Glory to Thee, O God," he yielded up his spirit.

The lads had much difficulty in procuring a grave. They laid him, shrouded in his blanket and coffinless, in his humble bed. He had been sick eight hours, and died in the forty-second year of his age.

A stone monument has been erected by the mission to mark the spot of his interment, bearing both in English and Mahratta the name, age, and office of their beloved fellow-laborer.

His character.

The writer saw Gordon Hall at his ordination in February, 1812, at Salem, but had no personal acquaintance with him, nor has he any recollection of his appearance. There is said to be no portrait of him. But his high qualities as a man, a Christian, and a missionary, made an impression on the Christian mind of his own and succeeding generations. He was one of the young men whose names will ever stand connected with the origin of the American Board. His self-consecration to the work of foreign missions dates back to his college life, and he was made for a leader in the enterprise.

Mental energy was the most prominent of Mr. Hall's natural qualities, and fitted him for great undertakings. It was more, however, the admirable combination of this with other excellent qualities, such as piety, industry, judgment, courage, and decision, that qualified him for the responsible station to which Providence assigned him. The Apostle to the Gentiles was his exemplar and study, whom however he resembled more in the strength and decision of his character, than in the gentler sympathies. He was more largely endowed with the diplomatic talent than any of his associates, and in favoring circumstances the rhetorical and logical exercise of this talent would have placed him in the front rank of diplomatists. The purpose of the India government to send him away from India, was met by a stronger purpose to remain; and the forcible and eloquent memorials which, through the divine blessing, ultimately secured the right to labor in India, are understood to have been from his pen. Severest among the trials of his faith must have been his toiling through twelve years with scarcely a hopeful convert. But he could appreciate the circumstances, and saw that he was laying the foundations of a magnificent structure to the glory of his Redeemer.

Mrs. Hall long survived her husband, and died in the year 1868, at Northampton, Massachusetts, in the house of her much respected son, who testifies concerning her, that she loved the American Board, and taught him to love it.

Death of Mrs. Hall.

CHAPTER IV.

MISSION TO THE MAHRATTAS.

1826–1834.

State of the Mission.

THE death of Mr. Hall made it necessary for Mr. Graves to reside in Bombay. The mission was now reduced to two members; and subsequently there were seldom more than two in that city at one time, who were able to converse with the people. In education there was a material advance. A separate school was established for girls, and with generous aid from English residents, the number of the schools was increased to ten, containing three hundred and eighty pupils. Among the more liberal contributors were Sir John Malcolm then Governor, and Mr. Elphinstone the late Governor, both of whom had witnessed the progress of the mission from the beginning. The government allowed the erection of school-houses in four unoccupied lots within the city.

Hopeful converts.

A teacher in one of the schools became a convert to Christianity, and gave pleasing evidence of piety on her death-bed. Her conduct in the near prospect of death, excited the attention of friends, and the mother came regularly to the chapel, and listened with much interest to the preaching. This she continued to do until health failed, and during her whole sickness she declared her strong faith in Christ as the Saviour of the world. Her prayers were addressed to Him, and her hope of salvation was in Him alone. Thus she died.

Messrs. Cyrus Stone and David O. Allen joined the mission in 1827, with their wives and Miss Cynthia Farrar. Mrs. Frost was married to Mr. Woodward of the American mission in Ceylon, and Mrs. Nichols to Mr. Knight of the Church Missionary Society on that island.

New missionaries.

A revised edition of the New Testament was published at the expense of the British and Foreign, and Bombay Auxiliary Bible Societies; also several religious tracts, and a revised hymn-book.

A revised New Testament.

A native superintendent of schools toward the close of 1824 requested admission to the church. The missionaries were hopeful concerning him, but not being fully satisfied as to his piety, adopted the somewhat novel expedient of associating him with other attendants on public worship in what they called a "Mission Chapel Congregation." The subscribers bound themselves to attend public worship, and regard the missionaries as their pastors; and the missionaries engaged to

"Mission Chapel Congregation."

watch over them, and minister to them in affliction as Christian pastors. I find no evidence that this arrangement lasted long. The first native admitted to the church at Bombay was from the Chapel Congregation. This was in November 1825.

Babajee, a brahmin convert.

Babajee, a brahmin, came to Bombay in 1823, and was employed as teacher in one of the schools. In the spring of 1828, the mission adopted a rule, that all persons in their employ should stand during prayer in the chapel. This was proper in itself, was practiced elsewhere, and not forbidden by the Hindû sacred books. But the brahmins of Bombay were afraid that so much compliance with Christian customs would lead to more, and in the end endanger the Hindû religion; so a combination was formed against it. All the brahmin teachers except Babajee left the service of the mission; and he was threatened with a loss of caste, should he comply with the rule. At least a thousand brahmins were believed to be present at one of the councils assembled to consider his case; and the penances imposed on him were so humiliating, that he retired for a season to the Deccan. The storm soon blew over. Other teachers were eager applicants for the vacated places, and many brahmins returned to the schools and conformed to the rule. Babajee came back, and resumed his duties as teacher, but of course with a diminished regard for brahminism. In 1831 he publicly professed his faith in Christ.

The girls' schools had their first public examination in the autumn of 1828. Somewhat more than three hundred girls were present, whose ages varied from six to eighteen. Mr. Graves examined them in reading, writing, and the catechism, and Miss Farrar exhibited specimens of plain sewing. The scene was full of interest and encouragement.

The girls' schools.

There were supposed to be not far from eighteen thousand Roman Catholics in Bombay. A few were descended from the Portuguese, but most were of Hindû origin, whose ancestors entered the Romish church two centuries before. Bombay was then a Portuguese colony, and great efforts were made by the Jesuits, aided by the whole power and patronage of the government, to multiply proselytes. These converts were left in nearly the same state of superstition and idolatry in which they were found. It is not known how far their long-continued isolation from Hindû social life was attributable to the enforcing power of caste. They were of course accessible to Jesuits on the revival of their efforts in India.

Roman Catholics.

The fourth annual meeting of the Missionary Union was held in October, 1828, and continued for several days. Encouraging reports were made from the several missions, sermons were delivered, important subjects relating to missionary operations were discussed, there was a gen-

The Missionary Union.

eral examination of the schools for females, a day of fasting was observed, and the Lord's Supper administered.

Nor was the press idle. The second edition of the

The press.

Mahratta New Testament was in progress, at the expense of the British and Foreign Bible Society. The characters for printing the native language were so large, that five thousand copies of the Testament cost six thousand dollars. An edition of Mahratta hymns was in press, and religious tracts were printed for the Bombay Tract Society. A monthly magazine in the English language, called the "Oriental Christian Spectator," was commenced at private expense, and edited for a time by the joint labors of an American and a Scottish missionary and two English laymen.

In 1831 a legacy of seven thousand rupees

Legacy and church building.

($3,500) was bequeathed by an English resident at Bombay for the support of public worship in connection with the American mission. Twenty-four years afterwards, this was applied to the building of a more commodious house of worship. A score of teachers, with nearly two hundred of the more advanced pupils, among them several brahmins, were accustomed to meet there for a catechetical exercise in the Scriptures. The school-houses were occasionally transformed into little

Preaching by the wayside.

sanctuaries. Much divine truth was also dispensed by the wayside, and in places of public concourse; and the hearers were sometimes as many as the speaker could reach with his voice. Early in 1830 Mr. Stone made a tour of eleven days on the continent; and Mr. Graves another of two hundred miles, in which he visited the grave of Mr. Hall, and erected a small monument to mark the place.[1]

Additions to the mission.

The additions to the mission in the six years following 1829, were Messrs. William Hervey, Hollis Read, William Ramsey, George W. Boggs, Sendol B. Munger, Henry Ballantine, Amos Abbott, William C. Sampson, Elijah A. Webster, and George W. Hubbard. Messrs. Sampson and Webster were printers, and Mr. Hubbard superintendent of schools. All were married men, and there were two single females, — Misses Orpah Graves and Abigail H. Kimball, the former of whom married Mr. Allen, and the latter Mr. Stone.

Popularity of girls' schools.

The power of the Gospel is nowhere more visible than among the girls and women of India. Nothing else could reach them. The twelve schools for girls in Bombay contained four hundred pupils, and their proficiency was securing much popular favor to the schools. Sir John Malcolm, the Governor of Bombay, presented the American missionaries with three hundred rupees for

[1] The author has the impression that, although more than forty years have elapsed, the last earthly resting-place of that remarkable man has as yet no fitting memorial.

them, and other English friends added twelve hundred more. The girls were learning to read printed books, but had a prejudice against needle-work as being mean and degrading, but Miss Farrar had so far overcome this prejudice that they were becoming fond of it, of course greatly to their advantage when they had families to care for. The boys' school at Nagotna, one of the best in the mission, contained thirty-five brahmin boys, and forty readers, most of whom had committed to memory the commandments and catechism, and understood the simple rules of arithmetic. In another place were two schools composed entirely of brahmin children.

Schools of brahmin boys.

It was obvious in 1831, that the field was growing in interest. Eighteen years before, the natives had never heard the Gospel preached. No part of the Scriptures had been translated. Nothing had been done to attract attention to the Christian religion. The missionaries were indeed in Bombay, but were without a knowledge of the language, without books, or printing press, or schools, without a place for preaching, without the favor of government, and wholly unknown to the native population. And when they contemplated the structure of society, so artificial, so bound up in the idolatry and laws of India which made the forfeiture of property the penalty for renouncing the Veda, or the Koran, they must have

Signs of progress.

regarded the visible results of their labors as certainly remote. But now the note of preparation was heard, the language was acquired, the New Testament and portions of the Old were translated and printed, elementary school-books were published, schools were established, a house of worship was built in the centre of Bombay, and opened regularly for all who would enter, the markets and other public places were frequented for conversation and preaching, journeys were made in the interior, and schools were multiplied. After a residence of twelve years, Mr. Hall declared that the facilities for making men acquainted with the Gospel had multiplied tenfold since his arrival in 1813. At the time of our present survey, there were eight missionary stations within the Presidency of Bombay, connected with five different societies, British and American, and the government protected the Christian missionary in every part of the country. The printing at Bombay from April, 1817, to the close of 1830, was about 10,000,000 of pages; in the last twenty-two months of that period it was nearly 3,000,000. The larger part of the expense was borne by the British and Foreign Bible Society. A lithographic press was received by the mission, and rendered valuable assistance.

Interesting cases.

In October, 1830, two members of the church died, one a native of Denmark, who had been recovered from a profligate life through the instrumentality of Mr. Hall, and another from Massachusetts, who had been hopefully converted at the Sandwich Islands. He was born in one of the most enlightened portions of the world, learned the preciousness of the gospel from missionaries in an island remote from his native land, and at the opposite side of the globe was received into the church by other missionaries sent forth by the same Society.

Mr. Garrett had charge of the press ten years. The close of his life, which occurred on the 16th of July, 1831; at the early age of thirty-four, was happy. On the day preceding, the score of native workmen in the office called to see him, and as he addressed them in Mahratta with appropriate exhortations, many of them sobbed aloud. His strength failing he bade them farewell, but they retired reluctantly from the room.

Death of Mr. Garrett.

Mrs. Hervey died of cholera on the third of May 1831, not long after her arrival. Her husband then removed to Ahmednuggur, and became a victim of the same disease on the 13th of the next May. They were lovely in their lives, and in their deaths not long divided. I remember the very expressive countenance of Mrs. Hervey, when taking her last look of friends in her native land while the ship slowly receded from the wharf. She was from Hadley, Massachusetts. The close of life was to her exceedingly joyful. Twice she repeated

Death of Mr. and Mrs. Hervey.

that beautiful stanza, "Jesus can make a dying bed." One who stood near her said, "O death, where is thy sting? O grave, where is thy victory? The sting of death is sin, and the strength of sin is the law." With animation she exclaimed, "But thanks be unto God, which giveth us the victory through our Lord Jesus Christ." Mr. Allen said he hoped the Saviour would be with her as she walked through the dark valley. "If this," she said, "be the dark valley, it has not a dark spot in it — all is light, light." At one time she wanted words to express her views of the majesty and glory of Christ. "It seems," she said, "that if all other glory were annihilated, and noth-nothing left but his bare self (as she expressed it), it would be enough, it would be a universe of glory."[1]

Mrs. Hervey's dying experience.

Mr. Hervey's illness accomplished its painful mission in a few hours, and such was its violence that he was scarcely able to express more than his confidence of soon meeting his Redeemer and Lord. He possessed a fine and well cultivated mind, was able to converse in the language of the country, and had awakened high hopes as to his future usefulness.

Death of Mr. Hervey.

Messrs. Allen and Read attended a meeting of the Missionary Union at Poona in 1831, where the Scottish missionaries had a station, and after-

[1] *Missionary Herald* for 1831, p. 379.

wards visited many parts of the Deccan to ascertain the most eligible place for an interior station. They selected the city of Ahmednuggur, and the station was commenced in the closing month of the year by Messrs. Graves, Hervey, and Read. Babajee was their native helper. The city is upon a plain twelve or fifteen miles in extent, about one hundred and seventy-five miles easterly from Bombay. Its population was not far from fifty thousand. Once a seat of Moslem power, its palaces, mosks, aqueducts, and numerous ruins show it to have been a place of much splendor. It was surrounded by a high wall of stone and clay four or five miles in extent, and there was a strong fort a mile east of the city, half a league in circumference, with a cantonment of English soldiers. In the vicinity were numerous villages easy of access. The climate was healthful. Before the end of the second year three natives of low caste, in whose conversion Babajee had been much interested, were received into the church, and the brahmin convert wept for joy. Before leaving Bombay he had been united in Christian marriage to a widow, whose husband, dying before they were old enough to live together, had left her to a forced life of solitary wretchedness.

Ahmednuggur selected for a new station.

Its advantages.

Babajee's marriage.

Another native helper transferred from Bombay to Ahmednuggur was Dajiba, mentioned in the missionary journals of 1830 as a reader of the Scriptures and candidate for baptism. He belonged to one of the higher castes, and said in view of impending persecution, "Let my caste take my life for embracing Christianity if they choose. Better to lose my life, than my soul." Some time after, returning home in the evening he was met by several men in a cart, one of whom recognized him and cried out, "There is the apostate." Three of them then jumped out, knocked him down, tore his clothes, and beat and kicked him till he was unable to walk home; and he was confined to his house for a week. The offenders immediately drove off and escaped.

Dajiba, another helper.

In the early part of 1833 a church was organized at Ahmednuggur. Babajee was made an elder, and Dajiba a deacon. The pastoral relation was sustained by Mr. Read, one of the missionaries. If they had had twenty years more of experience, Babajee would probably have been made the pastor. The members of the church formed themselves into a society for promoting Christian morals, and adopted a score of rules, drawn up by Babajee.[1]

New church and native officers.

The wife of Babajee was awakened by witnessing the peaceful death of Mr. Hervey, and was received into the church in 1832. She had learned to read and to sew, and, in the absence of

Remarkable native Christian woman.

[1] For these Rules, see *Report of the Board for* 1833, p. 57.

her husband and of Mr. and Mrs. Read, she daily read the Scriptures and prayed with the converts and others, who were accustomed to attend the family worship of the mission. On the Sabbath she assembled them in her own house at the customary hours, prayed with them, and read and explained the Scriptures as she was able.

Labors on the continent.

Most of the large villages on the shore of the continent had been visited by the missionaries, and some of them repeatedly, from Basseen thirty miles north of Bombay to Rajapûr more than a hundred miles south. In a number of villages, each with a population of from fifteen hundred to two thousand, Christian schools had long been supported and supplied with Christian books by the mission. They were all accessible by water from Bombay.

Public discussions with brahmins and others.

In the year 1832 the Rev. John Wilson, now Dr. Wilson, a member of the Scottish mission, engaged in a discussion with intelligent natives through the press. A learned Mahratta, conceiving himself able to refute all the objections brought against the Hindû religion, proposed a public discussion with Mr. Wilson. This was attended by a great number of brahmins and other respectable natives, some of whom gave much aid to the prime mover, and was continued six successive evenings, till the brahmins proposed its termination. The native disputant then published a treatise entitled "A Verification of the Hindû Religion," and challenged Mr. Wilson to write a reply, which was readily done. The same missionary, who was long since numbered among the learned men of India, also conducted a controversy with some leading Parsees, carried on chiefly in two native periodicals. The editor of one of the periodicals being furnished with copies of the Gospel of Matthew for each of his subscribers, went so far as to recommend the Gospel to their perusal.

Mrs. Allen died on the 5th of February, 1832, and Mr. Allen made a visit to the United States early in the following year, with his motherless son. He soon became so strongly impressed with the growing disposition among the churches at home to supply the heathen world with the Scriptures and other religious books, that he hastened his return to India, intending to itinerate four years as a Bible and tract distributor, and preach the gospel wherever he left the printed word.

Rev. D. O. Allen.

Mr. and Mrs. Boggs arrived in September, 1832, and proceeded to Ahmednuggur, where Mr. and Mrs. Read were then alone, with the native assistants Babajee and Dajiba. Mr. Read and Babajee visited more than fifty villages within a hundred miles of their station, not more than two of which were known to have been previously visited by a missionary. At one place, containing about twenty-five thousand inhabitants,

A new missionary.

Extensive preaching tours.

the native government published an order forbidding the people to hear them, and threatening to fine every person who should receive one of their books. The mandate of the government was openly disregarded by the people, all classes coming to obtain books and hear the preachers, and nowhere had they such large audiences. They parted with all the books they could spare, but were not able to supply the demand.

Death and character of Babajee.

Mr. William C. Sampson, a printer, arrived, with his wife, in May, 1833. In April of that year, the native assistant Babajee died at Ahmednuggur. Being by birth a brahmin, he knew the prejudices and superstitions of his people, and was familiar with their sacred books. He knew how proud yet degraded they were, how credulous yet suspicious, how wise yet ignorant, how religious and yet how ungodly. His appeals to the corrupt priesthood from which he came out, were as pointed arrows, prepared not in the spirit of rancorous bitterness but of divine love. They could not but respect him for the adroitness with which he used his weapons, though they hated him as a deserter from their cause. His devout deportment, the thousands of books he distributed, his exhortations and prayers, his frequent discussions with the brahmins, his preaching at Ahmednuggur, and in more than fourscore towns and villages in the Deccan, must have left an abiding influence.[1] His pious widow was in due time married to Dajiba.

Mr. and Mrs. Graves had visited their native land, as a last resort for the restoration of his health, and returned in 1833; and on the 7th of August Mrs. Atossa Stone died at Bombay.

Death of Mrs. Stone.

A change was made about this time in the native service of song at Bombay. The native tunes were found better adapted to the language and feelings of the people, than any in use among us. A collection of Christian hymns was therefore made to take the place of the hymns set to European music, and the singing of the native tunes attracted many to the sanctuary.

Change in the service of song.

The year 1833 was distinguished for itineracies. In January Mr. Read and Babajee visited nineteen villages northeast of Ahmednuggur, that had never before seen a missionary. In March Mr. Read crossed the country, two hundred miles, to the Mahabaleshwar Hills, going by way of Satara, the capital of a nominally independent Rajah. In December Messrs. Read and Ramsey spent fourteen days in visiting the mission schools on the continent, which they found in a prosperous condition. The same brethren, at the close of the month, commenced an extended tour in the Concan and Deccan;

Extensive preaching tours.

[1] A Memoir of him was prepared and published, both in Mahratta and English, entitled, in English, *The Christian Brahmin, or Memoirs of Babajee,* in two volumes, by Rev. Hollis Read.

going first along the coast one hundred miles to Tannah and Bhewndy; thence across the Ghâts to Ahmednuggur, two hundred miles; thence eastward to Jalna, northeastward to Aurungabad, northwardly to Ellora, and back to Ahmednuggur; in all, two hundred and fifty miles. Mr. Ramsey now returned to Bombay; and Mr. Read, with Mr. Allen, who had arrived at Ahmednuggur, proceeded to Panderpûr, one hundred and twenty-five miles southward; thence sixty-five miles westwardly to Phatan. Here the travellers separated, and Mr. Read proceeded to the Mahabaleshwar Hills, where Mrs. Read had been residing for the restoration of her health. The whole distance travelled by Mr. Read had exceeded seven hundred miles; and these tours, for preaching and distributing the Scriptures and religious tracts, were performed among the most energetic of the Hindû race. Mr. Read had travelled among a people not many years before addicted to plunder, without arms or a guard, the mode most becoming missionaries of the Gospel of peace, and had met with neither insult nor harm. His safety he attributed, under God, to the humble style in which he travelled, in the spirit of our Saviour's charge to his first missionaries.

New missionaries.

Messrs. Henry Ballantine and Elijah A. Webster and their wives joined the mission in October, 1835. Mr. Webster knew how to manufacture types and stereotype plates. Miss

Kimball had married Mr. Stone. Mrs. Ramsey had died suddenly of cholera; and Mr. Ramsey's health was so prostrated that, on the urgent recommendation of physicians, and with the unanimous consent of his brethren, he returned to the United States, taking with him his two little children; nor was he able again to return to India.

Death of Mrs. Ramsey, and her husband's return.

It is an interesting fact, which I state on my personal knowledge, that when Mr. Graves was informed by an eminent physician in Boston, that he could not recover, he requested, as a favor from the Prudential Committee, that he might return and spend the residue of his days, and be buried, where he had so delightfully spent his life as a missionary. That consent was cheerfully given, and he lived longer than he probably would have done in his native land; long enough to perform useful service as a translator of the Scriptures.

Missionary devotion of Mr. Graves.

The health of Mr. Sampson, the printer, had failed before the arrival of Mr. Webster, and he had embarked, with Mrs. Sampson, on a voyage for Singapore, hoping to arrest the progress of consumption, to which he was constitutionally inclined. Mr. Boggs accompanied them down the coast; but they could go no farther than Aleppie, where Mr. Sampson died.

Death of Mr. Sampson.

The amount of travel which Mr. Read performed

without apparent injury to his health, is surprising; but the constitution of Mrs. Read was delicate, and her life was repeatedly in great danger from attacks of serious illness. They therefore, with the advice of the mission, sailed for home in March, 1835; and the same cause which brought them home prevented their return to India. The active mind of Mr. Read has since found useful employment through the press. His departure made it necessary for Mr. Allen to spend much time at Ahmednuggur, where his preaching service on Sabbath afternoons was often crowded, though the brahmins tried him by their opposition.

Return of Mr. and Mrs. Read.

In the autumn of 1834, Mr. Allen visited Jalna, a hundred and twenty miles northeast of Ahmednuggur, in the dominions of the Nizam of Hyderabad, containing about seventy-five thousand inhabitants. The Nizam was a Mussulman, and the proportion of Mussulmans in the part of his dominions which fell under Mr. Allen's notice, was unusually large. The most singular occurrence at Jalna was the discovery of a native Christian society of forty or fifty members, without any pastor. Their origin reveals a possible mode of propagating the Gospel in India. The military force there of five or six thousand was composed of natives, excepting about one hundred English soldiers. These native Christians were connected with the officers as servants, and came from

Mr. Allen at Jalna.

A Christian society discovered there.

districts in the Madras Presidency, more or less under missionary influence. Two or three years before, one of them succeeded in getting a few to meet on the Sabbath for worship, which he usually conducted himself. A pious officer, hearing of the meeting, encouraged and assisted them. Meanwhile their number increased. Some persons belonging to the Roman Catholic Church united with them, and so did some of the heathen. As they became better known, an interest was awakened, a convenient place was procured for worship, and a native, who had been educated at Madras as a catechist, was procured to be their religious teacher.

Mr. Allen naturally came into connection with these people, and was greatly pleased with their appearance, and the apparent devotion of their worship. They had expected him, and gathered about him as a religious teacher. There was no chaplain there, and several were desirous of being baptized, and some wished to be married. They also earnestly requested him to administer the Lord's Supper before leaving them. With a view to ascertain the qualifications of different persons for the ordinances, he had frequent conferences with individuals, and attended several public meetings. He baptized four individuals, performed two marriages, and administered the Lord's Supper, in the native language, to fourteen communicants. Some of these persons were members of mission churches in different parts of

India; some had been educated in the Roman Catholic religion, and then, for the first time, commemorated the death of Christ in the manner prescribed to his disciples; and some had renounced the worship of idols. One had been notorious for dissolute habits and groveling vices, but for a year had given remarkable evidence of piety.

An interesting sacramental commemoration.

Mr. Allen preached in English to the European population on five of the ten days he spent at Jalna; and on the evening of the last Sabbath he administered the Lord's Supper to twenty persons, who, though of different denominations, united in commemorating the death of their common Saviour. He returned to Bombay by way of Aurungabad, about forty-five miles nearly west of Jalna, named after the famous emperor Aurungzebe; where is now a splendid mausoleum erected by him to the memory of his favorite wife. Aurungzebe died at Ahmednuggur, and his body was brought to Ellora, sixteen miles northwest of Aurungabad, a favorite place of Mohammedan sepulture, and was there buried, agreeably to his own request, without pomp or splendor. Being within a short distance of Ellora, Mr. Allen went out to see the celebrated excavations, said far to exceed anything of the kind in India; and a brief description of them, as given by him, may properly form a part of the history of missions in that portion of the Deccan.

The excavations at Ellora.

"These excavations," he says, "were designed as places of worship. The largest of them is called Kylas. Here a court is excavated in the mountain, the entrance into which is through a gateway on the west side, where the mountain gradually slopes away to the plain. This court is two hundred and forty-seven feet long and one hundred and fifty feet wide. The height of the walls, composed of the living rock, vary from thirty or forty to one hundred feet, where the mountain is highest at the east end of the court. In these walls are several large excavated rooms and halls, which were designed for purposes connected with the temple. A large mass of rock was left standing near the middle of the court, which was then cut down on all sides to the size of the temple. This was then completed internally by excavating the rooms requisite to complete the design. The external sides of the temple, even to the top, which is ninety feet high, are covered with images of gods, men, and animals of different sizes, all carved in the rock. The walls and pillars in the inside are also covered with images of various kinds and sizes, carved in the same manner. In the great hall four rows of pillars are left to support the immense weight of the rock above. Thus the temple, with all its images, is itself a part of the mountain. The ceiling of the great hall was once covered with cement, on which were drawn, in glowing colors, paintings descriptive of Hindû mythology.

"Near this are other excavations. Some of these are very large and contain images of gigantic size. In one place are three large excavations, one above the other. Of these the lowest one was designed to represent the Hindû hell, or lower world, the middle one this world, and the upper one the Hindû paradise. In these excavations the images were painted to make their appearance more beautiful or frightful, as the characters represented might require. The walls, pillars, and ceilings, where not taken up with images, were covered with paintings. Curtains which could be changed at pleasure were used to conceal different parts of the temples from view. In these gloomy recesses, surrounded with figures of gigantic size and frightful appearance, one seems almost to realize the descriptions of the infernal regions in ancient heathen poets. Here the rites and ceremonies of idolatry, partly exhibited and partly concealed, were performed in circumstances calculated powerfully to excite the feelings of a superstitious people."

There is no authentic history of these excavations, nor do any native traditions concerning them appear to be deserving of much credit. All agree that they antedate the entrance of the Mohammedan power into the country.[1]

[1] *Missionary Herald* for 1835, pp. 459, 460.

CHAPTER V.

MISSION TO THE MAHRATTAS.

1835–1847.

Mr. Allen made many missionary tours in the years 1833–1836.[1] He was again at Jalna, in the last of these years, and induced the native Christians to form a Christian society. This they did by adopting some regulations prepared by him in view of their peculiar circumstances.

Temporary station at Jalna.

After this he resumed his residence at Bombay, where he had the care of the printing establishment, and was also a member of the committee of the Bible Society. At the close of the year Messrs. Stone and Munger visited Jalna to ascertain whether a station could be formed there, and appearances were so favorable that they remained there during 1837. The Nizam, though a Mussulman, made no objection. The English residents had built a new house of worship, and gave them the use of the old one, but it was not found expedient to continue the station more than a year or two.

[1] For his journals see *Missionary Herald* for 1835, pp. 185, 211, 455; 1836, pp. 61, 298, 321; 1837, pp. 106, 206, 233, 332.

This was a time noted for commercial disaster. Upon receiving a circular from the Prudential Committee requiring reductions in the expenditure, ten boarding pupils at Ahmednuggur were dismissed, and six village schools were closed. The necessity of further reduction was prevented by the liberality of European residents. At Bombay the reductions were arrested in a similar manner. Miss Graves had charge of the female schools there. The printing from the beginning had amounted to 21,809,850 pages, the American and Bombay Bible Societies, the American Tract Society, and the Church Missionary Society, sharing in the expense.

Seasonable liberality.

Early in 1839 two brahmins, named Narayan and Haripunt, were baptized at Ahmednuggur. They were brothers, and the younger was the first to come to an open decision. The brahmin community was greatly excited, and declared that intercourse with the missionaries should subject any one of their fraternity to a loss of caste. Three of the schools of brahmin children were broken up. Both of the young men were deprived of their wives, but the wife of the younger brother returned to her husband before his baptism, and soon followed his example. Haripunt's connection with the mission, as teacher, catechist, licensed preacher, and pastor, continued till his death, twenty-five years. He had strength of character, was always ready

Baptism of two brahmins.

to do battle for the truth, and we shall have occasion to speak of him again. Narayan died in the year 1871. He was unemployed by the mission for many years, was bent on acquiring property, and was, for a time, under the discipline of the church. During his last sickness he gave pleasing evidence of penitence, and seemed to be a truly changed man.

Messrs. Ebenezer Burgess, Ozro French, and Robert W. Hume, with their wives, were added to the mission in this year. Mr. Hume was stationed at Bombay, and Mr. Burgess at Ahmednuggur. Mr. French formed a station at Seroor, thirty miles from that city.

New missionaries.

The first distinct mention I find of the Mahars is in 1816, in the journal of Messrs. Hall and Newell. Those living in Bombay were then described as the most degraded and vicious class of Hindûs, yet as forming a distinct caste, with rules and customs to which they attached much importance. The meanest of them, write the missionaries, would not eat with us, through dread of pollution and the loss of caste. In the Deccan they were more respectable, though low in the social scale. Many supposed them to be descendants of the original inhabitants. As with the hill-tribes, who are confessedly aborigines, the obstacles to their becoming Christians are far less than among the higher castes. Twenty years later the brethren at

The Mahars.

Ahmednuggur wrote thus concerning them. "Besides the brahmins, there is no class of Hindûs which affords so many religious teachers, or gûrûs, in this region, as the mahars. There are some noted gûrûs in this vicinity who boast of thousands of disciples, while among the higher castes, until you come to the brahmins, you seldom find a gûrû. Many of the mahar gûrûs are opposers of idolatry, discard the Hindû system of incarnations, and maintain the doctrine of one invisible God, who alone is to be worshipped, and whose favor is to be obtained by inward meditation upon his character and perfections. Many mahars, on hearing us preach, have exclaimed that this is just the doctrine taught by their own religious teachers; and it is only when we tell them of the Saviour of the world, that they perceive the difference between their system and ours; and even this does not excite in them that opposition, which it does in preaching to other classes of Hindûs."

Mahar gûrûs.

Seventeen natives were added to the Ahmednuggur church in 1842, twelve in the following year, and sixteen in 1844. A large portion of these were mahars. And it is worthy of note, that nine in the number last mentioned possessed property which made them independent of employment or assistance from the mission. Of twenty-two admitted in 1845, thirteen were men, and nine were women. Of the former seven be-

Additions to the church.

longed to villages from fifteen to forty miles distant, and most of them, though mahars, were substantial men of respectable character. Of the twenty-four who were admitted in 1846, eighteen resided in different villages, some of them considerably distant from Ahmednuggur, and all supported themselves. It should be further stated, that the mahars then formed a part of the official corps of every village. They kept the gates, were guides to travellers, conveyed burdens from village to village, and letters on public business, and formed a village police to guard persons and property against the attacks of robbers. In return, they were entitled to a certain portion of the proceeds of every estate belonging to their village, and had other perquisites. In consequence of their more extended intercourse with men, they are superior to the kûnabees, or cultivator caste, in general intelligence, though much lower on the social scale. A spirit of religious inquiry was evidently awakening among them, and the missionaries in their tours had frequent opportunities for public discussions, of which they give very pleasing accounts. The most promising district, at that time, was the one north of Ahmednuggur. A mahar gûrû of considerable influence was among the native assistants.[1]

Social position of the mahars.

Mrs. Allen, the sister of Mr. Graves, died at Bom-

[1] *Missionary Herald* for July, 1843, pp. 265–275.

bay June 5, 1842, "faithful unto death," and on the 24th of the same month Mrs. Burgess died at Ahmednuggur. She had been a successful teacher before her marriage, and exerted an excellent influence on the missionary schools.

Deaths of Mrs. Allen and Mrs. Burgess.

Mr. Graves finished his course at Malcolm-Peth December 30th of the following year. His missionary life of twenty-five years was one of uncommon singleness of purpose, and his end was peace. Just before his departure he said: "I covenanted with God, through Christ, long, long ago, to be his for time and eternity. Now I commit my all into his hands. Christ is all, *all*. The fear of death is gone." Mention has already been made of his request, when told by his physician in Boston that he would not recover, to return and die in India. Such men have no reason to fear death anywhere.

Death of Mr. Graves.

The year 1842 was made memorable by the removal of one of the barriers in the way of Christian toleration. The baptism of three girls in the boarding-school had been deferred on account of the opposition of their parents. At length the girls, fearing they would be taken from the school, urged that their baptism should be no longer deferred, and the missionaries, seeing no good reason for longer delay, received them to the church. Of course there was much excitement. The friends of one of the girls petitioned the gov-

Increased toleration.

ernment, and the case was investigated. As it appeared that she had embraced the Christian religion of her own free will, they were told that she was at liberty to do as she pleased. Thus the rights of conscience were secured to girls, even at the age of twelve years.

These girls belonged to the cultivator caste, which was numerous at Ahmednuggur and had social position, and this was the first case of conversion among them. They went in a body to the chief revenue officer of the district, and declared they would throw up their engagements with government and remove elsewhere, if the girls were not surrendered to them. The reply was, that the government would find other men to cultivate their grounds, but even if it could not, he would not be guilty of injustice. This firmness brought the disturbance to an end, yet the girls' schools were for a time considerably affected.

Of those who had most recently joined the church, one was a brahmin named Ramkrishnapunt, who proved a most valuable accession. He came from Poona, from a respectable family, and was employed as a schoolmaster. His manner was at first haughty and unpromising. He had been led to think of the folly of idol-worship by a heretical Hindû, a follower of the system of Kubeer, who taught that all the incantations and idols of Hindûism were false, and that God alone should be worshipped. Comparing what he had thus learned

Conversion of Ramkrishnapunt.

with what he found in the Christian school-books which he was daily using in his school, he was astonished at the agreement. While in this state of mind he made the acquaintance of Marûtee, a young man of the cultivator caste, who was also an inquirer after the truth. Ramkrishnapunt was the first to resolve fully. In order to obtain his wife before being baptized, he went to Poona, where his friends, learning his intention, put him under restraint, but the magistrate set him at liberty, and gave him a soldier to protect him a part of the way to Ahmednuggur, where he lost no time in connecting himself with the church. The communicants at that time were thirty-eight, of whom twenty-five were natives. Every one of the eight last introduced came from a different social circle, and so could exert an influence over a different class of persons. Marûtee was long associated with Mr. Fairbank, and became afterwards a teacher in the Normal school at Ahmednuggur. Of Ramkrishnapunt we shall have frequent occasion to speak.

Case of Vishnû.

The case of Vishnû, a younger brother of Ramkrishnapunt, though painful in its issue, affords an interesting specimen of brahmin domestic life. He seems to have sympathized with his brother, and renounced caste, professing his belief in Christianity. His father and mother, hearing of this, came to Ahmednuggur, and used their utmost endeavors to reclaim their children. The father, though greatly agitated, conducted with propriety; but the mother was frantic, and was at one time prevented from dashing her head against a rock only by being caught in the arms of her son. A company of brahmins endeavored to take the boy Vishnû away by force, but the native students in the seminary interposed. The magistrate was then called in, and finding it was the lad's decided wish to remain, ordered that he have liberty to do as he pleased. An older brother, a lawyer at Poona, petitioned the civil magistrate, alleging that Vishnû was yet a minor, under sixteen years of age. The youth sent in a counter petition, stating that though not sixteen, he was old enough to know that the Hindû religion was false, and therefore he claimed the liberty of worshipping God according to the dictates of his conscience; which was granted. I regret to add that his life was not always such as to justify the expectations awakened by his early history.

The Missionary Herald for 1843 contains interesting accounts of labors among the mahars northward of Ahmednuggur, chiefly from the journal of Mr. Ballantine.

The seminary and English school at Ahmednuggur were united in 1844, and placed in charge of Mr. Burgess, and Mr. Abbott was thus left more at liberty to engage in other kinds of labor. There were about fifty pupils. In this year, a mahar gûrû of the system of Kubeer, who had for some time been in training, was baptized and admitted to the church. He was a man of considerable influence among the mahars, and was clear and forcible in his addresses to the people on the great doctrine of the necessity of a Mediator. Mrs. Allen, wife of Mr. Allen, died at Bombay June 11, 1844. She had been connected with the mission of the Board in Borneo as Miss Condit, and had been at Bombay only a few months.

A mahar gûrû convert.

There is a lower depth in caste than the mahar. In the summer of 1845, Mr. French had the satisfaction, at Seroor, of baptizing a man of the mang caste named Bhagáji Kalokhe. Hitherto the great portion of the converts were from the mahar caste, which was so near the bottom of the Hindu social scale, that the mahars lost no privileges among their own people by becoming Christians, having found in the Christian church only those who were originally above them. But they had inveterate prejudices against the mangs, regarding them as hereditary beggars and thieves. Among the mangs, however, who called on Mr. French, he found many very intelligent men. Bhagáji proved himself to be higher and more noble in character and conduct than many who ranked themselves above him. He was among the most sincere of the native Christians, and was specially distinguished for love to his mother, making her a part

Conversion in the mang caste.

of his family, and bestowing upon her, till her death at an advanced age, all the attention which her circumstances required. The custom of his caste was to live very much by begging, but this did not suit him. He used to say that it was well for a man to obtain his food by his own labor, and then eat like a king. On this account he was treated with unusual regard, even by his own caste. It was no part of his motive in becoming a Christian, to get a living. For almost nineteen years, until his death in 1864, he lived the life of a consistent Christian, being exemplary in all his relations. During the last ten years he was deacon of the church. Twice a day he had his family devotions, and twice a day he retired for secret prayer.

Singular intolerance.

Much pains had been taken, before the public recognition of Bhagáji as a Christian, to instruct the church, not only at Seroor, but also at Ahmednuggur, as to what was due to the castes below them. Nor was it wholly in vain; for when the mang brother came to Ahmednuggur, the greater part of the church members, including all the native assistants, received him to their houses, and entertained him to the best of their ability, showing that they regarded him as a brother. But a violent outbreak of the caste feeling occurred a few days after he left. One young church member forcibly turned another out of his house merely because the latter had invited the mang convert to dinner. He also warned others, whose only fault was having dined with that Christian brother, not to enter his house; and he was supported in this by one or two other members of the church. Persisting in this course, he was suspended from the church. Others, not so bold, professed a willingness to do whatever the church should decide, and urged that the members should be assembled from the city and the villages, and determine by their votes what course to pursue. They were told that this was not a matter to be determined in that way, because the Lord required his people all to meet around his table as brethren. Meanwhile the communion season approached, and one or two of the communicants took occasion to leave Ahmednuggur a few days before. Some who had opposed remained and partook of the ordinance, having previously declared to the pastor that they would have no objection to communing with the mang convert. The young man was also present, though of course only as a spectator, and was deeply troubled, feeling that he had shut himself out from the company of God's people. The next day he came to the pastor and confessed his sin with the deepest humility; and afterwards, in a church meeting, he rose of his own accord, and gave such satisfactory evidence of repentance, that he was restored to the fellowship of the church. The trial had been useful to him.

Salutary discipline.

Mr. Munger, returning from a visit to his native land, was afflicted on the way by the death of his wife on the 12th of March, 1846, and she was buried in the Indian Ocean. Messrs. Samuel B. Fairbank and Royal G. Wilder, with their wives, arrived in India in September of that year, and were stationed at Ahmednuggur. Mr. Allen Hazen and wife arrived there in the following March. The station at Bombay was strengthened, in January, 1848, by the arrival of Messrs. George Bowen and William Wood and wife. Mr. French, after suffering much from the failure of his eyes, returned to the United States, with his family, in July, 1847, and was not long after released from his connection with the Board.

Death of Mrs. Munger.

New missionaries.

Return home of Mr. French.

The letters of Mr. Hume from Bombay contain a great amount of valuable information, for much of which the reader is referred to the Missionary Herald. A native magazine, called "The Dnyánodaya," or "Rise of Knowledge," was issued by the mission, and was regarded with interest both by friends and enemies. It had a considerable number of native subscribers, who, besides getting much useful information, took an interest in the discussions of religious subjects.

Native magazine.

The year 1847 was distinguished by the issue, on the first of March, of the entire Scriptures in the Mahratta language. Thus the whole

Publication of the Bible in Mahratta.

volume of inspiration became accessible to a numerous people in Western India. The New Testament was translated from the original Greek by the mission before the death of Mr. Hall. The Old Testament was also translated by American missionaries as far as 2d Chronicles, and also the book of Psalms. The version of the remaining books was made by the Rev. J. B. Dixon, of the Church Missionary Society, who also published a version of the Psalms.

The Bombay Bible Society appointed a committee in 1833, to prepare an improved version. The last years of Mr. Graves' life were devoted to this work; and this was the chief employment of Dr. Allen during the latter part of his residence in India.

The Gospel of Matthew was first printed in 1817, and several of the Gospels and the Acts were afterwards printed repeatedly. The New Testament was published entire in 1826. In 1830 a second edition of five thousand copies was issued, at the expense of the British and Foreign Bible Society. The types were large, and the cost of the edition was proportionally so. The size of the letter was afterwards reduced, and of course the cost of the volume. The printing of the entire Bible in one volume, was completed in 1855. The newly revised edition of the New Testament was completed in the same year; and this all the missions in the Mahratta country united in using. Nearly the whole printing of the sacred volume was done at the press of the American mission.

The printing establishment of the Board at Bombay was one of the most complete in Western India. It included a bindery and foundry, seven hand printing-presses, a lithographic press, an embossing press, two standing presses, two cutting machines, seven furnaces, moulds and matrices for three fonts of English type, for seven Mahratta fonts of the Baldodh, for a Mahratta font of the Modh character, for three Gajeratee fonts, and for one Zand font. It employed more than a hundred workmen, and had cleared by its job printing 93,000 rupees, or $46,500. There was no longer a need of the Board's maintaining so large a printing establishment in that part of India. Nor was it expedient to do so for the sake of pecuniary profit, when the department, which was the source of gain, had an absorbing influence on the time of a clerical missionary superintendent. The portion required for English job printing was therefore sold in 1855. Three years later, it appeared that other presses in Bombay could do all the work needed by the mission, and the printing establishment was sold; it being the usage of the Board not to be encumbered with such establishments, except where they are a necessity.

The printing establishment.

Its reduction.

According to Mr. Hume, there were fifteen periodicals printed at Bombay in 1847, for the native population, most of them published weekly. He also says: "Without enumerating either the European printing establishments, or the native offices in which type is employed, there are some forty-five or fifty lithographic presses engaged in printing native works, which obtain considerable circulation, and which must exert a very extensive influence." Special exertion was now made to put books and tracts in circulation by sale, rather than by gratuitous distribution.

Increased efficiency of the native press.

CHAPTER VI.

MISSION TO THE MAHRATTAS.

1847–1854.

THE difficulty of personal access to the people in the early stages of the mission, and so making converts, naturally suggested a resort to boarding-schools, and seventeen of the forty-one natives received into the Bombay church were from the schools of this kind for girls. Such schools were also deemed needful to raise up Christian schoolmasters, catechists, preachers and pastors; and for common schools there was an additional reason in the belief, that they would greatly aid in securing stated congregations. In 1851, Bombay reported eighty girls and three hundred boys in the free schools, and twenty-six in the girls' boarding-school. Satara reported two hundred boys in the free schools. Ahmednuggur reported forty in the seminary, twenty-three in the boarding-school for boys, thirty-seven in the one for girls, and six hundred in the free schools, eighty of them girls under the care of Miss Farrar. Seroor reported eighteen in the boys' boarding-school, fourteen in

Results of boarding-schools.

that for girls, and one hundred and twelve in the free schools, and there were ninety-five in free schools at the out-stations. Thus there were, in all, eighty-one boys and seventy-seven girls in the boarding-schools, and thirteen hundred eighty-seven pupils in the free schools.

On no part of the missionary operations in Bombay did the blessing of God seem to rest so much as upon Mrs. Hume's boarding-school for girls. It was discontinued in 1854 in consequence of her return to the United States, there being no one to assume the care of it. A part of the pupils were taken by Mrs. Mitchell, of the Scotch Free Church mission at Poona. Eleven had been received from Mrs. Hume's school into the church during ten years, and several were in stations of usefulness.

The condition of the schools in the Ahmednuggur branch was less satisfactory. The Christian parents had somehow come to entertain the notion, that their children were all entitled to be educated at the expense of the mission, and the boarding pupils were nearly all their children, and only two were connected with the church. In reorganizing this branch of the mission, it was deemed expedient to discontinue the boarding-schools as then constituted, and all the free schools which had heathen masters.

The mission compound.

The church at Ahmednuggur, previous to 1855, was made up chiefly of converts from villages in the surrounding country, some thirty or forty miles distant, and there was a tendency, especially among the mahar converts, to migrate from their villages with their families, and occupy cottages in the compounds around the houses of the missionaries, where their children had free access to the mission schools. Not less than two hundred, old and young, from one cause or another, were found to be residing on the mission compounds at Ahmednuggur in the year 1854.

The only effectual means of keeping the village converts at their homes, was to establish village churches, with pastors of their own race, wherever there was a suitable number of natives belonging to one village, or to several adjacent villages, in circumstances to meet regularly for religious worship on the Sabbath, and to perform the duties of a church of Christ; the native pastors of these churches to be responsible, with the church members, for the government and discipline of the church.

In March, 1848, Haripunt and Ramkrishnapunt were licensed as preachers of the gospel, and the latter was stationed at Newàse, lately opened by Mr. Wilder. At Pimpalgaum, a small village ten miles from this place, Mr. Wilder baptized Yesûba with his four children. Yesûba was a man of considerable property and unusual energy. He had carried on a profitable trade in cattle for many years, and, though con-

Licensed preachers.

An interesting convert.

vinced of the truth of Christianity, had resisted the conviction that he ought not to frequent the cattle-market, held on the Sabbath in the vicinity of Ahmednuggur. Being at length resolved, he returned home, and was baptized. He became an interesting Christian, and remained such, though greatly persecuted by his heathen neighbors.

New station at Satara.

As the health of Mrs. Wood required a removal from Bombay to the Deccan, Mr. Wood was authorized to form a station at Satara, the capital of what was formerly the kingdom of that name. The city is fifty miles from the western coast, and more than two thousand feet above the sea, with a position singularly beautiful.

The law Christianized.

Hitherto, in Western and Southern India (and in Bengal up to 1832), there had been no special law for the protection of Christian converts. Hindû law being applied to Hindûs and Mohammedan law to Mohammedans, converts from those classes were still considered as liable to be tried by the same laws to which they had been amenable before conversion, laws which pronounced them outcasts, and deprived them, as such, of all right to their property. Many were thus subjected to great losses. No court in India would put them in possession of any property to which any other heir laid claim. This state of things was extremely trying, and various efforts had been made by Christians in India to obtain legislation that would secure them equal rights. At length, in 1850, the following Act was passed by the Governor-general in council: "So much of any law or usage now in force, within the territories subject to the government of the East India Company, as inflicts on any person forfeiture of rights or property, or may be held in any way to impair or affect any right of inheritance, by reason of his or her renouncing, or having been excluded from, the communion of any religion, or being deprived of caste, shall cease to be enforced as law in the courts of the East India Company, and in the courts established by royal charter within the said territories."

This enactment was received with gratitude by all who were interested in securing the extension of the Gospel of Christ.

The seminary for boys at Ahmednuggur, in consequence of Mr. Burgess's ill health in the fall of 1849, was placed under the charge of Mr. Wilder. The girls' boarding-school, because of a visit of Mr. Ballantine and his family to the United States, passed, about the same time, into the hands of Mrs. Burgess. Mr. Fairbank removed to Bombay in the hope of improving the health of his wife. Mr. French suffered for many months from the failure of his eyes, and tried in vain the influence of a protracted visit to his native land. Apprehending the effect of a return to India, he felt constrained, in 1851, to take a release from his

Changes in the mission.

connection with the Board. The Rev. Samuel Bissell and wife arrived this year, and were stationed at Seroor. Mr. and Mrs. Burgess removed to Satara at the close of the year, and Mr. Hazen to Ahmednuggur, where he was associated with Mr. Ballantine, who returned from the United States in 1852. Mr. and Mrs. Wilder commenced a new station at Kolapûr, an eligible situation seventy miles south of Satara. Mr. Munger remained at Bhingar, near Ahmednuggur. The most hopeful part of the field, at that time, was doubtless northward of Ahmednuggur, where the missionary usually found large and attentive audiences in the villages, whom he could address as long as he thought proper. There was consequently much touring in the cool season, though wisely restricted, in great measure, to portions of the country which had often been visited.

Lesson in mission policy.

Mr. Burgess about this time developed an idea which had not been sufficiently considered by the Board, or its missionaries. It was, that every missionary should have, as far as possible, a separate and distinct department of labor; and that, even in large cities, it might not be possible, for a time, to secure regular preaching stations for more than a very few. The most united, most happy, and most efficient missions were generally where every man had his own appropriate sphere of labor.

The health of Dr. Allen had been good during most of his five-and-twenty years in India, but indications of a change in his constitution now appeared, that threatened serious results; and he was advised by his physicians and by the Prudential Committee, to return home for a time. This he did in 1853, and was never able to resume his missionary labors. He died at Lowell, Massachusetts, July 19, 1863, aged sixty-three years.

Retirement and death of Dr. Allen.

Dr. Allen possessed a strong mind and sound judgment, and there were great industry and thoroughness in the use of his powers. The work he published in 1856, on "Ancient and Modern India," a solid octavo of more than six hundred pages, is creditable to him in every respect. He was familiar with the Mahratta language, and during the twenty years of his connection with the Translation Committee of the Bombay Bible Society, one half of which time he was its Secretary, he performed a most important service in the revision of the Mahratta Scriptures. The printing had advanced through the second book of Samuel when he left Bombay, and arrangements were made for progress in the work during his absence. The present Mahratta version of the Bible owes much to his labors. His associates were impressed with the value of the influence he exerted, through the press and otherwise, on the general mind of the Mahratta people.

Mrs. Wood died at Satara on the 13th of August, 1851, leaving two sons. Though earnestly desirous of doing more for the salvation of the people, she submitted cheerfully to the Divine will. Mrs. Fairbank closed her pilgrimage on the 21st of August, 1852. Her health gave way in the autumn of 1846, within six months of landing at Bombay, and most of her remaining days she spent as an invalid; the first three years in the Deccan, the rest of the time at Bombay. After finding that she had no prospect of living long in India, she decided still to remain; happy in thus enabling her husband to continue in the missionary work, and making a pleasant home for him; a decision, which was to the last a source of comfort to her and her associates. A brahmin, well acquainted with Mrs. Fairbank, said with great earnestness, when looking on her face sweet even in death; "The religion must be true, which secures a death like this."

Death of Mrs. Wood.

And of Mrs. Fairbank.

Mrs. Burgess went to Satara soon after the death of Mrs. Wood, and acted the part of a mother to her children. But she too was called from her earthly cares on the 26th of April, 1853, and left a field in which she had been eminently useful, for higher service in another world. Peculiarly fitted for her work, and especially for the training of children; always rejoicing in a sense of God's love and favor, and carrying joy with her

Death of Mrs. Burgess.

wherever she went, she was the life of the circle in which she moved. Not only were the two families at Satara deprived of their only female associate, but the other families in the mission were deeply afflicted by her death.

Mr. Wilder removed, with his family, to Kolapûr late in 1852. The excitement among the people, awakened by his arrival, sensibly diminished as mistaken views and apprehensions gave place to a more correct understanding of his character and object. Mr. and Mrs. Barker arrived at Ahmednuggur in 1853.

New station at Kolapûr.

The Government of India has, within a few years, introduced railways and the electric telegraph on a large scale. It will be convenient to indicate them here, some fifteen years before their completion. The "East India Railway," in the valley of the Ganges from Calcutta to Delhi, a distance of a thousand miles. The "Great India Peninsular Railway" connects with the one in the Ganges valley at Allahabad, about five hundred miles above Calcutta, crosses the Deccan plateau, and descends thence to the Concan and Bombay, and from Bombay it proceeds to Madras. The whole length of the line is twelve hundred and sixty-six miles. The ascent of the Ghâts, on the line from Bombay, required the labor of seven years, with occasionally as many as forty thousand laborers employed upon it at one time. "Beginning

A vast system of railways.

its ascent along a spur thrown out from the main range, this incline continues its upward winding way through long tunnels piercing the hardest basalt, across viaducts spanning ravines of great width and depth, often along what is simply a large notch cut in the face of a precipice."[1] The "Madras Railway" crosses from Madras to Calicut, a port on the Malabar coast, eight hundred and twenty-five miles. The "Bombay, Baroda, and Central Railway" goes northward from Bombay to Surat and Ahmedabad, three hundred miles. The "Punjaub Railway" extends from Delhi through Lahore, the capital of the Punjaub, and thence westward to Mooltan on the Indus river, five hundred and sixty miles. The "Southern Indian Railway" is in progress from Madras, and will probably extend through the Madura and Tinnevelly provinces to Travancore, on the western side of southern India.

These railways, as will be seen, make Bombay, and not Calcutta, the sea-gate through which the postal communications of India, Europe, and America are to pass. Their cost cannot have been less than five hundred millions of dollars. And they are as important in a missionary point of view, as in their relation to the civil, political, and commercial interests of India. Under the orderings of Divine Providence, they were built as really for the Church,

[1] *North British Review*, 1868, p. 177.

as for the world, though designed only for the promotion of worldly interests. The saving they will make to the Church, in the work of evangelizing India, will be immense, in travel, labor, time, expenditure, health, and life. Bombay, and not Calcutta or Madras, will now be the great place of landing and departure for missionaries, and how much more easy, economical, and safe will be the access to every section of the country.[1]

As the desire for education was increasing, so the government was enlarging its grants in aid of the same. They were made in 1853 to the amount of nearly a hundred thousand dollars, and the people were never so ready to contribute for the support of schools. The most remarkable of the changes was in regard to female education. The most influential natives now subscribed for girls' schools, sent their daughters to be educated, and were present at the examinations. Mr. Hume attended a meeting in the Town Hall at Bombay for distributing prizes to the pupils of eight girls' schools, established and superintended by a society of native young men. Six hundred pupils were reported as in attendance. In several of the larger towns in the interior similar schools were also found, supported by natives, and the number was increasing. The native periodical press was gradually becoming more able and in-

Government patronage of education.

Increasing interest in schools.

Native periodical press.

[1] *Foreign Missions*, p. 205.

fluential. Several periodicals had been started at different times for the purpose of reviling and opposing Christianity, but they had all been short-lived. Though the existing Mahratta periodicals were not just what the missionaries desired, their influence on the whole was salutary, in diffusing useful information and destroying confidence in prevalent superstitions. The periodical published by the mission, once in two weeks, exerted a great and happy influence on the community.

Mrs. Hume was now the only lady connected with the mission at Bombay, and her labors were most valuable. Mention has already been made of the select boarding-school for girls, which she had in her own house.

Retirement of Mr. Burgess.

The health of Mr. Burgess obliged him to return to America early in 1854, bringing with him his three motherless children, and those of Mr. Fairbank. He was afflicted during his passage by the death of one of his children. Mr. Wood sought relief from his bereavement and solitude in a tour of five weeks among the villages. The removal of Miss Farrar to Satara afforded the proper supervision for the girls' and boys' schools there. Mrs. Graves, now aged and infirm, made her home at Mahabalishwar, where she had a school, which received a liberal support from English residents on the Hills. Mr. Wilder's report of his first year of labors at Kolapûr, at the close of 1853, shows that he felt much encouraged.

Mr. Hume's health, after fifteen years of faithful and valuable service, had become so impaired in 1854, that a visit to a colder climate was apparently the only means of preserving his life. He accordingly embarked on the 20th of September, with his family, for the Cape of Good Hope, in an English ship, there being no American vessel then in port, intending to go thence to the United States. He was not permitted, however, to visit the home of his early years, but died at sea on the 26th of November, and was buried in sight of the coast of Africa, just a week before the ship arrived at Cape Town. Mrs. Hume and her children received much kindness from the Rev. Mr. Thomson, of the London Missionary Society, and others, while detained at the Cape, and reached Boston on the 11th of April, 1855.

Voyage and decease of Mr. Hume.

The author's recollections of Mr. Hume are chiefly as a correspondent; and he was not excelled, in the extent and value of information thus given, by any one of his brethren in India. He appreciated his position in the commercial centre of India, which was soon to become, as he believed, through a magnificent system of railways, the door of ingress for all the Christian nations of the West. The conversion of India, through the Gospel of the Lord Jesus, was his one governing object through the fifteen years of his missionary life; nor was he disheartened by disappointments

His character.

however great, nor by difficulties however unforeseen. Where many would have been cast down he was calm and cheerful, trusting in the Lord and seeking direction from Him. He was a firm believer in divine Providence, and in the prosecution of measures once deliberately commenced, he carefully observed providential indications, that he might be the more profoundly assured of the divine approbation. He was greatly respected by the English and native community of Bombay, and his loss was deeply felt by the native church, the general missionary circle, and the different benevolent and religious societies with which he had been connected. A fitting memorial of him may be seen at Bombay, in the "Tract Society Building" of three stories, erected by funds which he, as Secretary of the Society, collected near the close of his life.

And here I cannot withhold a beautiful illustration of native sympathy in the hour of his departure from Bombay. I give it as it was related by Mrs. Hume, soon after her arrival, to a lady in Boston.[1]

A native memorial of him.

Mr. Hume being entirely prostrated at the time of his embarkation, was carried on board the ship in a palanquin and laid in a berth.

[1] The statement was placed by the lady in the hands of the Rev. David Stoddard, of the Nestorian mission, then in the United States, and temporarily editing the *Youth's Dayspring*, and was inserted by him in that work. See *Youth's Dayspring* for June, 1855, pp. 81, 82.

He and his family having brought many of the people to the knowledge of Christ, the day of his departure was to them a day of sorrow. The ship was anchored at some distance from the shore, but so eager were the people to be with their beloved teachers as long as possible, that many went off in boats, and quite a crowd collected on the deck, lingering till evening. One woman was allowed to remain; and after the children had retired, while Mrs. Hume was sitting alone in the cabin, this woman came and sat down beside her on the floor, embraced her feet, kissed them, and wept. Then looking up into her face, she said, "Madam Sahib, (a term of great respect) once there was a great tree, a beautiful tree, and God was pleased to raise its head higher than any of the trees. It had many great branches, many little branches, and many, many blossoms. All the people round about gathered under its shade. The fowls of the air and the little birds built their nests, and laid their eggs, and hatched their young among these branches, and here they sang and were so happy, oh! *so happy.*" Here she stopped and wept. Lifting her head again she continued, "But it pleased the Lord to send a great storm, and to lay this tree low. Its branches were cast upon the ground, all the people were scattered, the birds hovered around making a mournful cry, not knowing where to find a resting-place, the eggs were broken, and all was distress." Here she again stopped and wept. Then, with the most affectionate and tender expression, she took hold of Mrs. Hume's arm, and pointing toward the inner cabin, where Mr. Hume was lying, she said, "Madam Sahib, THERE LIES THAT TREE."

JAFFNA
Seven miles to one inch.
PALK STRAIT
Point Pedro
Oodoopitty
Kaddaiveli
Atchuvaly
Tellipally
Panditeripo
Mylitti
Sangany
Mallagam
Puttur
Karadive
Oodooville
Manepy
Batticotta
Varany
Koppay
Nallur
Kaits
Vanuarpanny
TOWN
Chavugacheri
Chundikkuli
Katchay
Navatkuly
Velany
Mugamaly
Tampagamam
Nyanative
Pongortive
Mullipattu
ELEPHANT PASS
GULF OF MANNAR
Delft
Punari
MAIN LAND OF
CEYLON

CHAPTER VII.

THE TAMIL PEOPLE.

CEYLON MISSION.

1815–1822.

CEYLON was brought before the Board and the American churches by the communications of Mr. Newell, who, in his presumed exclusion from Bombay, found a quiet residence on that island. In December, 1813, he wrote to the Corresponding Secretary of the Board recommending a mission there. Among the reasons assigned was the friendly disposition of General Brownrigg the Governor, of Sir Alexander Johnstone the Chief Justice, of the Hon. and Rev. Mr. Twistleton and Rev. Mr. Bisset the Chaplains, and indeed of all the influential men at the seat of government.

Origin of the mission.

Mr. Newell landed at Point de Galle, on the southern extremity of Ceylon, on his way from the Isle of France, and went thence by palanquin eighty miles to Colombo, by an excellent road along the shore, through beautiful groves of palmyra trees. Governor Brownrigg gave him a friendly reception, and every facility for visiting Jaffna, the northern province. While there, he enjoyed the hospitalities of J. N. Mooyart, Esq., to whose personal kindness the mission was afterwards much indebted. He became acquainted with the Rev. Christian David, a native of Tanjore, who had been a pupil of Schwartz, and had charge of a Protestant native congregation. The only other person of like mind in Jaffna known to him, was a lady of Dutch extraction, who spoke the Dutch, Portuguese, and Tamil languages, and was a true missionary to the native people. "Here," wrote Mr. Newell, "there is every facility for spreading the Gospel among these pagans. The Governor is desirous that they should be instructed, and would encourage every attempt of this nature. The people have no particular objection to the Christian religion, and will not molest missionaries, and the government will protect them. Perhaps no portion of the heathen world possesses so many advantages for spreading the Gospel."

In view of Mr. Newell's statements, the Prudential Committee resolved, soon after the proclamation of peace with England, to send a mission to Ceylon, believing that in this they followed the divine leading.

The mission.

Messrs. James Richards, Edward Warren, Benjamin C. Meigs, Horatio Bardwell, and Daniel Poor, constituted this second mission of the Board. They received ordination in the

Presbyterian church at Newburyport on the 21st of June, 1815. The house, one of the largest in the commonwealth, was thronged, not only during the ordination services, but at the subsequent celebration of the Lord's Supper. Pastors and delegates from ten churches, with Professors from the Andover Theological Seminary, composed the Council, which had been assembled by invitation from the Prudential Committee. This was the customary mode of inviting councils for the ordination of Congregational missionaries down to about the year 1830; after which it was deemed expedient to leave the matter with the missionary candidates and the churches to which they belonged.

These missionaries, all of them married except Mr. Warren, sailed from Newburyport October 23d, in the brig *Dryad* for Colombo in Ceylon. What was familiarly known then and afterwards as "the embarkation," until the substitution of steamships for sailing vessels, was thus described at the time; and the memory of these seasons of thrilling interest ought not utterly to perish. "The day was pleasant. A large concourse assembled on the wharf where the vessel lay, on adjoining wharves, and wherever was a near view of the scene. The vessel's deck was filled with visitors, mostly ladies, the particular friends of the missionaries, assembled to bid them a last farewell. Just before the tide was most favorable for sailing,

The embarkation.

Dr. Spring addressed the throne of grace. The utmost stillness and solemnity pervaded the multitude. A missionary hymn was sung. Many were bathed in tears. The visitors immediately stepped on shore, the vessel left the wharf, spread her sails to the breeze, and quietly entered on her voyage, followed by the gaze of many deeply interested spectators."[1]

The arrival.

The company arrived at Colombo on the 22d of March, 1816, and the Governor gave full consent to the commencing of a mission in Jaffna. An opposing monsoon delayed their departure from Colombo several months, but all were together in Jaffnapatam before the end of the year, except Mr. Bardwell, whose knowledge of printing made it desirable that he should join the mission at Bombay.

The field to be occupied.

The field to be occupied by these brethren was unlike that among the Mahrattas. Jaffna had been missionary ground of some sort, perhaps to its disadvantage, for more than three centuries.[2] It was first occupied by the Roman Catholics; next, by the Dutch; and then by the English. The Portuguese divided the province into thirty-seven parishes, and provided each with a church of coral, and a glebe for the residence of a Franciscan priest. Some of

Previously occupied by the Portuguese.

[1] *Panoplist* for 1815, p. 533.

[2] From 1544, when Francis Xavier spent a year in Jaffna.

the churches were very spacious, and their ruins attest the care and cost of their construction. In Jaffnapatam there was a church and college of Jesuits, a church and convent of Dominicans, and a convent of Franciscans. When the Dutch made themselves masters of the fortress in 1658, Baldæus, the Dutch historian, saw from forty to fifty ecclesiastics — Jesuits, Franciscans, and Dominicans — marched out; and it is asserted on apparently good authority, that while Jaffna was occupied by the Portuguese, almost its entire population, including even the brahmins, submitted to the rite of baptism.[1]

As occupied by the Dutch.

The Dutch seized all the Portuguese possessions in Ceylon about the middle of the sixteenth century, and established the Reformed Church of Holland in the colony. They had suffered so cruelly themselves in their own country from the Catholics, that they banished the Romish priests from Jaffna under the severest penalties. But many of them contrived to remain, and large bodies of the natives are said to have adhered privately to the papal religion. The failure of the Dutch mission in Jaffna is instructive. Like that of the Portuguese, it was intimately connected with the government. The Dutch repaired the churches erected by the Papists, and put a large school in each, which became the nucleus of the congregation; and the attendance of pupils was enforced by

[1] Sir James Emerson Tennent on *Christianity in Ceylon*, p. 13.

fines upon the parents. The instruction was gratuitous, but superficial. One of the earliest and ablest of the Dutch missionaries testifies to the small amount of religious instruction he found it expedient to require for admission to church membership. The converts in Jaffna, only five years after the conquest, were estimated at 65,000, and, twenty years later, at 180,000. How feebly the doctrines of Christianity were inculcated is evident from the fact, that the instruction was imparted almost wholly through interpreters. Of ninety-seven Dutch clergymen in Ceylon, between the years 1642 and 1725, only eight could preach in the native languages, four of them in Tamil, and four in Singalese. In 1749, there were but five Dutch clergymen in all Ceylon, and of these only one understood the language of the natives. The celebrated Christian Frederick Schwartz spent the year 1759 in Jaffna. School children were seldom taught more than to read and write their own language; and it is to be feared that their teachers were no better Christians than their parents. Even this small amount of teaching was discouraged by the supreme authorities at Batavia, who regretted the charge it made on the Netherlands East India Company. "At the close of their ministrations," says Mr. Tennent, "the clergy of the Church of Holland left behind a superstructure of Christianity, prodigious in its outward dimensions, but so unsound internally, as to be distrusted even by those who had been instrumental in its erection; and so unsubstantial, that it has long since disappeared almost from the memory of the natives of Ceylon."[1]

England dates her possession of Ceylon from 1802. Among the first efforts of her officials was an attempt to revive the educational system of the Dutch; and for some years the Presbyterian Church, according to the forms of the Church of Holland, was practically the ecclesiastical establishment of the colony. But the Presbyterian clergy gradually diminished in number, though Scotland was appealed to for aid; and so small was the government allowance for education, that nearly fifty schools were discontinued in Jaffna in one year.[2] As religious conformity was not required by the English, and the possession of offices no longer depended on an outward profession of Christianity, the number of nominal Christians rapidly declined. In 1802, the Protestant Christians in Jaffna were estimated at 136,000. Four years later, Dr. Buchanan described the fine old churches erected by the Portuguese as decaying, and the only missionaries in the District as Romanists from the college at Goa.[3] The neglect of the government to prevent the natives from returning to heathenism, made known doubtless by the publications of Dr. Bu-

Occupied by the English.

1 Tennent, p. 71.
2 Tennent, p. 81.
3 Buchanan's *Researches*, p. 60.

chanan, awakened complaint in England, and Lord Castlereagh, the Secretary of State, exhorted Sir Thomas Maitland, the Governor, to attend to the matter. Three English missionaries who had arrived in 1804, now received special favor from the local authorities. One of them, the Rev. Mr. Palm, connected with the London Missionary Society, was stationed at Tillipally in Jaffna. He remained there only a few years, and when the American mission arrived, was connected with a Dutch church at Colombo.

Sudden relapse to idolatry.

One cannot but wonder at the rapid renunciation of even the name of Christianity by the people of Jaffna, after the departure of the Dutch. It should be borne in mind, however, that the chains of caste had never been broken, and that the doctrines of Christianity had been too superficially taught to make much impression on the reluctant minds of the natives. Very few of the Dutch ministers, moreover, had command of the vernacular language, and therefore preached through the cold medium of interpreters.[1] Their numbers were too few. In 1722, there were in all Ceylon only fourteen clergymen for half a million of nominal Christians, and almost no native ministry, and the education imparted in their schools was "infinitesimally small." To all this it should be added, that the people, accustomed to a system of religious

[1] Rev. Mr. Palm, as quoted by Tennent.

compulsion for nearly two centuries, expected a continuance of the same rigor on the arrival of the British, and were prepared to accept any prescribed form of Christianity. But finding that its outward profession was no longer required for holding government offices, and that they were no longer to be paid for their hypocrisies, the number of nominal Christians began rapidly to decline; until Dr. Buchanan described the Protestant religion in 1806, as being extinct in Jaffna. Catholic priests, flocking in from Goa, had induced great numbers to join the Roman Catholic communion; and the large residue rebuilt their heathen temples, and publicly resumed their idolatrous rites. The heathenism of Jaffna is Hindû, the same with that which prevails on the neighboring continent. In the Singalese or southern provinces of Ceylon, the heathenism is of the Buddhist form, such as prevails in the Burman empire.

The province of Jaffna is a cluster of islands at the northern extremity of Ceylon, separated from each other by narrow channels, and rising but little above the level of the sea. The ruined old churches in this province belonged to the Government, which allowed the American missionaries to occupy the buildings and glebes at Batticotta and Tillipally. The remains of the one at Batticotta were the finest in the district. The roof was gone; but its walls of coral, four feet

Jaffna described.

Favor from the government.

thick, were standing, and enclosed a space one hundred and sixty-three feet long and fifty-seven wide. Two rows of ten pillars, each ten feet in circumference, had divided the interior into three aisles. Two thirds of such a building was large enough for a place of worship, and the remainder was ultimately used for school-rooms and other purposes. There were also the walls of a dwelling-house more than one hundred feet long, and of five small out-buildings, all without roofs or windows. In the rear of all was a garden of nearly two acres, enclosed by a high coral wall, and containing three wells for watering it in times of drought. On the premises were sixty trees, twenty-nine of which were fruitful palmyras capable of supporting a native family. The buildings at these two stations were repaired by the mission, and the Government afterwards granted the church buildings in six other parishes.

Opening of boarding-schools.

It being found that many parents would put their children under the care of the missionaries for education, if the mission would support them, it was decided to open a boarding-school for boys at Tillipally, where the estimated annual cost of each would be about twelve Spanish dollars. Placing the boys in a building erected for the purpose in the garden, they were in good measure kept from the influence of heathen society, and were steadily employed in useful studies. They were also instructed in the principles of the Christian religion as fully as if they had been the children of Christian parents.

The Tamil language is not easy of acquisition, and the preaching, for a time, was necessarily through interpreters; but in October, 1817, just a year after settling at Tillipally, Mr. Poor commenced preaching in the native language; and so did Mr. Meigs at Batticotta.

Preaching in Tamil.

Painful apprehensions had arisen before this time, as to the health of Messrs. Warren and Richards. The climate of Jaffna, though one of the best, was found too bracing for them, and Mr. Warren was prostrated by a hemorrhage. They repaired first to Colombo, and then to Cape Town, Governor Brownrigg granting them a free passage in a public vessel. The voyage was beneficial till near its close, when they were driven back to sea by tempestuous weather, and both of the invalids took severe colds. They arrived at Cape Town on the 11th of July, and were received with distinguished kindness by Christian friends, especially by the Rev. George Thom, of the London Missionary Society. Mr. Warren died on the 11th of August, 1818, at the age of thirty-two. Though young in the service, his brethren bore united testimony to his eminent devotedness to the holy cause, his well-directed zeal, his diligence in labors, his equanimity in sufferings, his

Failure of health.

Visit to Cape Town.

Death of Mr. Warren.

wisdom in counsel, and his prudence, kindness, and heavenly mindedness. His exemplary resignation, during his lengthened illness, and his conversation were in a high degree edifying. He was heard to say faintly, just before departing, "Is this death? Yes, this is death. Come, Lord Jesus, come quickly." Such were his last words. Mr. Richards returned to Jaffna with somewhat improved health, and his life was prolonged several years.

Return of Mr. Richards.

On the 8th of June, 1819, Messrs. Levi Spaulding, Miron Winslow, Henry Woodward, and John Scudder, M. D., sailed for this mission from Boston with their wives, in the brig *Indus*, Captain Willis, bound to Calcutta. Persons are living who remember the remarkable religious awakening on board the *Indus* during this voyage, embracing the greater part of the crew. The mission families had some afflictive experiences at Calcutta; but there, and at Trincomalee, Galle, and Colombo, they found missionary friends to help them on their way, and all reached Jaffna early in the following year. Their arrival was opportune, as the health of Messrs. Poor and Meigs was beginning to fail. Considering the decidedly oceanic character of the climate, it is singular that the cases of illness thus far had all been pulmonary.

The mission reinforced.

The parishes under the particular care of the mission were eight, namely, Tillipally, Batticotta,

Oodooville, Panditeripo, Manepy, Mallagaum, Milette, and Changany. The repairs of the old church buildings were somewhat expensive, yet were they deemed of great advantage to the mission. The total number of pupils at the close of the year 1818, was about seven hundred. The mission had an efficient assistant in Maleappa, a native of Malabar about twenty years of age, the son of a native preacher supported by government at Negombo. He had been in Christian David's school at Jaffnapatam, and was instructed by the first members of the mission while delayed at Colombo. About a dozen girls attended worship on the Sabbath and recited the catechism, and about the same number of women were present. The dress of the native children, and of the men generally, was of the most simple kind; consisting of a piece of plain India cotton a yard in width and two or two and a half in length, wound round the person. The practice was soon introduced of giving names to the beneficiaries in boarding-schools, according to the wishes of patrons in America.

The mission stations.

The schools.

Those who have been familiar with the financial operations of the Board only since 1831, when it began to remit funds to the missions through the Messrs. Baring of London, can hardly imagine the embarrassments growing out of the delays and uncertainty of remittances while

Difficulties in remitting funds.

the Board was young in years and little known. Of what avail would it have been to draw bills on the Board, unless the Board had a recognized existence in the commercial world? Meeting the exigency with Spanish dollars was expensive, their seasonable arrival was uncertain, and if sent long in advance there was the loss of interest. The difficulty was in part overcome, for a time, by the kind and generous agency of Messrs. Arbuthnot, De Monte, & Co., of Madras, and Edward A. Newton, Esq., of Calcutta.

A printing establishment not allowed.

A printing-press having been given for the mission, types were ordered from Calcutta, and Mr. James Garrett, a printer, was sent out to take charge of the establishment. He arrived in August, 1820, and the consent of the government was requested for his residence on the island. There was every reason to presume it would be given. Sir Robert Brownrigg, Sir Alexander Johnstone, and Archdeacon Twisleton had done everything to encourage the mission, and official permission had been given to their having a printing-press, "subject to the censorship of the government." Under what unfavorable influences Sir Edward Barnes, the Lieutenant-governor who succeeded Sir Robert, had been educated, is not known; but when the arrival of Mr. Garrett was communicated to him, as it was without delay through the venerable Dr. Twisleton, and permission was requested that their newly-arrived brother might be associated with them in labor, Sir Edward directed his secretary to reply, that government did not deem it proper to allow any increase of American missionaries in Ceylon; and that Mr. Garrett could not be permitted to reside in Jaffna, but must leave the island within three months from August 24th, the date of the letter. Surprised by such a communication, the missionaries supposed the Governor must have been under some misapprehensions, which a full exhibition of the facts would remove. They prepared a memorial, therefore, in which they called his attention to the inoffensive nature of their mission, to its freedom from all political intent, to the approbation received from the late Governor and the leading men around him, to the schools which the missionaries had established, to the expenses incurred in repairs at the different stations, and to the official permission they received in 1816 to the setting up of a press. They asked, that Mr. Garrett might remain with them at least until the pleasure of the king's government could be known.

The printer banished.

The Governor's reply to this, dated September 22d, may be found, with the memorials from the mission, in the Appendix to the Report of the Board for 1821.[1] It was a strange document. And when an appeal was made to his benevolence, on the ground that no passage for the

The governor inexorable.

[1] pp. 168–176.

United States could be obtained nearer than Calcutta, and that, during the rainy season, then at hand, it was almost impossible to proceed to that port by water on account of the monsoon, or by land in consequence of heavy rains, and they humbly requested that the time for his departure might be prolonged at least two months; this was refused. Mr. Garrett therefore proceeded to Negapatam, on the Coromandel coast, wholly uncertain as to his future destination.

Action of the government at home.

It is unpleasant to be obliged to add, that Sir Edward Barnes' decision against an increase in the number of American missionaries in Jaffna was, some time afterwards, affirmed by the home government, and continued in force until the year 1832.

Supposed call for a new mission.

The Jaffna brethren were led at that time to inquire, whether they ought not to extend their operations to the people on the adjacent continent speaking the same language. Indeed they designated two of their number to take measures for occupying a station on the Coromandel coast, but relinquished the project on hearing that the departure of Mr. Bardwell from Bombay had created a call for Mr. Garrett to that place.

Excellent spirit of the Danish missionaries.

The Danish missionaries at Tranquebar received Mr. Garrett most kindly, and hailed the coöperation of American Christians in the work as an event joyful in itself, and most encouraging to those who had previously entered the field.

Death of Mrs. Poor.

The death of Mrs. Poor, on the 7th of May, 1821, was a sore affliction to the mission, as well as to her husband and children. Her illness was regarded as dangerous from the first, but her intellectual powers were in vigorous exercise during the whole fortnight of its continuance, and her death-bed was a scene of victory and exultation. It was edifying and animating to those around her to witness her clear and satisfactory views of the Gospel scheme of salvation, and of her own interest in the Saviour, and her lively anticipations of heavenly realities. Her surviving friends could not but rejoice with her, and go forth to their several labors consoled and strengthened.[1]

Mrs. Poor was a faithful helper to the mission, and endeared to all her associates. She was an invaluable friend to the children of the heathen, whose spiritual interests she habitually consulted. A short account of her life and death, circulated among the natives, was believed to have been a means of blessing to many.

[1] *Missionary Herald* for 1822, pp. 94–96, and 121–127.

CHAPTER VIII.

THE TAMIL PEOPLE.

CEYLON MISSION.

1820–1832.

Development of schools.

THE Ceylon mission was gradually working itself into that system of schools, which for nearly half a century formed one of its prominent features. The facility with which heathen children were obtained for Christian training was remarkable. Doubtless the access which a moderate knowledge of English gave to lucrative positions in government offices, plantations, and mercantile houses, promoted, to a considerable extent, this readiness to learn.

The schools were of two classes, the village free schools, and the boarding-schools. The free schools were commenced at once under heathen masters, no others being attainable. Mainly through conversions in the boarding-schools, this evil gradually diminished, and the schools went on prosperously. The first boarding-school for boys was commenced by Mr. Poor at Tillipally, soon after his arrival.

Girls were also obtained as boarders as early as 1818. All received Christian names, proposed by patrons in America, and were pleased with them as tokens of approbation and pledges of support; but among their heathen friends they were known only by their old names.[1] In 1823 there were boarding-schools at most of the stations.

Proposal for a college.

The missionaries at this time projected a College, in which the course of study should occupy six years. In giving their reasons for such an institution, they said: "Those unacquainted with the existing state of things in India cannot understand the hindrances to the reception of the Gospel in that country. Not one of those evidences, on which Christianity rests its claims at home, can be fully apprehended here. The internal evidences from the excellence and sublimity of the sacred Scriptures are little understood, and the external evidences cannot be apprehended at all. If we speak of prophecies which have been fulfilled, the history of the times when they were spoken and when accomplished is alike unknown. If of miracles, we are told of unnumbered miracles vastly more marvelous than any of which we can speak. Besides, the belief that miracles constantly occur, even now, hinders their being received as a divine attestation to the truth of Christianity. Before these evidences can be appreciated by the people of

[1] *Missionary Herald,* 1820, p. 136.

India, they must first understand something of history, and enough of true science at least to know what a miracle is. They must learn to bring their credulous belief in everything marvelous to the test of reason, and understand the difference between truth and fable, and think, compare, reflect; things which the great mass of people in India never do. General knowledge must be disseminated. It might easily be shown, that so contrary to fact are the principles of Geology, Natural Philosophy, and Astronomy, as laid down in their sacred books, that even a superficial acquaintance with these branches of science would explode their systems, and materially affect the credit of the books which contain them."

That there were good reasons for the liberal education of translators and teachers, will not be questioned. But the reflecting mind, looking upon the actual influences of the Gospel, will see that it has, and must have, through the agency of the Holy Spirit, a more direct access to the heart where it is faithfully presented, than can be secured by any other agency, whatever the amount of ignorance to be removed, or the influence of false systems to be overcome.

Adverse position of the government.

Subscriptions for the proposed College were obtained to some extent in India; but the Government of Ceylon would not sanction such an institution in connection with the American mission, alleging that a College, if instituted, should be under teachers sent from England.

Sir Edward Barnes doubtless communicated his views to his government at home; for when the Prudential Committee, at the beginning of 1826, through the kind aid of Mr. Wilberforce, opened a correspondence with the Home Government on the subject, the reply was, that no increase of the number of American missionaries in Ceylon would be permitted, and that a College, if established, should be under instructors from Great Britain.

Central boarding-school at Batticotta.

It was still possible, however, to have a high school, which should give an education nearly or quite equal to what was then possible for a college in so remote a province. Permission was obtained from the subscribers to apply the funds already pledged in India to the central boarding-school at Batticotta, and the needed buildings were erected. The principal building, sixty-four feet by twenty-nine, with a veranda on each side, designed for library, apparatus, lecture rooms, and examinations, was called Ottley Hall, in honor of Sir Richard Ottley, Associate Justice of Ceylon, who had shown a deep interest in the mission, and had rendered valuable aid by his personal influence and donations. A dining-hall was also erected, with rooms for study and devotion. And as they were not permitted to look for professors to America, the Seminary was to furnish, as fast as possible, a faculty for itself. Twenty-two out of its fifty-three students were members of the church, and eighteen more were received from the preparatory school. Seventy candidates presented themselves for examination, to take the places of the eighteen thus promoted, and of these thirty were received.

English schools.

The station boarding-schools for boys were followed by what were called English schools, intended to prepare lads to enter the Batticotta Seminary at small expense while residing at home with their relatives. The English language was taught in their schools, but the pupils all pursued a thorough course of study in the vernacular. They had previously become familiar with the catechisms, Scripture history, and Bible reading taught in the native free schools, though a further acquaintance with these Christian lessons was required to enter the Seminary. The Bible was read daily both in English and Tamil. Almost all the schools had Christian teachers, and they were usually so near the residence of a missionary as to be under his eye and influence. The largest number of these English schools was sixteen in the year 1848, with six hundred and eighteen pupils.

Central boarding-school for girls.

A boarding-school for girls was commenced at Oodooville, in the year 1826. Sixteen of its first pupils had previously been under the instruction of missionary ladies at the different stations. Its design was to take girls away from the heathen influences of their homes, and so provide suitable companions for the graduates of the Batticotta Seminary. The school was for a time under the care of Mr. and Mrs. Winslow, and, after several changes, under that of Mr. and Mrs. Spaulding. The prejudices against female education were everywhere very strong, and had come down from ancient times. Mr. Meigs could hear of only three respectable females in Jaffna in 1816, who were able to read and write. A certain amount of education was given to those who were to become dancing girls in the native temples, and to sing the dissolute songs connected with the temple worship.

For twenty years, it was deemed necessary to retain pupils in this school until marriage, except in cases of misconduct, and that they should receive clothing as well as board. When married with the approval of the mission, they received a dowry of about twenty-five dollars. After that time, however, no pledges of dowry were given, and in two years more the term of residence became limited. At the end of another two years, a portion of the pupils were required to pay something towards their board. Yet the applicants for reception continued to be more than could be admitted. The ages at which pupils could enter the seminary varied from six to ten years. They were from different castes, though neither from the highest nor the lowest, and very few were from wealthy families. The whole number of pupils, up to the year 1854, was two hundred and ninety-five, of whom one hundred and seventy-five became church members; and not more than twelve of these dishonored their profession.

The firmness with which the graduates of this school adhered to their Christian profession, was remarkable. When in Ceylon, the author saw many of them as wives and mothers, at their own homes and elsewhere. They were intelligent, thoroughly Christianized, cordial in their manners, and evidently a blessing in their families, and in the community.

The schools as converting institutions.

Children in the boarding-school were separated from the outside world for a time, and brought under religious influences; but were somewhat in the situation of green-house plants in winter. Whatever the view subsequently taken of the defects of boarding-school training as a means for providing efficient helpers in the Christian work, it became an interesting study as a converting agency.

REVIVALS OF RELIGION.

Anticipating the chronological order of events, it may be well to notice several of the revivals connected with the schools in a continuous series.

In 1821, there was special seriousness at Tillipally. Nicholas, a native helper, came one day to

Mr. Poor, to ask how he should converse with persons anxious for their salvation. His eldest sister, he thought, was trusting in Christ, and he had heard Tappan, a boy only ten years old, addressing boys smaller than himself on the subject of Christ's coming to judge the world. Of seven girls who called on Mr. Poor, two seemed to be truly converted. In August, three young men were received into the church, and two of them became useful helpers. Other young men had been received previously, one of whom is living to this day, and has ever maintained a Christian character.

At Tillipally.

Early in 1824, Mr. Woodward saw that some of the boys at Tillipally were peculiarly affected under preaching. Thus encouraged, he appointed meetings for the afternoon and evening. Next day, being himself unwell, he sent for Mr. Winslow, who attended the evening meeting, and found a large room nearly filled with boys and others. It was not long before all the forty members of the school, with two or three schoolmasters and the domestics of the family, were among the inquirers.

On Mr. Winslow's return to Oodooville, there was a similar movement at his station. The preaching on the Lord's day drew tears from many eyes. The same hallowed influence was extended to Manepy, Panditeripo, and Batticotta. Special meetings were held by the brethren jointly at different stations, and the interest soon became

At the stations.

general. The quarterly meeting of the brethren at Oodooville, was the most interesting that had been held in the mission. "The conversation through the day," writes one of the missionaries, "was on the means of promoting the work of God among us. It was a season of weeping for joy, as well as brokenness of heart for sin. The Redeemer was with us, and his banner over us was love." On the 25th of February, there was a general meeting of the schoolmasters and superintendents of schools connected with the mission. All the brethren of the mission and Mr. Knight of the Church Missionary Society attended. The schoolmasters from Nellore, Mr. Knight's station, were also present. In all there were seventy men, with many of the older boys in the schools. A meeting was first held with the masters, in the veranda of the house, at which several of them expressed hope in Christ and readiness to forsake all for Him, and about thirty testified their belief in Christianity as the only true religion. In the afternoon a general meeting was held in the bungalow. This was attended by the more thoughtful lads from Tillipally and Panditeripo, and by both boys and girls from the schools at Manepy. An interesting account of the revival at the different stations was given by Philip Matthew, and those present who were willing to leave all for Christ were called upon to testify their purpose to do this. More than sixty responded. On the 30th of March nearly all the boarding children in the mission, about one hundred and seventy, assembled at Manepy, and ninety-two of them expressed a hope in Christ; but the evidences of conversion were not in all cases satisfactory.

The result.

As the result of this awakening, forty-one were gathered into the church on the 20th of January, 1825, of whom thirty-six belonged to the boarding-schools. The meeting was in a rude building erected for the purpose in the central village of Santillepay, and from twelve to fifteen hundred natives were present. The Church Missionary and Wesleyan brethren were there. Thirty-three were baptized. The candidates stood in a semicircle fronting the pulpit, and came forward in sections, each missionary taking part in the joyful service. The communicants were eighty-two. At the close of the service, more than a hundred, not connected with the church, testified their belief in the Christian religion, and their purpose to embrace it. Some of these were among the hopeful converts. The audience gave good attention till the end, notwithstanding the great length of the exercises.

A second religious awakening.

In October there was another religious awakening, preceded by an unusual spirit of prayer in the mission, and there was special seriousness at all the stations. The hopeful converts were chiefly from among the boarding scholars and schoolmasters. The report of the seminary at Batticotta speaks of three seasons of special religious interest in that institution during this year, in which those who had been previously awakened but had become comparatively thoughtless, obtained more impressive views of divine truth, and gave more satisfactory evidence of genuine conversion.

A third awakening.

Another religious awakening occurred near the close of 1830. It began at the monthly concert, and the effects of it were first seen in the families of the missionaries. The native churches were all revived. The members of the church at Batticotta were moved to confession and prayer, and to labor for those around them. The studies of the seminary were nearly suspended for a time, and it was cheering to behold the little rooms for prayer in the Seminary building lighted up till a late hour in the evening. At a stated quarterly meeting, more than one hundred teachers and superintendents were present, besides the members of the Seminary. The interest was thus extended, and there were tokens of the divine presence at all the stations, but especially in the boarding-schools at Tillipally and Oodooville. In November a meeting of all who could read in the free schools was held at Oodooville. At least eight hundred were present, and there was evidence that considerable progress had been made in the knowledge and belief of Christianity.

Thirty-four were received into the church in April of the year 1831, as the fruit of this awakening. Of these, eighteen were members of the seminary, four belonged to the preparatory school, two to the boarding-school for girls, seven were schoolmasters, and three were women not connected with the schools. This reception of converts was at Oodooville, and Mr. Winslow thus describes it: —

"The candidates, standing in a semicircle in front of the pulpit, gave their assent to the articles of faith; and then all advancing, one by one, kneeled, and received baptism. After this they entered into covenant with the church, and the members, rising, entered into covenant with them." In the July following, twenty-seven others were received, including the two oldest children of the mission. Ten were from the seminary, and eight were schoolmasters, the ages varying from twelve to sixty. The number added to the church as a consequence of this revival, was sixty-one. Of the two hundred and four who had been admitted to Christian communion since the commencement of the mission, one hundred and seventeen were boarding scholars, thirty were schoolmasters and superintendents of schools, and fifty were villagers. Thirty were more than forty years of age, thirteen were over fifty, one was above seventy, and one over eighty. In March, 1832, twenty-two were received as church members, very much in the proportions already stated. The seminary had then more than fifty pupils, who were in good standing as church members.

Still another.

Still another season of refreshing was enjoyed at the close of 1834. The majority of the students at Batticotta were more or less affected, and the influence extended to the seminary at Oodooville and then to the other stations, at all of which protracted meetings were held. The effect of these was very salutary. An impression was made on some hundreds in the native free schools. Among those received into the church from the Seminary was Breckenridge, since favorably known as principal of the Native English High School. The accessions to the church as a consequence of this revival, were sixty-seven.[1]

The boarding-schools an auxiliary.

The reader will have noticed, in these brief descriptions of the visitations of divine grace previous to 1835, that the favoring circumstances of the boarding-schools were powerful auxiliaries to the preaching of the Gospel, and consequently the revivals stand connected both with preaching and with education as instrumental causes. It is a fact worthy of special attention, that no general and vigorous opposition appears to have been aroused among the heathen parents and friends of the pupils in the schools during these revivals.

[1] See an interesting account by Mr. Poor in the *Missionary Herald* for 1835, pp. 285–290; also, 1836, pp. 85–88, and 140.

Returning from this digression we resume the narrative of events in their proper order. Dr. Scudder received ordination in the Wesleyan chapel at Jaffnapatam in May, 1821, and Mr. Chater a Baptist missionary and Mr. Roberts a Wesleyan missionary, united with their American brethren in the ordaining services. In the same year, Gabriel Tissera, Francis Malleappa, and Nicholas Permander, native converts who had pursued a course of study preparatory to the ministry, were licensed as preachers of the Gospel. Gabriel was the first convert received into the church. His talents were of a superior order, and he had an ardent thirst for knowledge. His remarkable command of the English language was shown in a long letter to the Corresponding Secretary of the Board, and in a still longer and beautifully written journal, which were published at the time.[1] His exhortations in religious meetings were earnest, and he was acceptable as a leader in all departments of social worship. He died rather suddenly on the 9th of February, 1838, and his loss was deeply felt. Francis Malleappa was a native of Malabar, the son of a native preacher supported by the government at Negombo, and born about the year 1800. He was one or two years in the government school at Jaff-

Ordination of Dr. Scudder.

Native preachers.

Gabriel Tissera.

Francis Malleappa.

[1] *Missionary Herald* for 1820, pp. 138–142; and *Report of the Board* for 1823, pp. 147–172.

napatam, under the care of Mr. David, and was six months in a school taught by American missionaries while detained at Colombo. He served as interpreter at Tillipally, had much facility in addressing the people, and delighted in preaching. Nicholas Permander was spoken of in 1820 as admitted to the church in the presence of four hundred natives. He rendered valuable service to the mission as schoolmaster, catechist, and general assistant, but withdrew from it in 1827, in the hope of obtaining higher wages in the service of the government. For this reason his license as a preacher was revoked.

Nicholas Permander.

In April, 1822, Nathaniel Niles and Jordan Lodge were received into the church, and in August, Ebenezer Porter, Whelpley, and Valen, the last a slave of the Covia caste, who received the Christian name of Onesimus.

Other assistants.

About this time a marriage occurred which was an inroad upon ancient customs, and a bold violation of the laws of caste. A young man of heathen parentage, who lived much in the family of Mr. Richards, had recently been admitted to the church. He was known in the mission by the name of Daniel Smead, and was nineteen years of age. Certain gross vices to which he was addicted when he first came to live in the mission were abandoned, and not long after he gave evidence of conversion. Though of the Vellale caste, he de-

An influential marriage.

termined to marry an educated Christian woman of a comparatively low caste, and with scarcely half the dowry he might receive with a heathen wife. She had received the name of Miranda Safford, and was one of the most advanced scholars in the school. In direct opposition to the popular sentiment, he assigned her good education as a reason for his choice. But his most offensive innovation was eating at the same table with his wife. Even the Roman Catholics had not ventured on such a departure from the customs of the country. The immediate effect was so favorable, that three girls of high caste from the village where Miranda lived, applied for admission to the school.[1]

Death and character of Mr. Richards.

Mr. Richards, after lingering about five years with a pulmonary disease, died on the 3d of August, 1822, at the age of thirty-eight. It is believed that he was the first, after Samuel J. Mills his classmate in Williams College, to dedicate himself to the work of Foreign Missions. At the Seminary in Andover he labored with Mills and several others, in promoting the spirit of missions among the students, and by the distribution of books in the community. The reason why his name did not appear in the memorial presented to the General Association was, that four were thought a sufficient number to be presented in the first instance as devoted to foreign missions, and the others,

[1] Tracy's *History of the Missions of the Board*, p. 116.

being his seniors in the Theological Seminary, would be sooner prepared to leave their country. He spent nearly two years in the Medical School at Philadelphia. Declining a call to settle as pastor of a people, who had been divided but were united under his ministry, he married Miss Sarah Bardwell of Goshen, Massachusetts, and embarked for Ceylon. The failure of his health, and his consequent visit to the Cape of Good Hope in 1818 with Mr. Warren, have been already mentioned. After the departure of this brother to a better world he returned to Ceylon, and to the surprise of all labored on till June, 1822, when his last illness commenced. His sufferings were often very severe, but they roused the faculties of his soul to vigorous exertion. The Lord was pleased to manifest himself as a being every way worthy of supreme affection. So desirable did it appear to him that God should be glorified by all his creatures, that he was willing his sufferings should be continued and even increased, if that were necessary to promote the designs of his Heavenly Father; and since his sufferings were the means of revealing to him such views of God, he regarded them as a proper occasion for thanksgiving. Certainly his experience was a means of good to his brethren of the mission, and to the native Christians around him. "The pains, the groans, the dying strife," are descriptive of his last days. They were filled also with the triumphs of faith, and the end, as he saw it approaching, was welcomed with holy joy. Among his last words were, "I still feel that I see through a glass darkly, but very soon face to face!" Those around his bed, when they saw that he was gone, united in a hymn and a prayer expressive of their mingled emotions of joy and grief.[1]

Early in the year 1823 Mr. Poor was married to Miss Knight, a sister of Mr. Knight, Church missionary at Nellore. The friendly attentions of the Church missionaries had been specially marked and encouraging during the interdict placed on the mission by Sir Edward Barnes.

Marriage of Mr. Poor.

Slavery, as it then existed among the natives, was a great barrier to social intercourse. At the commencement of the mission, one slave might have as many as fifty masters. Slaves were the property of families, rather than of individuals. If a man needed the assistance of his slaves he supported them while thus employed, which was often but a few days, and then dismissed them leaving them to provide for themselves. Some slaves were employed but little by their masters. In the year 1818, Governor Brownrigg had taken measures for having all the slaves in the district divided and registered, so that each should have but one master. He also made the humane regulation, that if a slave wished to be free and would apply to the

Slavery in Jaffna.

[1] See Memoir of Mr. Richards, *Missionary Herald*, 1823, pp. 241–246, and 1824, pp. 233–236.

provincial court, he should be appraised by five men, two appointed by the owner, two by the slave himself, and one by the government, and if the slave should pay the sum at which he was valued, with ten dollars more for stamp duties, he should be freed. In this way Cornelius and Danvers, promising brothers in the boarding-school, were freed, to their great joy, by Mr. Poor. The former was valued at twenty-two dollars, and the latter at eighteen.

Attendance on public worship.

Public worship was now regularly attended at the stations every Sabbath, at which the mission families, domestics, school-boys, and other natives attended. The average attendance at Tillipally was about three hundred, the greater part of whom were children. Prayers were offered in the church morning and evening through the week, with reading of the Scriptures, at which the pupils of the schools were present. Dependence on interpreters gradually ceased. It is said of Messrs. Winslow and Woodward, as it had been of Messrs. Poor and Meigs, that they preached in Tamil in less than a year after they became settled on mission ground.

Deaths.

The widow of Mr. Richards had been married to the Rev. Mr. Knight, but on the 26th of April, 1825, she died; and Mrs. Woodward followed her on the 24th of November.

Flourishing condition of the schools.

There were sixty-seven students in the Batticotta Seminary in 1827, of whom somewhat more than half were church members. Mr. Poor was aided in the Seminary by Gabriel Tissera and ten other natives. Of free schools there were ninety-three, containing 3,378 boys and 942 girls, and the attendants at public worship on Sabbath mornings were about two thousand. The whole number in all the schools, at the close of this year, was 4,500.

Twelve years had wrought a great change in the Jaffna schools. A class of fifteen graduated from the Batticotta Seminary in 1828, and there were not less than two hundred applicants for admission to the new class, whose claims were urged by relatives and friends, but only twenty-nine could be received. The whole number under instruction in the mission in 1829, was 3,436.

Bearing of education on the brahminic philosophy.

The improved system of education was attracting the attention of all classes of men. The Seminary especially was made to bear on the question, whether the popular idolatry was true. The systems of geography and astronomy taught by the brahmins are parts of their religious system, and as such claimed infallibility, and if overthrown it would seem that the whole must fall. The brahmin cannot admit that the earth is a sphere, or that it moves, and a slight knowledge of geography shows that many of the mountains and seas mentioned in the histories of their gods, have no existence. Eclipses are said to be caused by two monsters, sometimes called serpents, who attempt to devour the sun and moon. These were perhaps intended, originally, as emblems of the ascending and descending nodes, called, even in some of our almanacs, the "dragon's head" and "dragon's tail," near which alone eclipses can take place; but modern brahmins teach, that they are actual serpents or monsters, and when an eclipse occurs the people call earnestly upon the gods to deliver the endangered luminary. Still, strange as it may seem, their learned men can calculate the time when it will please Rahoo, one of the monsters, to seize the moon, how much of it will come within his grasp, and how long the struggle will continue.

Vesuvenather, whose ancestors had been astronomers for nine generations, and who was the most learned native astronomer in the region, had published his annual almanac, in which he predicted an eclipse of the moon on the 21st of March, at twenty-four minutes past six P. M., which would obscure five eighths of the moon's disc. According to calculations at the Seminary it was to commence at nine minutes past six, and to obscure only three eighths of the disc. There was also a difference of twenty-four minutes in the predicted duration of the eclipse. Hearing of the difference Vesuvenather, assisted by his brethren, carefully reviewed his calculations and reaffirmed their correctness. As the time drew near, a leading brahmin grew deeply interested in the affair, and ran from place to place calling the attention of the people to the decisive evidence about to be given of the superiority of their religion over Christianity. The evening came. At six o'clock Mr. Poor and his students and the Pandarum[1] and his friends were all assembled. The telescope was ready, and the nicely regulated watch. They turned to the east, but a small cloud was rising which threatened to conceal the object of their anxiety. At nine minutes past six the cloud was still there. In another minute the moon appeared. A small spot was visible on her northeastern limb, but "it was the cloud, certainly it was the cloud." In two minutes more the cloud was gone, but the spot had grown and the eclipse had certainly begun. The Pandarum was silent for a while, and then began to abuse the native astronomers for "imposing upon the people." Mr. Poor defended his acquaintance Vesuvenather, on the ground, which a believer in the infallibility of their system could not admit, that even the most learned men are liable to mistakes. He then led the way to his school-room, and delivered a lecture on eclipses. By means of an orrery, putting a lamp in the place of the sun, he showed them the heavenly bodies as they had seen them at sunset, and then extinguishing all the lamps but that which represented the sun they saw how the shadow of the earth eclipsed the moon. The Pandarum himself was gratified, and the company generally expressed their delight at seeing the two

[1] Priest of the Temple.

great serpents changed into two shadows, that of the moon and that of the earth.

But, after all, might not the time-pieces be wrong and the native astronomers right? Two other tests remained, the magnitude and the duration of the eclipse. These were watched with intense interest, but it was certain that less than half of the moon was obscured, and that the duration was just what had been predicted at the Seminary. The Hindû system was seen to be incorrect. There could be no doubt about it, and there were great reasonings among them as to what would be the result. A few days afterwards Dashiel, one of the students at the Seminary, called on Vesuvenather. The old man brought forward an ancient book, which he said was written more than two hundred years ago, and which contained the true theory of eclipses. He said he had long been acquainted with that theory, and knew it to be the true one. Being asked why he did not make it known to the people, and especially to the learned in the district, he replied that "the people would not believe it, nor could they be made readily to understand it."

Perplexity of an old brahmin.

Does the reader ask, what was the result of all this? Not a single instance of conversion, for astronomical truth cannot change the heart; but the learned were compelled to regard and treat the Seminary and the mission with more respect than formerly. The words of the missionaries

The result.

had more weight with people of every class; their preaching had better access to the minds of men; the confidence of the people in the brahmins was also weakened; and in every way the influence was favorable to the dissemination and candid reception of that truth, by which the heart is changed.[1]

Popularity of the higher schools.

The government commissioners for inspecting schools visited the Seminary at Batticotta in September, 1830, and bore most decided testimony in its favor, and one of them placed twenty pounds in the hands of the Principal to be distributed in prizes for the best translations of useful essays into English. About the same time, an application was received from a missionary of the English Society for Propagating the Gospel, residing at Trichinopoly, for fifteen pupils to be employed as catechists among the Tamil people on the continent. Also, as soon as it became known that there were twelve vacancies in the girls' school at Oodooville, there were not less than seventy applicants for admission.

A destructive fire.

The mission buildings at Manepy were consumed by fire in March, 1831. They were a dwelling-house, church, study, and a large bungalow. Being thatched with leaves, the conflagration was exceedingly rapid, and Mr. and Mrs. Woodward, though aided by Mr. and Mrs. Roberts, Wesleyan missionaries who happened to be present,

[1] Mr. Tracy's *History of the Board*, p. 216.

were able to save scarcely any of their effects. The loss, including private property, was estimated at between three and four thousand dollars. The heathen exulted, as if it were a victory of their god Ganesa, whose temple formerly stood on the mission premises, over the God of the Christians. But the house of worship was rebuilt in six months.

A large-hearted bishop.

Bishop Turner of Calcutta was there a few days after the fire, and subsequently obtained a thousand rupees at Madras, and almost twice that sum at Bombay. If the like benevolent effort was not repeated by him at Calcutta, it was because the excellent prelate was called to rest from his labors soon after returning to that city. The annual Report of the Board mentions others, who were specially active in collecting money to repair the loss.

Bishop Turner devoted a day to an examination of the Seminary at Batticotta, together with the preparatory and female central schools, both of which were assembled for the purpose. He expressed the gratification he felt on the occasion, and assured the students of his readiness to coöperate with the conductors of the Seminary. He also declared to the members of the mission his full concurrence in their plans of procedure. The brethren were strongly reminded, by what they saw of this prelate, of the description of true bishops drawn by the pen of inspiration. His decease took place at Calcutta on the 7th of July following.

In the year 1832, Sir Robert Wilmot Horton, having succeeded Sir Edward Barnes as Governor of Ceylon, granted official leave for missionaries to be sent from America until reference could be made to England; and Lord Goderich, Secretary of State for the Colonies, appears to have lost no time in giving the assent of the Government. Accordingly Messrs. George H. Apthorp, William Todd, Samuel Hutchings, Henry R. Hoisington, James R. Eckard, Nathan Ward, M. D., and Eastman S. Minor, were on their way in 1833. Mr. Ward was a physician, and Mr. Minor a printer.

Sir Robert Wilmot Horton removes the injunction from the mission.

Reinforcement of the mission.

CHAPTER IX.

THE TAMIL PEOPLE.

CEYLON MISSION.

1832–1853.

Batticotta Seminary.

THIRTY-EIGHT, or nearly half, of the scholars in the Batticotta Seminary were church members at the opening of the year 1832, and the weight of character and influence in the institution was decidedly Christian.

Death of Mrs. Winslow.

Mrs. Harriet Lathrop Winslow died January 13, 1833, about three months after hearing of the decease of an only and promising son in the United States. During the three hours of her sickness she was unable to speak; but not a word was needed to assure her surviving friends of the blessedness of the change, which thus suddenly came upon her. Her missionary life, commenced in 1819, had been a continual series of diligent, active, useful labors in the cause of her Redeemer. Three of her sisters afterwards joined the mission, and two of them died in Ceylon, and rest with her in the pleasant repository for the missionary dead at Oodooville.[1]

[1] *A Memoir of Mrs. Winslow,* prepared by her husband, was pub-

After this, Mr. Winslow made a visit to the United States, bringing with him his three children, and seven other children from different families in the mission. Much interest was taken in this little company, and all readily found guardians and homes. Mr. Spaulding now removed to Oodooville, Mr. Meigs to Tillipally, and Mr. Woodward to Batticotta. Dr. Scudder commenced a station in the eastern section of the district. Mr. and Mrs. Woodward were obliged to repair for health to the Neilgherry Hills on the continent. Lord William Bentinck, Governor-general of India, and Sir Frederick Adam, Governor of Madras, being there, he obtained leave for a mission in the Presidency of Madras. Mr. Spaulding had already made the needful explorations preparatory to such a mission. Mr. Woodward perceiving his strength to be rapidly failing, set his face toward Jaffna hoping to reach Madura. He was able to go no farther than Coïmbatoor, near the foot of the mountains, and there, in the hospitable family of the Rev. Mr. Addis of the London Missionary Society, he was taken to his heavenly home. He died on the 3d of August, 1834, in the thirty-eighth year of his age, having been a member of the mission somewhat more than fourteen years. His body was deposited in the burying ground at-

Children of missionaries.

Sickness and death of Mr. Woodward.

lished in this country by the American Tract Society not long after her decease, and republished in England. 16mo, pp. 480.

tached to the mission chapel. Mr. Spaulding arrived in a few days from Madura, and accompanied the bereaved widow to Jaffna.

Mr. Woodward was a good missionary, though often embarrassed by illness. His first wife died in November, 1825. His second was the widow of Mr. Frost, who with commendable zeal resolved to continue her mission in India; as was stated in the history of the Mahratta mission. The death of Mr. Woodward did not shake her purpose, and she remained in the Ceylon mission, though with the care of three fatherless children. In December, 1836, she was married to Mr. Todd, and removed to Madura, where she died in June, 1837.

Mrs. Woodward.

One of the later communications of Mr. Woodward contained a striking illustration of the benevolent spirit of the Gospel, as contrasted with the hard-heartedness of heathenism. While the throng of worshippers of Ganesa were engaged in getting rice for an offering, one of them in drawing water fell into the well. As soon as they heard of it, the priest of the temple and the crowd rushed to the spot, and, after gratifying their curiosity, returned; not one of them showing the least concern for the man, who was then struggling in the water. They chatted about him, but no one seemed to think that assistance ought to be rendered. One of the head men came at length to the

Gospel benevolence illustrated.

spot, and exerted all his influence to induce some one to dive into the water, which any person accustomed to swimming might have done with perfect safety, but his efforts were in vain. He sent for the priest, who was known to be an expert swimmer, but he excused himself, saying that he could not be absent so long from the duties of the temple. Just at this moment an unknown man arrived, and, as soon as he learned that a fellow-being was drowning, threw aside his garment, and leaped into the well. After repeatedly diving, he recovered the body. When the noise had subsided, a whisper passed through the crowd, "Who is that good man?" and the idolaters were not a little confounded, when told that it was Azel Backus, a Christian. Mr. Woodward regarded this event as having done not a little toward stopping the mouths of some, who were arrayed against Christians.

Messrs. Todd and Minor joined the mission in 1834, and Messrs. Perry and Lawrence in the following year. They were married men.

In the summer of this year the church and schoolhouse at Tillipally were destroyed by fire, set, as was believed, by an incendiary. Nearly all the Tamil books and tracts belonging to the station were consumed.

A destructive fire.

The demand for the services of natives acquainted with English had so increased, as to awaken the fear, that few who were educated in both Tamil and English would resist the temptation to leave the mission for the sake of greater wages than it could afford to pay. To avoid this, it was proposed to instruct a large proportion of those who should be admitted into the Seminary in Tamil only. A class of twenty-two was admitted on this plan in February, 1834, but years elapsed before the mission was able to check this evil. The reasons for teaching the English language are stated in a letter from the instructors of the seminary, published in the "Missionary Herald" for 1836.

Consequences of teaching the English language.

The following is a tabular view of the schools at the close of the year 1835: —

	Free Schools.	Boys.	Girls.	Preparatory school.	Totals.
Tillipally . .	30	1,500	156		1,656
Batticotta . .	29	1,005	157	37	1,199
Oodooville . .	15	340	137		477
Panditeripo .	14	448	58		506
Manepy . . .	18	402	279		681
Chavagacherry .	32	862	227		1,089
Varany . . .	7	175	15		190
	145	4,732	1,029	37	5,798

The seminary contained one hundred and forty-eight members, not including thirty-seven in the preparatory school. A fifth class of forty pupils had been received in October, and the prospects of the institution were never more encouraging. The instructors were Mr. Poor, the Principal, and teacher in astronomy and the higher branches of mathematics; Mr. Hoisington, teacher in the English language; Dr. Ward, teacher in natural philosophy and medicine; Nicholas, Martyn, Warren, Hassleton, and Volk, teachers of the native classics; Dashiel, teacher of Sanskrit, native arithmetic, and astronomy; Ropes, medical assistant; and White, teacher of the preparatory school. The central boarding-school for girls at Oodooville was under the care of Mr. Spaulding, Mrs. Spaulding, and Mrs. Hutchings. There was also an infant school at Batticotta of one hundred and twenty pupils, which had been established by Mrs. Eckard, and was then under the superintendence of Mrs. Ward, aided by two seminarists.

Mr. Poor goes to Madura for a season.

At the close of 1835, Mr. Poor, with the approbation of his brethren, resigned his station as principal of the Batticotta Seminary that he might labor for a time in the new mission on the continent. The seminary now came under the superintendence of Mr. Hoisington, and his scholarly attainments and habits, while he gave great prominence to Biblical instruction, did much to develop the desire for scientific knowledge. None of the missionary teachers, however, had the facility of Mr. Poor in the use of the native language, and the strong tendency among the students to make English the universal medium

Succeeded by Mr. Hoisington.

of communication embarrassed the new missionaries in their efforts to acquire a free use of the Tamil.

Disastrous reductions in the schools.

The year 1837, memorable for its wide-spread commercial distress, had such an effect on the receipts of the Board that the Prudential Committee, not then fully experienced in such matters, required the several missions to make large reductions in their expenditures. The facilities for remitting funds to distant missions were by no means then what they are now, and information of the embarrassments when received by the missionaries, combined with a delay in the arrival of funds, was distressing in its results beyond anything that would be experienced now, or that could then have been anticipated by the Committee. One hundred and seventy-one free schools and as many schoolmasters were discharged. The dismissed pupils exceeded five thousand, and the remarks of Mr. Spaulding on parting with the children were read at the time in this country with the most painful interest.

An affecting scene.

"After my usual lessons with the readers in the schools yesterday," he says, "I gave to each a portion of the Bible as a present. I told them the reason, exhorted them to read it and not to enter into temptation, to keep the Sabbath holy, prayed with them, commending them to the Friend of little children, and then sent them away from me, from the Bible-class, from the Sabbath-school, from the house of prayer, to feed on the mountains of heathenism with the idols under the green trees, a prey to the roaring lion, to evil demons, and to a people more ignorant than they, even to their blind, deluded, and deluding guides; and when I looked after them as they went out my heart failed me. What an offering to Swamy — five thousand children!"[1]

Deaths of Mr. and Mrs. Perry.

The letter giving the painful results was written by the Rev. John M. S. Perry, who had joined the mission with his wife, September 24, 1835, and on the 13th of March, 1837, only ten days after the date of the letter, he was removed by cholera in a very sudden manner. Three days later he was followed by Mrs. Perry, a victim of the same disease. She was sister to the first Mrs. Winslow, and one of three sisters whose bodies rest among the native churches of Jaffna.

Seasonable aid from the government

The Seminary at Batticotta had been reduced to one hundred students by turning away forty-five, and eight girls were removed from the Oodooville school. The two seminaries would have suffered greater reductions but for a seasonable donation of a thousand dollars from the government of Ceylon. Indeed every department of labor suffered more or less under the depression, and the Prudential Committee, on learning the results, lost no time in withdrawing the restriction,

[1] *Annual Report,* 1838, p. 99.

an act that was soon indorsed by larger receipts. The mission, on receiving notice that the churches had enabled the Committee to relieve them from their embarrassments, kept a day of special thanksgiving. The government of Ceylon soon after made a second appropriation for the schools like the above. But so great a ruin could not be repaired at once.

New missionaries.

Three female teachers were added to the mission this year in compliance with its request; namely, Misses Eliza Agnew, Sarah F. Brown, and Jane E. Lathrop. The health of Miss Brown permitted her to remain but a short time.

Admissions to the church.

The admissions to the church from August 4, 1816, to May 19, 1839, were 492. Dividing this period into two nearly equal proportions, some will be interested to see how the two parts compare with each other. This is shown in the following table: —

Ages.	First Period.	Second Period.
10 to 20 years	68, or 1-2	246, or 2-3
20 to 30 years	28, or 1-4	67, or 1-5
30 to 40 years	15, or 1-8	28, or 1-13
40 to 50 years	6, or 1-20	18, or 1-20
50 to 60 years	4, or 1-30	5
60 to 70 years	5	1
70 to 80 years	0	0
80 to 90 years	1	0
	127	365

The excommunications in the first period were

nineteen, and in the second twenty-four, all between the ages of ten and fifty.

A continuous statistical history of the schools from year to year, though necessary in successive annual reports, would be out of place in a history extending through a series of years. The general reader will be content with occasional summaries, and the same may be said of the operations of the press, and the additions to the churches.[1]

Necessary abbreviations.

A Tamil Dictionary, commenced by Mr. Knight of the Church mission, was continued after his death by native assistants under the supervision of Mr. Spaulding, and published in Ceylon early in 1842. Mr. Knight also commenced a Tamil and English Dictionary, and this was committed to Mr. Hutchings, who removed to Madras mainly for the purpose of carrying it through the press. In addition to these an English and Tamil Dictionary was prepared by Mr. Spaulding.

Tamil Dictionaries.

"By these three dictionaries," Mr. Spaulding writes, "the Tamil language is not only in a great measure settled in respect to orthography and definition, but brought within the reach of the Tamil and English student in our villages and seminaries, and of those engaged in translations of the Bible, book-makers, and preachers."

[1] A Tabular View of the Missionaries, and a General Summary of the Publications, in the several missions, may be found in the Appendix.

Mr. Edward Cope and wife joined the mission in 1840, and in the next year Mr. Poor returned to Jaffna from the Madura mission, where he had labored five years. He was received with a cordial welcome. In April, 1842, the mission was reinforced by Messrs. Samuel Whittelsey, Robert Wyman, and John C. Smith, all married men. Mrs. Smith must have carried with her the seeds of consumption, and she died of that disease at Batticotta on the 9th of May. In the autumn of the next year, Mr. Smith married the widow of Dr. John Steele of the Madura mission.

Painful developments in the Seminary.

Early in the year 1843 very painful developments were made by young men connected with the Seminary. It appeared that attendance on heathen dances, the practice of unnatural vice, and lying and deception, had become prevalent, and it greatly increased the grief of the missionaries that some of the church members, and many of the select class, and a portion of the native teachers had connived at these practices, and some had even taken a leading part in them. The measures adopted were prompt and efficient. The select class, and sixty-one from the other classes, were sent away, and the offending teachers were dismissed.[1] This severe discipline of course occasioned murmuring at the time, but was satisfactory in the end, both in its effect upon the young men, and upon the

[1] *Annual Report*, 1844, p. 173.

interests of the mission. It increased the confidence of the native community in the conductors of the institution.

Mr. Hoisington was absent during this time on a visit to the United States. He returned in 1844, bringing with him a valuable scientific apparatus. The instruction was now divided into three departments, Scientific, Biblical, and English; and Mr. Whittelsey was assigned to the Biblical department, hoping that, with his proficiency in Tamil, he would succeed in creating a sufficient enthusiasm in that direction to counterbalance the tendencies toward the study of the English and the sciences.

Reconstruction.

Early in 1844, Mr. and Mrs. Apthorp removed from Varany to Valvetty, near the sea, for the benefit of her health. A few months later Mr. Apthorp was attacked by typhus fever, and died on the 8th of June. His last words, within an hour of his departure, were, "Precious Saviour, come, come quickly." His afflicted widow, though not in good health, decided to remain in the mission, and took the oversight of schools at Manepy.

Death of Mr. Apthorp.

Messrs. Spaulding, Scudder, and Hutchings being in the United States in 1845, the Prudential Committee held a protracted consultation with them, mainly to ascertain why greater progress had not been made in obtaining a native ministry, and how that important result could

Consultations with returned missionaries.

best be promoted. The inquiry involved many of the vital principles and many details of the missionary work, and was afterwards further prosecuted among the missionaries then on the ground.

The organization of the churches in Ceylon had been more and more with a view to their training for self-government. Mr. Spaulding said, that they never used authority to influence a vote, and always took care not to break with the church, but to carry it with them. At their best estate, the churches always had great weaknesses when first gathered from among the heathen, and could not stand alone. It took a long time for them to rise above the inveterate habit of lying, and dishonesty, and the not less inveterate prejudices and habits of caste. That these churches might spread themselves beyond the stations, under a native ministry, and exist independently of the mission, it was important that every church member should come as soon as possible to have a mature and well-balanced Christian character. Yet it was obvious that all who gave satisfactory evidence of being regenerated by the Holy Ghost, ought to be received into the visible fold of Christ as soon as they gave such evidence, so that the principles and influences of the Gospel might be brought to bear upon them with their greatest force. In this way the standard of practical religion would be progressively raised, and along with it, by an obvious process, the standard of qualifications for church membership.

The Christians in Jaffna lived among the heathen, often in the same house; and though the ultimate good results might thus be greater, this commingling of the two elements must have a tendency to weaken the power of the Christian life in its professors. The children, moreover, of the native Christians must thus be in very great danger of imbibing heathen ideas, prejudices, and customs. But there seemed no way of avoiding this evil. We must sow beside all waters, and preach the Gospel to all as we have opportunity, leaving it for the Head of the Church to work out the great result.

Value of the schools.

The testimony of the brethren as to the value of the schools in their own mission, was united and strong. The religious instruction given in the Seminary at Batticotta they represented as being greater, than is given in any of the colleges in the United States; but the instructors desired some one to be associated with them, who by long preaching in the native tongue would be better prepared with language and experience, than any of the instructors then in the pastoral and theological departments.

Value of the native helpers.

The brethren, in giving their testimony before the Committee, described the native helpers of the Ceylon mission as possessing fine talents. They excelled as mathematicians. One of the native preachers was said to be as well qualified for the ministry, as one half of the young clergymen in this country; and he and another of the preachers were thought to be fully equal in the pulpit to some of our American preachers of acknowledged eloquence. In seasons of revival the native helpers have manifested a lovely spirit; and some of them, when sent to the continent, have gone thither with a missionary spirit. They sometimes appeared to think very little of money, and the brethren were unitedly of the opinion that the native Christians strongly resembled some of the best Christians at home, placed under similar circumstances.

In the absence of Mr. and Mrs. Spaulding, the female seminary at Oodooville had the care of Mr. Whittelsey, and enjoyed its usual prosperity. Seventy pupils had been married from this institution since its commencement. All but two or three of them were regarded as hopefully pious, and only three or four had conducted badly.

The Oodooville seminary.

The printing establishment at Manepy had four presses in operation, and during the year 1845 printed 23,744 volumes, and 145,000 copies of tracts, including a series for children. The whole number of continuous pages was 1,894, and the total of pages printed was 6,156,768; of which 1,200,000 were portions of the Scriptures, and 4,050,770 were religious tracts.

Amount of printing.

Mr. Wyman died at sea, soon after commencing a homeward voyage on account of his health. Messrs.

William W. Howland and Adin H. Fletcher joined the mission with their wives in 1846. In the next year, Mr. and Mrs. Spaulding returned with recovered health, from their visit to the United States, and resumed their station at Oodooville. They were accompanied by Messrs. Eurotas P. Hastings and William W. Scudder, a son of Dr. Scudder, and were followed by Samuel F. Green, M. D.

The mission strengthened.

At Tillipally the experiment was tried by Mr. Poor of forming a Christian congregation in connection with the church, but the people seem not to have been prepared for it.[1]

Mr. Whittelsey, while journeying for health in southern India, was seized with an inflammatory fever, the result, as was supposed, of fatigue and exposure on his way from Madura to Dindigul, and died at the latter place on the 10th of March, 1847. When drawing near the close of his exemplary and useful career, he witnessed this good confession, "I would rather be a missionary in this dark land pointing these ignorant heathen to Christ, than to be enjoying all the pleasures of a civilized and Christian country."

Death of Mr. Whittelsey.

The persecution experienced by a convert among the Roman Catholic fishermen, is thus described by Mr. Howland: "Soon after he began to come to us, his Roman Catholic neighbors

Roman Catholic persecution.

[1] See *Report* for 1847, p. 152.

commenced persecuting him for leaving their religion, and they still trouble him in every possible way. They at one time secreted salt in his yard; and, bringing an officer, seized him upon the charge of making salt contrary to law; but his terrified relatives, by paying money to the parties concerned, arrested the prosecution. His enemies then threatened to take him to court, and, by swearing that he was a robber, obtain his imprisonment; which, in this land of crime and perjury, could easily be done. At other times they have tried to instigate his relatives against him, and again they have threatened to beat him, so that he was obliged to stay away from the bungalow for several Sabbaths for fear of disturbance. One of the principal men in his village told him, not long since, that if it were not for fear of the law, he would kill him for bringing disgrace upon the Roman Catholic religion. During all this persecution he has stood firm. He does not seem anxious that we should use our influence to prevent it, but rather the contrary, saying, "I must trust in God; even though they destroy my body, they cannot destroy my soul."

Dr. Poor arrived in the United States with his wife in September, 1848, and his addresses during the two years of his visit are among the cherished memories of many in different sections of the country. Messrs. Joseph T. Noyes, Cyrus T. Mills, and Thomas S. Burnell, printer, with their wives, joined the mission in March, 1849.

New missionaries.

On the 11th of the same month Mrs. Catherine E. Scudder, wife of Mr. William W. Scudder, and daughter of Dr. Thomas Hastings of New York, died of cholera on board a small native vessel while returning, with her husband and infant child and a brother missionary, from Madura to Jaffna. Death in such circumstances might well have seemed a fearful messenger. "After speaking of her affection for me," says her husband, "she added, that she hoped I would not grieve too much on account of her death, but strive to live a devoted missionary. I asked her if she were happy. She replied, 'Yes, for Jesus is with me.' We then united with brother Hastings in a short prayer. When he had closed she commenced praying. She thanked the Lord that we had all been permitted to live so long, and asked that we might spend the remainder of our lives in his service, and be at length received into glory. She paused for a moment, and then commended her babe to the kind care and protection of her heavenly Father. When she had finished praying, I asked her if she had not a blessing to ask for me. She said, 'Yes, that you may be a devoted missionary.' Shortly after this she left messages for a few of her friends, and then added: 'I know that my parents will never regret having given me up to the missionary work.' I asked, 'Do you regret it yourself?' She replied, with unusual emphasis, 'No.' Being asked, if she were afraid of death, she said,

Death of Mrs Scudder.

'No, for my Saviour is with me.'" The vessel was then anchored off Annapatum, a town on the continent. In a coffin of rough boards, the best that could be obtained, her mortal remains were deposited beneath a grove of thorn trees, looking out upon the ocean, there to await the resurrection of the righteous dead.

Mr. and Mrs. Cope were obliged to return home this year, and so were Mr. and Mrs. Hoisington, and Mr. and Mrs. Fletcher. Mr. Mills was appointed principal of the Seminary. Just before this, the price of board was raised in that institution, and due notice of the fact was given, and that all must pay in advance for at least one term. The mission expected to get a class, but was not prepared for a rush as on former occasions. But when the day arrived, the premises were crowded with candidates and their interceding friends. There were not less than forty who were fitted and ready to pay, and many others were as well prepared for entrance as those formerly received, thus indicating an advanced state of public sentiment on the subject of education. Among the fathers and friends of the candidates were some of the most influential men of the land. One fact came distinctly to view, that the people felt their sons to be safe in the Seminary as to their moral habits.

A good omen.

"How changed!" exclaimed Mr. Hastings' moonshee, on observing how earnestly these

The change.

heathen parents were pleading for the admission of their sons into a Christian boarding-school. "I seem as one born blind, and now just made to see. These men, when young, would refuse even a plantain from the missionary, and if they came to his house they would purify themselves by bathing before going to their own home. I used to do so. When I taught the missionaries I always stopped at the tank on my way home and bathed, else my friends would not have received me. But now, how changed!"

Death of Mrs. Apthorp.

Mrs. Apthorp lived five years after the death of her husband, until the 3d of September, 1849. Her remains were deposited by the side of those of her husband in the mission burial-ground at Oodooville. Though much of the time a sufferer from bodily infirmities, she had been an active and faithful laborer, spoke the language of the people with ease and correctness, and made the Gospel known to not a few of her own sex. It was her deliberate purpose, if such were the will of God, to die among the heathen.

Testimony of the Governor.

The Governor of Ceylon, after returning from a tour in the province of Jaffna in the early part of 1850, published the following notice of his visit: —

"His Excellency cannot omit to dwell, with peculiar satisfaction, on the pleasure afforded him by his personal inspection of the great educational establishments which are the distinguishing characteristic of the northern province. To those noble volunteers in the cause of Christianity and education, the gentlemen of the American mission, who by their generous self-devotion in a foreign and distant land have produced so marked an improvement in the scene of their labors, His Excellency feels that he should pay a special tribute of grateful acknowledgment. He is glad to hail, in this dedication of American enterprise and American charity to the work of civilizing and enlightening a distant dependency of the British crown, one more tie of kindred with the great nation that sends them forth — one more pledge that between the Old and the New England there can henceforth be only a generous rivalry in the cause of knowledge and truth."

Return of Mr. Minor.

Mr. Minor the printer was obliged, after a residence of seventeen years, to return with his family to his native land, where he arrived in July, 1851, nor was he able to resume his work.

The medical department.

The patients registered by Dr. Green during the year ending April 1, 1851, were 2,217, not including those visited at their own houses. They came to the dispensary at nine in the morning, and were instructed in the truth by Dr. Green, or his assistants. The number reached by the Gospel in this way, in that one year, must have been more than three thousand. Five young men, all of them professing Christians, were receiving instruction as a medical class. Dr. Green was preparing a Tamil nomenclature for anatomy, physiology, and hygiene, expecting soon to put the elements of these sciences into the native language. Some work of this kind he thought might do much good, not only as introducing more medical knowledge and a better system of medical practice, but also as helping to undermine superstition, with which the practice of the native physician is intimately connected.

Accessions and changes.

It was in the year 1852 that Mr. Marshall D. Sanders and his wife joined the mission. Mr. Noyes was transferred to the Madura mission in the next year, for the improvement of Mrs. Noyes' health, where she found great benefit from their near proximity to the Pulney Hills. The health of Mrs. Mills having failed, she and her husband were obliged to return to the United States in 1853, and Mr. Hastings took charge of the Seminary. Mr. and Mrs. Mills were afterwards connected for some years with the Oahu College, on the Sandwich Islands. The Rev. Nathan L. Lord and wife arrived in June, 1853.

CHAPTER X.

TAMIL PEOPLE ON THE CONTINENT.

THE MADURA MISSION.

1834–1853.

Southern India delineated.

SOUTHERN India has no great alluvial plains. Along the eastern shore from Cape Comorin, there is a strip of sandy waste, extending three or four miles from the sea, beyond which the land rises so imperceptibly as to give the appearance of an almost level plain quite back to the base of the mountains. Here and there detached hills and groups of mountains rise abruptly from the plain, with their upper parts clothed with forests. The Madura Collectorate has about nine thousand square miles. It is watered by rivers running from the mountains to the sea, which are filled by the annual rains. The waters are stored within strong artificial dikes on the river sides, and are thus made available for the needed irrigation.

The Collectorate is bounded on the north by Coimbatore, Trichinopoly, and Tanjore, on the east by the Bay of Bengal, on the south by the Gulf of Ma-

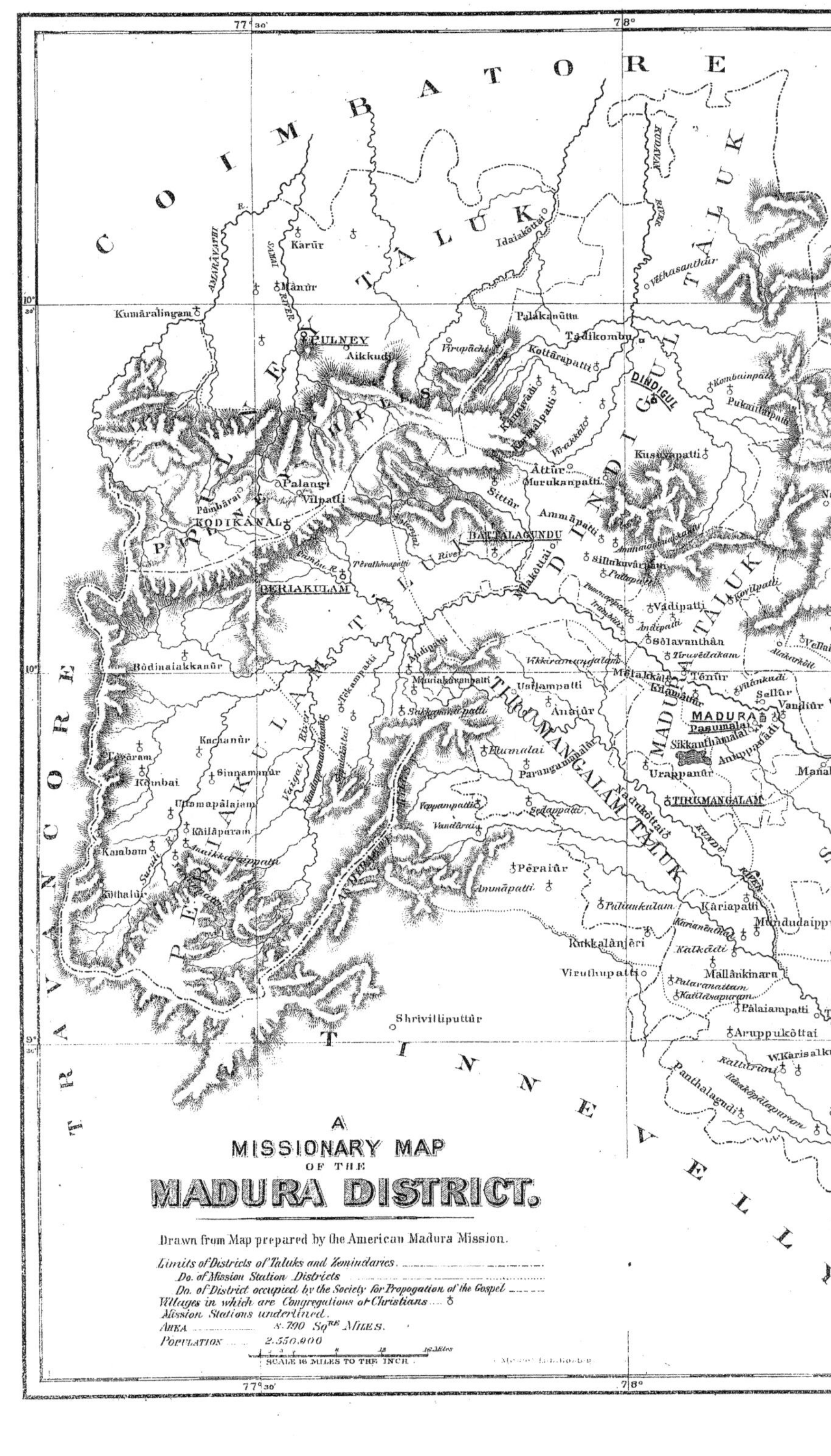
A
MISSIONARY MAP
OF THE
MADURA DISTRICT.
Drawn from Map prepared by the American Madura Mission.
Limits of Districts of Taluks and Zemindaries.
Do. of Mission Station Districts
Do. of District occupied by the Society for Propogation of the Gospel
Villages in which are Congregations of Christians
Mission Stations underlined.
AREA 8.790 Sq^RE MILES.
POPULATION 2.550.000
SCALE 16 MILES TO THE INCH.
77° 30'
78°
COIMBATORE
TRAVANCORE
TINNEVELLY
TÂLUK
PULNEY
DINDIGUL TÂLUK
PERIAKULAM TÂLUK
TIRUMANGALAM TÂLUK
MADURA TÂLUK
Kumâralingam
Kârûr
Mânûr
Aikkudi
Palakanûttu
Tâdikombu
Kottârapatti
Idaiakôttai
Palangi
Vilpatti
Pambârai
KODIKANAL
Attûr
Murukanpatti
Sittûr
Ammâpatti
BATTALAGUNDU
Kusavapatti
Sillukuvârpatti
PERIAKULAM
Vâdipatti
Sôlavanthân
Bôdinaiakkanûr
Tônûr
Usilampatti
Anaiûr
MADURA
Pasumalai
Sellûr
Vandiûr
Sikkanthâmalai
Urappanûr
Elumalai
Parangamanalûr
Kachanûr
Sinnamanûr
Tevâram
Kombai
Uttamapâlaiam
Kailâparam
Kambam
Kûthalûr
TIRUMANGALAM
Pêraiûr
Ammâpatti
Palankulam
Kâriapatti
Mundudaippu
Kukkalânjeri
Viruthupatti
Mallânkinaru
Pâlaiampatti
Aruppukôttai
Shrivilliputtûr
W. Karisalkulam
Panthalagudi
Manalûr
Vellaiampatti
Vithasanthûr
Kombainpatti
Pukaiilaipatti
Vaigai River
Sarali R.

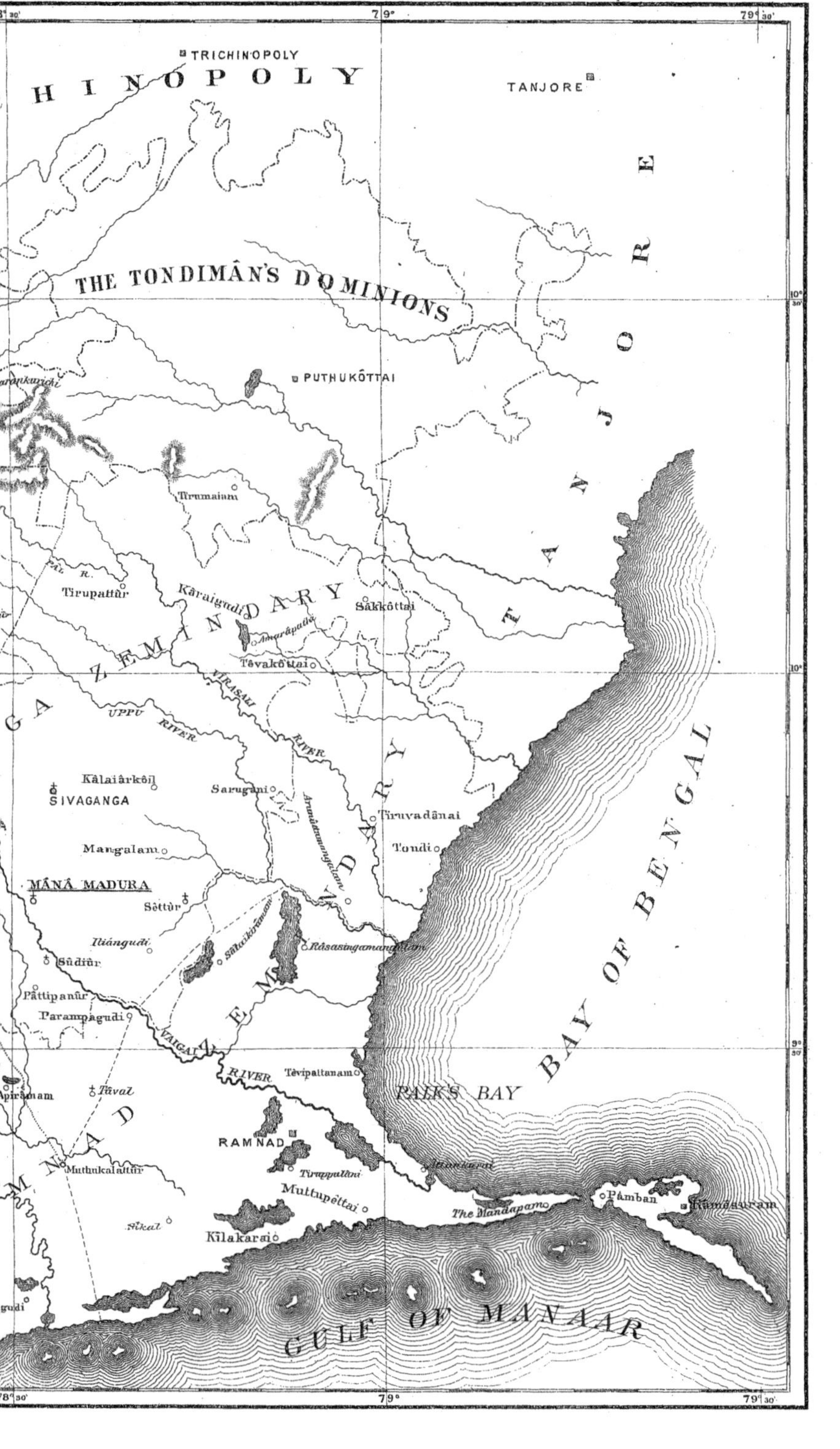

TRICHINOPOLY
HINOPOLY
TANJORE
THE TONDIMÂN'S DOMINIONS
PUTHUKÔTTAI
TANJORE
Tirumaiam
Tirupattûr
Kâraigudi
Sâkkôttai
ZEMINDARY
Têvakôttai
UPPU RIVER
VIRASALI RIVER
Kâlaiârkôil
SIVAGANGA
Sarugani
Tiruvadânai
Mangalam
Tondi
MÂNÂ MADURA
Sôttûr
Iliángudi
Râsasingamangalam
Sûdiûr
Pâttipanûr
Parampagudi
VAIGAI RIVER
Têvipattanam
PALK'S BAY
BAY OF BENGAL
Tâval
RAMNAD
Muthukalattûr
Tiruppullâni
Muttupêttai
The Mandapam
Pâmban
Râmêsuram
Kilakarai
GULF OF MANAAR
79°
79° 30'
10°

naar and Tinnevelly, and on the west by the native kingdom of Travancore, and lies between the latitudes 9° 05′ and 10° 45′. The principal spur of the Ghâts, known as the Pulney Hills, is in the north-western section of the District, and upon these is the Sanitarium of the Madura Mission, situated on a large plateau, seven thousand feet above the level of the sea.[1] The thermometer ranges from 20° to 25° below that of the plains, and the climate is very salubrious, being elevated above the reach of the ordinary malarious fever of India, and drier and more equable in temperature even than the Neilgherries.[2] The District, though hot, is free from sudden changes, and is healthy. A score of missionaries have spent nearly twenty years in the mission, with no other relief than an occasional resort to the Hills. The population of the District is now about two and a half millions. Mohammedans and Roman Catholics are scattered in the towns and villages, but the mass of the people are pagans.

Why made the site of a new mission.

As it was contiguous to Jaffna, and unoccupied by missionaries, while two English Societies had each a mission in the Jaffna District, it was natural for the brethren in Ceylon to look to the Madura District when in search of a field for a new mission.

Accordingly Mr. Spaulding, early in 1834, was

[1] The height of Mount Washington, N. H., is 6,214 feet.

[2] Nelson's *Manual*.

commissioned by his brethren to visit the continent, and ascertain where it would be advisable to commence the mission. Taking three native helpers, and a large number of tracts and portions of Scripture, he visited Ramnad, Palamcotta, Nagercoil, and the city of Madura. Madura had been the abode of the ancient Tamil kings, and the chief seat of brahminical pride. It was also the grand centre of Jesuit missions in the seventeenth century. Mr. Spaulding selected it as the most eligible location. Palamcotta, Nagercoil, and Tinnevelly were already occupied by English Societies. It has been stated that Mr. Woodward of the Ceylon mission, when on the Neilgherries for the restoration of his health, obtained the consent of the Governor-general of India and the Governor of Madras for an American mission in Southern India. Messrs. William Todd and Henry C. Hoisington were introduced to this new field by Mr. Spaulding in the following July, accompanied by three of the older pupils from Batticotta. Jaffna is comparatively crowded with villages, and Mr. Hoisington felt some disappointment on his way to Madura; the villages seemed so far apart and small. The population of the Madura District was then estimated at one million three hundred thousand, and the Tamil people of the continent numbered six or eight millions. The city of Madura had between thirty and forty thousand inhabitants, and was sur-

The preliminary measure.

Commencement of the mission.

rounded by double walls, with numerous bastions and a broad ditch. The walls have since been leveled, and the ditch filled up. Mr. Hoisington speaks of it as a city of temples, the largest of which has a wall half a mile in circumference, containing as many as ten thousand stone pillars, on which are carved curiously wrought images of every description.

Mrs. Todd lived but a short time, her death occurring, after a painful sickness, in September of the following year. Early in 1835, Messrs. Hoisington and Eckard made an exchange of labors, Mr. Eckard removing to Madura. Messrs. Alanson C. Hall and John J. Lawrence, and their wives, reached Jaffna in the same year, and went with Messrs. Poor and Todd to Madura, arriving in October after a journey of twelve days. Mr. Poor expected to spend three months in missionary labors at Madura, and his preaching at once excited much attention. Mrs. Todd had died September 11, and Mrs. Hall followed her on the 2d of the following January. Both of these devoted women departed in great peace of mind, rejoicing that they had gone to India on such an errand of mercy. Mr. Hall's health failed so that he soon after returned to the United States, and at his own request received an honorable dismission. The health of Mrs. Eckard required the return of herself and husband back to the Ceylon mission.

Mr. Poor's removal to Madura.

The three months spent by Mr. Poor at Madura had so impressed him with the value of the field, and the desirableness of having those on the ground who could preach in the native language, that, with the concurrence of his mission, he resigned the care of the Batticotta Seminary and removed to Madura in March, 1835. "Regarding the missionary premises as a centre," he writes, "there is within the compass of a single mile, a greater amount of population, than is to be found in the whole extent of the field of our labors in Jaffna. The population consists principally of idolaters, the worshippers of Siva and Vishnu. Madura is the principal seat of idolatry in southern India. It is indeed a stronghold. Idolatry seems to be the all-engrossing subject, and wears a bold front. There are circumstances, however, which render even the Fort of Madura a more inviting field of labor than Jaffna. Many of the brahmins, some of the highest standing, are in the service of government, consequently they are detached in an important sense from the temple service, and comparatively indifferent to its interests. These are of course more accessible than those connected with the temples. The brahmins are extremely numerous, but learning among them is in a low state. The friends of idolatry rely mainly upon the outward pomp of their numerous festivals to captivate the imaginations of the people, and hold their minds in bondage." A leading object with Mr. Poor was to ascertain what were the obstacles to the seminarists as native assistants, and how those obstacles might be overcome.

Schools and helpers.

Thirty-five schools were then connected with this mission, containing more than a thousand boys, and nearly a hundred girls. Nine of the schools were in the city of Madura. A more advanced school was opened there, in a set of rooms loaned for the purpose by the collector, in the arcades of the old palace of the Pandian kings. Eight of the native helpers were educated at Batticotta, two came from Tranquebar, one from Trichinopoly, one from Palamcottah, and six belonged to Madura. The English Society for Propagating the Gospel sent a missionary to Madura, another to Dindigul, and a third to Ramnad, but soon decided to withdraw from all these places, except the last.

Enlargement of the mission.

Mr. Robert O. Dwight and wife joined the mission in April, 1836, and near the close of the year commenced a station at Dindigul. Messrs. Henry Cherry, Edward Cope, Nathaniel M. Crane, Clarendon F. Muzzy, William Tracy, F. D. W. Ward, and Dr. John Steele, with their wives, were added to the mission in the year 1837. The second Mrs. Todd, formerly Mrs. Woodward, died June 1, and Mrs. Cherry on the 4th of November at Chavagacherry in Ceylon. The second Mrs. Cherry, sister of the first, and also

Deaths.

of Mrs. Winslow, died January 19, 1844, four years after her marriage.

Absurd reports.

The schools at Madura suffered from an absurd report raised by a native, that the missionaries privately compelled the children to drink a dose prepared to bewilder their minds, and so make them Christians. Parents also feared lest their children, if they entered the schools, would be made slaves, or soldiers, or be transported beyond the seas.

Seasonable aid from government.

This was the year so memorable for commercial disaster in the United States; and the schools of the Madura mission must have suffered, as did those in Ceylon, had not the Madras government made a grant of fifteen hundred dollars toward their support.

Death of Dr. Steele.

The mission entered upon the year 1839 with five stations, — Madura, Dindigul, thirty-eight miles northerly from Madura, Tirupuvanam twelve miles southeast, Sivaganga twenty-five miles easterly, and Tirumangalam twelve miles southwest. Mr. Todd's health constrained him to return home. Dr. Steele was seriously threatened with consumption but partially recovered by means of a voyage to Singapore. He died on the 6th of October, 1842. As a physician, a man of business, and a missionary, he won the esteem and confidence of all his associates, and greatly endeared himself, by his kind and prompt attention and his endeavors, even beyond his strength, to administer relief in times of sickness. The native population loved and respected him. His end was peace. "After five years acquaintance with him," wrote Mr. Dwight, "I do not recollect a word or an action which I could wish different."

Francis Asbury, a promising native, was licensed to preach the Gospel. Most of the native helpers were educated at Batticotta. Two weekly meetings were held with them at Madura; one for receiving their reports, the other for giving them instruction in theology. Expository preaching, with a free use of interrogatories, was found to be the most useful. Mr. Poor returned to Jaffna in October, 1841, after an absence of six years.

The native helpers.

The East India Government had heretofore the control of the revenue arising from a tax upon pilgrims visiting the sacred places, and also from certain funds connected with the temples. As the disbursement of these gave an official support to idolatry, an order was promulgated, about this time, to dissolve all such connection with the system. A brahmin, formerly much opposed to Christianity, called soon after on Mr. Tracy, who thus writes: "In the course of conversation, I mentioned the rumor that the government was about giving up to the people the care of the temples, and asked if he could tell me anything about it? He replied, he was very sorry to say it

The government connection with idolatry dissolved.

was too true. Why? I asked. Because, said he, 'the government took very good care of the temples, but now they will go to ruin. The government ought not to resign this charge of the sacred places.' 'But,' said I, 'the government have often been charged with approving of heathenism because they took care of temples, and there was some reason for such a charge. Now they show that the charge was unfounded. As it would be wrong for the government to compel any to become Christians, so it would be wrong for them to support heathenism. If the people love their own religion, they will support it; and if they do not, then let it go to ruin.' 'Ah,' said he, 'there is the difficulty. The people do not love their religion for its own sake; scarce a single brahmin could be found who would do anything from real love to it. It is a desire to make a living, which influences them all. Here in Madura the temple is under the care of four men, two of whom are among the highest brahmins. Now commit the funds of the temple to their hands, and those funds will quickly disappear. Each one will appropriate something to his own use, till in a short time all will be gone. And the same is true of the other temples.'"

Native estimate of the brahmins.

Mrs. Steele having married Mr. Smith, of the Ceylon mission, removed to Jaffna; and the departure of Mr. Poor made it necessary for Mr. Dwight to remove to Madura. On the 7th of

January, 1844, he was attacked with the cholera, which proved fatal on the following day. In the same house, Mrs. North died on the 13th, and Mrs. Cherry on the 19th; and there also Mrs. Dwight and her children, and Mr. Muzzy, and the children of Mr. North lay sick with the same disease. The native population were dying at the rate of fifty or sixty a day, and the atmosphere was tainted with the odor from the funeral piles. The annual meeting of the mission had been appointed at Madura on the day of Mr. Dwight's death, and all the members of the mission had been thus brought together, to pass through these scenes of affliction. Their danger was enhanced by the fact that they were then without a physician, Dr. Ward having been transferred to Madras. Mr. North had arrived from Singapore only a few days before. The loss of Mr. Dwight was greatly felt. There was in him a combination of qualities, that promised great usefulness, and his presence in the mission seemed never so much needed. His end was characterized by Christian peace and hope. The Rev. Horace S. Taylor and wife joined the mission this year.

Deaths of Mr. Dwight and others.

The course of the mission for the next twelve years was one of gradual but nearly uniform progress. It differed from the Danish Protestant mission at Tranquebar, Trichinopoly, and Tanjore mainly in its treatment of caste, and the principles on which professed converts were admitted to church fellowship.

THE TRANQUEBAR MISSION.

The Tranquebar mission was established by Ziegenbalg and Plutscho in 1706, and Trichinopoly and Tanjore were branches of the same. The Scriptures were translated and printed by these missionaries, and a native pastor was ordained in 1733, probably the first in India, but they did not venture to ordain one of a low caste. The most prosperous period of their mission was about the time of its jubilee in 1756. At least three of the eight missionaries then in the field were men of great ability. Swartz was then one of the junior brethren, having been there but six years. The number baptized during these fifty years was about eleven thousand. The missionaries were all from Halle, and though supported by the English Christian Knowledge Society, looked to the celebrated Augustus Francke as their spiritual head. They were remarkable for the length of their missionary services. Weidebrook labored nearly thirty years, the first Kohlhoff fifty-three years, Zeiglin forty years, Klein forty-five years, Dr. John forty-three years, Dr. Rottler sixty years, Dr. Coemmerer forty-seven years, Gerické nearly forty years, and Pohle forty years. Fabricius died at the age of eighty-one.

Extraordinary length of missionary services.

I have stated these facts, gathered from Dr. Joseph Mullens' account of the Missions in South India, in justice to the pioneers of Protestant missions there, and for the same reason I make the following quotation from the same author.

"Before the close of the century the churches at Tranquebar, Cuddalore, and Madras had begun to fade, and when Swartz and Gerické were dead those of Tanjore and Trichinopoly followed them. A missionary or two remained at each place. Dr. John and Dr. Coemmerer continued at Tranquebar. Pohle and Kohlhoff presided over the church of Tanjore. Dr. Rottler was at Vepery. No younger missionaries followed them to take their place as they grew old. The Evangelical Church at Halle, whence the strength of the South Indian Mission had been drawn, itself decayed and at last expired. Some of the later missionaries brought neology with them, and thus the missions lingered on and on, till each of the old men was dead. Three of them survived till 1837, and one of them, Caspar Kohlhoff, died as late as 1844. The total number of missionaries that had joined these several stations during the first hundred years of their history is just about fifty, and their converts amount to more than fifty thousand. Whatever deficiencies there were, we must remember that the Lutheran missionaries were the very first to occupy the land, the first to find out what Hindûism really is, the first to oppose caste, the first to exhibit the peculiar character of the Hindû converts, the first to meet the difficulties by which the work of Christ in India is beset. To these men, then, we must render high honor, as we admire the fidelity, consistency, and perseverance, with which they carried on their labors. They lived not in the days of missionary reports and platform speeches. No magazines chronicled their difficulties, or sought sympathy on their behalf. Scarcely a man of them ever returned to Europe. They came to India young, in India they lived, in India they died. They lived amidst wars and raids, amidst plunder and confusion; they lived in an age of gross irreligion, and they fought their part manfully and to the last. Peace be to their ashes; honor to their memory."

Era of modern missions.

The era of modern missions began in England and America, just as the light of the Tranquebar missions was fading away.

The Leipsic mission.

Since the year 1840, the churches and stations originally established by Ziegenbalg have been under the charge of missionaries supported by the Leipsic Missionary Society.

Consequences of a higher evangelical policy.

The experience of the American missionaries in the Madura District must needs differ considerably from that of the Tranquebar and Tanjore brethren. The American missionaries, before their twentieth year, had ceased from compromises with caste, and from the first insisted on credible evidence of piety for admission to the

Lord's Supper, nor were any except church members to offer their children for baptism. Nor did temporal advantages, to any considerable extent, result from a profession of the Christian faith, but the contrary, until equitable changes had been made by the government in the law of inheritance. Yet the progress, though gradual, was constant. Six years after the arrival of the first missionaries Mr. Spaulding, on his second visit, reported five stations, nine missionaries, eighty free schools, four boarding-schools, and fifteen native assistants. Five years later the free schools had increased to one hundred and fourteen, with more than three thousand pupils; there was a Seminary with thirty pupils, four boarding-schools for boys, distinct from the Seminary, and two for girls containing more than one hundred pupils, five select schools with two hundred and nine pupils, and eighty-seven church members.

Leading object of the mission.

The leading object of the mission was to gather self-governing churches; and people in more than forty villages had been induced in 1846 as a step in this direction, to place themselves under Christian instruction. These were first called Christian Villages, but afterwards Christian Congregations.

Christian congregations instituted.

This new step resulted from an application of the people, occasioned in some cases by the extortion of their priests, in others by the expectation of obtaining the assistance of the missionary, and thus improving their worldly prospects. Some had been led to see the folly of idolatry by the portions of Scripture distributed among them. At least three families were deemed needful to form the congregation, and these were supposed to have deliberately renounced idolatry, or Romanism, and to have adopted the Christian religion. They were to meet on the Sabbath, and at other times as they were able, for instruction and worship. The number of families embraced in these congregations, in the first two years, was four hundred and twenty. In the third year, the congregations were sixty-nine, containing seven hundred families and two thousand six hundred individuals. In these villages were fifty-nine schools, containing nine hundred children. Religious services were regularly held on the Sabbath in fifty-eight of the villages, with an average attendance of about six hundred persons.

Mrs. Dwight was married to Mr. Winslow of the Madras mission in March, 1845. Messrs. James Herrick, John Rendall, and Edward Webb, with their wives, joined the mission in April of the next year, and Mr. George W. McMillan and wife in the following July. Dr. Scudder returned to India this year, and spent a year as missionary physician at Madura, but without transferring his relation from the Madras mission. Mr. Lawrence died at Tranquebar, after twelve years

Additions to the mission.

Death of Mr. Lawrence.

of missionary labor, December 20, 1846, at the age of forty. He had been a faithful servant of Christ, and the thought was pleasant to him that his body would rest by the side of the early missionaries of Tranquebar. Mrs. Muzzy also died on the 3d of December. She had been ten years in India, and such was the impression made by her on the natives, that many came from Tirumangalam and Tirupuvanam to see her remains, and some hundreds of persons attended her funeral.

Death of Mrs. Muzzy.

As it was desirable to have the Seminary nearer the central station, it was removed to Pasumalai, two miles southwest of Madura, where convenient buildings were erected for the principal, the teachers, and students, on a lot of land secured to the mission. The number of students had increased to sixty, of whom sixteen were members of the church. All of the graduating class became helpers in the mission. The object of the Seminary was not to raise up clerks for the government offices, but helpers for the mission, and pastors for the native churches. On this account the patronage of the government, kindly offered about this time, was respectfully declined.

New location of the Seminary.

Why government patronage was declined.

The girls' boarding-school at Madura had seventy-two pupils, nine of whom were admitted to the church during the year. Four of the stations had each a boarding-school for boys, and

The schools.

these were regarded as nurseries for the Seminary. They contained one hundred and fifty-five pupils. There were three select day-schools, one for boys and two for girls, each at a different station; the pupils residing at their homes. Of village free schools there were one hundred and twenty-five, containing three thousand and eight hundred pupils. The native churches received ninety-seven members during the year. Thirteen Christian marriages were reported. Madura was visited this year by an agent of a native society of pagans at Madras for the promotion of Hindûism. Besides putting in circulation the tracts of his society, this agent delivered addresses twice every Sabbath to large audiences, assembled to hear him in the great temple. These were not so much a defense of idolatry, as deistical objections to the Bible, gathered chiefly from Paine's "Age of Reason;" and he dealt largely in ridicule of Christianity and its adherents, especially the missionaries. Absurd reports were put in circulation, which were so extensively received, that the Collector, fearing the consequences, made public proclamation, that any one found guilty of uttering such things against the missionaries, without proving the truth of the charge, should be called to an account. Such an organized opposition to the Gospel was really among the proofs of its progress.

Churches and marriages.

A pagan missionary.

The mission made decided opposition to caste in

the year 1847, and seventy-two who persisted in adhering to it, were, on one occasion, debarred from the privilege of coming to the Lord's table when the assembled mission commemorated his death. Thirty-eight of these were catechists.

Opposition to caste.

The mission was enlarged in this year by the arrival of Messrs. John E. Chandler and George Ford and their wives, and of Rev. Charles Little and wife in the following year, and of Dr. and Mrs. Shelton in March, 1849. Dr. and Mrs. Scudder returned to Madras soon after. Mrs. Little's labors were closed by death on the 4th of July in the year of her arrival.

New missionaries.

A station at Puthukotai, formed by the "Indian Church Missionary Society" at Madras, was transferred by that Society, in the year 1846, to the Madura mission, with its lands, schools, and catechists. It was about sixty miles northeast from Madura, on the road to Tanjore, and within the territory of a native prince, who was independent of the British government. But after two years, owing to its distance and the consequent difficulty of superintending native helpers, together with the limited amount of funds that could be appropriated to that station, the mission voted to relinquish it. This they did with regret, since appearances were as promising there, as in other parts of the field.

Transfer of a station to the mission.

Why relinquished

Dr. Shelton, the missionary physician, reported eighteen hundred applicants for medical treatment in 1849. To all these, and to their friends who accompanied them, the Gospel was preached. Some of the patients came sixty miles.

Medical treatment.

In that year, the Seminary at Pasumalai was blessed with a spiritual awakening. The apparent origin of this was intelligence of awakenings in the seminaries among the Nestorians of Persia. Several of the most unpromising students were deeply affected, and hopes were entertained of the conversion of a considerable number. Nine were admitted to the church at the close of the year. The native church was much quickened. Its members became more humble, more watchful against sin, and more diligent in laboring for the good of others.

Revival in the Seminary.

We read, about this time, of students called "Preparandi." These were promising young men under the personal instruction of missionaries. It was a step in the direction of a native ministry.

Preparandi.

Mr. Cherry returned to the United States in 1850, and was released, at his own request, from his connection with the Board. Mr. Taylor commenced a new station at Mandapasalai, thirty miles south of Madura, it being more central in respect to his village congregations. He organized a church, making the tenth in the mission.

A new station.

For the year 1851 the missionaries reported, that they had travelled more than six thousand miles in preaching the Gospel. One missionary reports having visited two hundred and thirty-five different villages. The number of persons connected with the village congregations was 2,471. The want of more laborers was severely felt, and gave rise to earnest appeals.

Itinerant preaching.

The mission had now extended itself so as to cover a territory more than one hundred miles in length, and over sixty in breadth. But the stations and village congregations were too much scattered, and the native catechists and readers were too limited in their education. Seventy-two persons were received by profession to the churches during the year 1852, of whom fifty-six were adults in the village congregations. A class of twelve was received at Pasumalai, nearly all from the congregations, making the number of students thirty-seven, of whom twenty were church members. There were also sixteen young men, members of the Preparandi class. They lodged in a room by themselves, but took their food with the members of the Seminary. Bringing them together from the different stations was believed to be a wise measure. Thus there were fifty-three students at Pasumalai, taken from different castes, living together in harmony. Four boarding-schools for boys,

Extent of the field.

Admissions to the church.

Students for the ministry.

Other schools.

at as many different stations, contained eighty-eight pupils, nearly all of them children of parents connected with the village congregations. The girls' boarding-school at Madura contained thirty-seven pupils, all of whom except one were from native Christian families. Sixteen hundred patients applied for medical treatment, during the year, at the dispensary under the care of Dr. Shelton.

The medical dispensary.

Two men were licensed to preach the Gospel in 1853, one of whom was the first to be ordained, two years later, as a native pastor. A Native Evangelical Society, formed in October, 1853, commenced active operations in January, 1854, under favorable auspices.

THE JESUIT MISSION.

Here, two centuries and a half ago, was the seat of the most remarkable of the Jesuit missions in India; and a brief account of their efforts is needful to a full understanding of the field as occupied by the American missionaries.

In 1606, Robert de Nobilibus, a Portuguese Jesuit, mastered the Sanskrit language, and the manners and usages of the brahmins; and fortified by a written document, which must have been forged by some one, he entered Madura, not as a Portuguese, but as a brahmin of high sanctity from the west, come to restore the ancient forms of the Hindû religion. His success was not promising at first.

The chief of the brahmins charged him, in a large assembly convened for the purpose, with being an impostor, who sought to deceive the people by lies, in order to introduce a new religion. Whereupon Robert de Nobilibus produced his written scroll, and protested, under an oath in the presence of them all, that he had verily sprung from the god Brahma. Several brahmins then arose, overpowered by the evidence, and persuaded their brethren not to persecute a man who called himself a brahmin, and proved that he was so by written evidence and solemn oaths, as well as by conformity to their manners, conduct, and dress. Having passed this ordeal, he gave himself out as a Sunniási, or devotee, and kept up the pretense for the remainder of his life. His single daily meal was a little rice, a little milk, and some bitter vegetables; and his only garments were a long yellowish robe, a veil, a turban, and a pair of clogs. In token of his religion and caste, he wore a cross suspended from his neck by five threads, three of which were of gold and symbolized the Trinity, while the other two were of silver, and symbolized the body and soul of our Lord. Having obtained a piece of land in the brahmins' quarter, he built a church upon it, and lived there for a time in the strictest seclusion, attended by brahmin servants alone, and observing, in the minutest particulars, the customs of those in the midst of whom he sojourned. His fame was soon noised abroad. Hindûs of all classes thronged the gates, in the hope of being admitted; and the few who were successful found him seated cross-legged on a divan covered with a red cloth, before which were spread a carpet and a handsome mat. They were charmed with the affability and politeness of the distinguished teacher of religion; and at the same time astonished at the purity of his Tamil accent, the profoundness of his oriental learning, and the versatility of his intellect. His popularity soon became established in Madura, the number of his visitors increased, and the king sent repeated messages inviting him to the palace, but he respectfully declined. Brahmins, priests, rajahs, courtiers, professors, men of the best castes, humbly implored the great Roman gûru to point out to them the way of salvation.

It is difficult to imagine what directions Robert de Nobilibus could have given them. The gûrûs suffering a great loss of customary fees from the conversion of so many of their disciples to the new faith, a cloud of persecution gathered around the mission, but it soon passed away, Robert having the protection of a nobleman who took great delight in his society.

After about five years, information of his extraordinary proceedings were conveyed to Rome, and he was suspended from his office by the Pope, and not permitted to resume his labors for ten years. The mission was carried on, in this interval, by men of inferior ability and enterprise.

Meanwhile the mission was by no means inactive, nor did it change its method, and in 1623, when Robert de Nobilibus resumed his labors, a new spirit was infused into it. He himself preached in all the more important towns of the kingdom, making many converts, some of them high chiefs, and the other Jesuit missionaries, stimulated by his success, devoted themselves to the work of proselyting. Robert appears to have left Madura in the year 1648, after forty-two years of service in the mission, of which he might be called the founder, broken in health and nearly blind. He was removed first to Ceylon, and then to the neighborhood of Madras, where he died. To the last he claimed to be a brahmin of high rank. And his associates and successors down to the year 1741, through considerably more than a century, were able to keep up the deception. Among these were the martyr De Britto, one of the more distinguished; Tachard, Bishop Lainez, Bouchet, also distinguished, Martin, Turpin, De Bourges, Mouduit, Calmette, De la Fontaine, Pere le Gac, and Beschi, the last and most learned of the Jesuit missionaries.[1]

The chief object of this mission was the conversion of brahmins, but in this they had only a very partial success. They gained a considerable number of Sûdras, but the bulk of their converts were Pariahs, and, for prudential reasons, great precaution

[1] Nelson's *Manual.*

was used in their intercourse with the lower castes. The utmost regard was paid to caste. The Pariahs had separate catechists, and separate churches, and if they presumed to enter churches of a higher caste, they were violently driven out. Even when Pariahs were dying, the Christian Sunniásis refused to enter their dwellings, and the dying were dragged into the open air, or to the nearest church, that the Sunniási might administer the last rites of the Church without contamination.[1] Yet they reckoned their converts among the masses by tens of thousands, and the number was greatly exaggerated by counting every baptized dying child among their converts, though baptized by catechists or women, as most of them were, and without the knowledge of their parents. The missionaries dressed, bathed, ate, and demeaned themselves like real brahmins, wore the sacred thread, put ashes on their breasts and foreheads, wore the native wooden shoes, and slept upon a tiger skin. They allowed their converts the same cars and idolatrous processions as before, the Virgin Mary taking the place of the Hindû god. Nor was there any material change in the marriage customs, or in the religious formulas observed in their bathing.

It should be added that the Popes from the year 1623 to 1741, during more than a hundred years, tried in vain to put an end to these abuses of the

[1] *Calcutta Review*, vol. ii. p. 95.

Jesuits. At the close of that period, as a consequence of wars between the French and English, the natives discovered the Roman Sunniásis to be no other than Feringees, or Franks. The discovery of the fraud enraged and disgusted the heathens, and put an immediate stop to conversions, and their converts rushed by crowds into apostasy. Twenty years later, and soon after the suppression of the Society of Jesus, those who still professed to be Christians in Madura were described by a Papal writer as living in the lowest state of superstition and ignorance. The account he gave of their morals, especially of the catechists and native clergy, is too gross for transcription. Their number had greatly declined. In 1776, Fra Paolino da San Bartolomeo found only 18,000 in Madura and 10,000 in Tanjore.[1]

The generations have long since passed away upon whom these brahmin Jesuits operated, and it is not easy to estimate their influence upon the Tamil people of the present time.

[1] *Calcutta Review,* vol. ii. pp. 95 and 115.

CHAPTER XI.

TAMIL PEOPLE ON THE CONTINENT.

THE MADRAS MISSION.

1837–1864.

Origin of the mission.

THIS mission grew out of representations by Mr. Winslow, while on a visit to the United States in 1834, as to the probable demand for books and tracts in the Tamil missions. He sailed from Philadelphia in the next year, accompanied by the Rev. Robert O. Dwight, and by several missionaries of the Presbyterian Board. Messrs. Winslow and Scudder were subsequently designated by the Ceylon Mission to commence the mission at Madras, it having been ascertained that the proposed mission would not interfere with the published plans of either of the English Missionary Societies already in the field. The population of the city then exceeded four hundred thousand. Mr. Winslow arrived in August, 1836, and Dr. Scudder in September, and it was arranged that Dr. Scudder should reside at Chintadrepettah, a suburb southwest of the walled town, and Mr. Winslow at Royapûram on the north. Mrs. Winslow became a victim to the cholera in September, 1837. She was gifted with a superior intellect, refined by education and travel, and had ample means for living at home in comfort. But she went joyfully on her mission, and when death came suddenly, in one of his most distressing forms, he was regarded as a messenger from her Lord, and she regretted none of her sacrifices.

Death of Mrs. Winslow.

Dr. Scudder labored fraternally with Mr. Smith of the London Missionary Society, and a revival of religion was the consequence. The mission had sixteen schools containing five hundred pupils, and the government made a grant of six hundred dollars to sustain them through the commercial distress of 1837. Besides this, the Governor and seven others gave fifty dollars each. While Dr. Scudder devoted himself chiefly to preaching tours and the distribution of books and tracts, Mr. Winslow was mainly employed on a revision of the Tamil Scriptures, and in conducting a magazine in that language. The committee of the Auxiliary Bible Society, of which he was a member, had completed a revision of the Tamil New Testament, and had begun upon the Old Testament, in the translation of which Mr. Rhenius, of the Tinnevelly mission, had previously made considerable progress. The number of distinct publications then existing in the Tamil language, was estimated at about two hundred.

Early proceedings.

An opportunity was unexpectedly offered, in the year 1838, for the purchase of a printing establishment belonging to the Church Missionary Society. It consisted of eight iron printing presses, a lithographic press, a hydraulic press, a type-foundry, a book-bindery, fifteen fonts of Tamil, Telûgû, and English type, and one in Hindûstanee. Mr. Phineas R. Hunt arrived as a printer in 1840, and took charge of the establishment. The profits of the job printing in such a place as Madras were considerable, and soon repaid the purchase money. The printing in native languages from June 1838 to 1841, was 33,750,000 pages, a large part of which were selected portions of Scripture, printed at the expense of Bible and Tract Societies.

Purchase of a printing establishment.

Amount of printing.

In the spring of 1840, the two brethren made a tour to Conjeveram, a sacred place forty-six miles southwest of Madras. In the summer, Dr. Scudder performed another tour in the Cuddalore and Tanjore districts, two hundred miles south. In the autumn, Mr. Winslow journeyed west of Madras into the Mysore, one of the Protected States, governed by a Rajah. This immense terrace of table-land, three thousand feet above the level of the sea, Mr. Winslow describes as a splendid country, much superior to that on the coast, and cooler by many degrees than the plains below. But the Tamil language was less prevalent than the Cana-

Preaching tours.

rese, and several places were already occupied by English missionaries.

It was probably, in 1841, that Dr. Scudder made a visit to Vellore, of which we have an account in an extract from his journal. There, on one occasion, he took his position at a gateway before seven o'clock in the morning, and did not leave it until six in the evening. This laborious service was performed in accordance with his rule, not to give a copy of the Scriptures until the recipient presented a ticket showing that he was able to read. He used two kinds of tickets, one testifying to an examination as to the ability to read, the other a permit to receive books. To avoid pressure from the crowd, it was necessary to give out his tickets from a seat above the people. Fifteen hundred Gospels and a large number of tracts were thus distributed at Vellore.

Labors at Vellore.

Protracted journeys in a debilitating climate at length broke down the vigorous constitution of Dr. Scudder, and his physician advised him to visit America as affording him the only hope of life. Previous to this, however, in order to accomplish an object which greatly interested him, he crossed the Neilgherries. Some part of the journey subjected him to perils from wild beasts, and, worse than all, from the pestiferous atmosphere of the jungle. He contracted the jungle fever, and his life was so seriously threatened that

Perils in the wilderness.

intelligence was sent to Mrs. Scudder. The heroic woman, though in no condition personally for such a journey, provided herself with a tent, palankeen, and provisions, and travelled night and day with only a faint hope of finding her husband alive. "In the worst part of the jungle road, as night drew on, the palankeen bearers, frightened by the noise of wild beasts, fled, leaving Mrs. Scudder and her little son exposed to a horrid death, with none to protect them but Daniel's God. What could she do? She held her little one by the hand, and spent much of the night in prayer. She heard the heavy tread of wild elephants, which could have trampled her and her son to death. Then came the growl of ravenous beasts, the sound approaching and then receding. They seemed to be circling round the little spot; but God held them back. So they passed the night. Morning came, and the cowardly bearers returned."[1]

Visit to America.

The voyage to America was unexpectedly beneficial, and Dr. Scudder resolved, on his arrival in 1842, to devote himself to an unremitted effort for awakening a missionary spirit among the rising generation of his native land. For three years he was constantly employed in this work, until he had addressed over a hundred thousand children.[2] The interest thus awakened in the

[1] *Memoir of Rev. John Scudder, M. D.*, p. 178.

[2] *Ibid.* p. 178.

youthful mind of the country, and its results, can be fully known only when the secrets of all hearts shall be revealed.

Twenty-one natives were admitted to the church at Madras in 1841 and 1842, making the whole number twenty-eight. About this time, a church edifice was erected at Royapûram, chiefly by donations in the city and vicinity. Mr. Hutchings removed from Ceylon to Madras to assist in the preparation and publication of a Tamil and English Dictionary, which had been begun by Mr. Knight of the Church Missionary Society. Mr. Hutchings took charge of Royapûram, and Mr. Winslow removed to Chintadrepettah, where he opened a boarding-school for girls of the higher castes. Mr. Ferdinand D. W. Ward removed from the Madura mission to Madras in 1843, and Mr. Hutchings, with health seriously impaired, proceeded to the United States. His place at Madras was supplied, in the following May, by Mr. Henry Martyn Scudder, eldest son of Dr. Scudder. He was the first missionary son sent forth by the Board. His birth-place was in Ceylon, and having spoken the Tamil language in his boyhood, it returned to him like a forgotten dream, so that he was preaching to the natives five months after his arrival. Mr. Winslow had married Miss Anne Spears in the year 1838, daughter of a gentleman connected with the Madras medical service. After

Admissions to the church.

Literary and other labors.

The first missionary son.

an exemplary life, she was suddenly removed by death on the 20th of June, 1843.

Productions of the press.

More than seven millions of pages were printed in that year, and the number from the beginning was 53,697,766. The demand for printing was on the increase, not only in the Tamil language, but in the Telûgû and Canarese, spoken by large communities north and west of Madras. Among the published works were a newspaper and magazine, both in the Tamil language. The latter was at first monthly, then semi-monthly. A uniform edition of six thousand copies of the Tamil Scriptures, in one volume, was completed at the close of 1844, with the headings and chronology according to the English authorized version, and with references.

Conflict with caste

Early in the following year, the mission took measures to test the power of caste in the church, and it was found necessary to suspend five of the male members. Their wives were also members, but did not follow them, and the men all came forward, after some months, and agreed to renounce the distinctions of caste.

Heathen opposition.

Among evidences of the advancing power of Christian truth, was the increased opposition from the heathen. This was occasionally seen in the breaking forth of riotous conduct, carried as far as a fear of the magistrates would permit. An anti-Christian society existed at

Madras, and, by means of a newspaper, tracts, lectures and agents, exerted much influence on the interior villages. It was a deeply interesting fact, however, that the government was adopting a more humane and liberal policy. It declared that all religions professed by its subjects would be equally tolerated and protected; and, contrary to what had been the law of the land, that the Hindû might embrace Christianity and break caste without the forfeiture of property, or any of his civil rights.

Enlightened policy of the government.

Dr. and Mrs. Scudder returned from the United States to Madras in March, 1847, and went immediately to Madura, as was related in the history of the Madura mission. A generous subscription of nearly two thousand dollars was made by English residents at Madras toward the erection of a house of worship at Chintadrepettah, which was opened for use in 1848. The congregations at the two stations were each estimated at five hundred, but many must have been children from the schools. The Rev. John W. Dulles, who had married a daughter of Mr. Winslow, arrived at Madras in 1849, and in the same year Dr. and Mrs. Scudder returned from Madura. Henry Martyn, their son already mentioned, had been residing at Madras as a missionary since the year 1844.[1]

The mission reinforced.

[1] Six others of the sons became missionaries in the land of their birth, and the two daughters married English gentlemen residing on the Neilgherries.

On the 19th of November Mrs. Scudder died, after a brief illness. She was a rare woman, and her husband hardly recovered from the shock occasioned by her decease. She had been thirty years connected with the India missions.

Death of Mrs. Scudder.

Henry had qualified himself in a government institution to assist his father in the medical department. Renting a house in the most populous portion of the city, they preached in the yard or in the street to such as could be induced to listen, and thus proclaimed the Gospel to many thousands. They also put in circulation a great number of Tamil and Telûgû books and tracts.

The father and son.

Mr. Winslow spent five hours each day, during four months of the year, with a committee of revision on the historical and prophetic parts of the Tamil Scriptures, and the greater part of the remaining time, twice a week, with one of the members of the committee, on the poetical books. When not thus engaged, he was occupied three hours daily with a moonshee, on the Tamil and English Dictionary already mentioned.

Mr. Winslow's labors.

The new version of the Tamil Bible was completed in November, 1850. It had been in hand three years, and for two years the united labors of Messrs. Percival and Spaulding of Jaffna, Brotherton of the Church of England, and Winslow of Madras, had been devoted to it, most of the time daily except on the Sabbaths. It was

New version of the Tamil Bible.

thought, in accuracy, conciseness, elegance, and idiomatic correctness, to be a great advance on anything that had gone before. Printed in new small pica type, in one royal octavo volume, it was much admired.

In March, 1851, the younger Dr. Scudder commenced a new station at Arcot, seventy miles west of Madras, on the road to Bangalore, and was then the only missionary between Madras and Bangalore, a region full of cities, towns, villages, and hamlets; and he found it an interesting field.

New station at Arcot.

Mr. Isaac N. Hurd and wife joined the mission in July, 1852, but Mrs. Hurd died in the January following. Failure of health obliged Mr. and Mrs. Dulles to return to the United States in the autumn of 1852. The missionary labors were similar in each succeeding year. There were four places for stated preaching, with congregations at two of the stations of from two hundred to four hundred and fifty. The membership in the two churches was forty-five. The printing, in 1853, was 27,813,246 pages, nearly half of them pages of the Bible. The free vernacular schools were twelve, with three hundred and twenty boys and one hundred and seventy-five girls. The English and vernacular school contained two hundred pupils. The children of the schools all attended public worship and Sabbath school instruction.

Summary.

The elder Dr. Scudder had become so reduced in health, that in the summer of 1854 he was induced to try the effect of a voyage to the Cape of Good Hope. He was accompanied by his son Joseph, who, with Henry and William, had commenced a separate mission at Arcot. In the salubrious region of the Cape his health was apparently much benefited, and he commenced preaching with his usual earnestness to the children, crowds of whom flocked to hear him. He had engaged his return passage, when, on the 13th of January, 1855, he passed while sleeping into an apoplectic state, and soon slept in death. He was in the sixty-second year of his age, and the thirty-sixth of his missionary life.

Death of Dr. Scudder.

Nothing more need be said to illustrate the life and character of Dr. Scudder, as a missionary. His aim was single, his labors indefatigable, and it is presumed his energies could not have found a more ample scope.

Mr. Winslow's health was so impaired in the year 1855, that his brethren of the Deputation, then at Madras, advised him to visit his native land, which he did early in the next year. Mr. Hurd now took charge of the English high school; and being able to give more time to the school than Mr. Winslow had done, the number of students increased, and there was greater activity both in teachers and pupils. In April there were five additions to the church.

Mr. Winslow visits the United States.

It had been arranged, in 1855, to sell the English portion of the printing establishment; and its continuance was soon after rendered impracticable by the large wages offered to English type-setters by the government press.

Reduction of the printing establishment.

Mr. Winslow returned to his post early in 1858 with his wife. They were married in Boston just before their departure, and were cordially welcomed by their missionary and native friends. The degree of Doctor of Divinity had been conferred upon him by Harvard College.

Both Dr. Winslow and Mr. Hurd now found, that the policy of the government in giving both an English and vernacular education to the Hindûs in that Presidency, seriously affected the mission schools. Many boys came only to commence English studies preparatory to entering the government school, and then to become qualified, after two or three years, for some position under government. It was observed, too, that the lads in the school took much less interest in the study of the Bible. Mr. Hunt, the printer, represents the change of the press, making it a purely missionary institution, as exceedingly gratifying to himself and to all the friends of missions in that region. The Madras Bible Society bore testimony to "the important service it had rendered to the circulation of the Bible by the improved typography of the vernacular Scriptures; a result entirely due to the ex-

Influence of the press.

ertions of Mr. Hunt, its indefatigable superintendent." The printing of the Scriptures in that year amounted to 14,353,536 pages in Tamil, and to 3,440,000 in Telûgû. The "clear, correct, and beautiful editions of the Tamil Bible, each edition excelling the previous one, called forth the admiration and merited the gratitude of all native Christians."

The Tamil Bible.

Dr. Winslow had the pleasure of seeing the Tamil and English Dictionary completed in 1862. It contained nearly a thousand pages, and 67,452 words; 30,551 more than Rottler's Dictionary, and 900 more than the Tamil Dictionary published in Jaffna. It was said to be the most elaborate and complete Dictionary hitherto prepared in any of the languages of India, next to the Sanskrit Lexicon of Professor Wilson.[1]

Completion of a Tamil and English Dictionary.

A pocket edition of the whole Tamil Bible was issued about this time, in fine morocco binding, and was in great demand. A popular edition of the New Testament had prepared the way for it.

Pocket edition of the Bible.

The time had now come when the Head of the Church saw fit to call to Himself the venerable originator and only clerical member of the mission. After fruitless endeavors at the Hills to recover health, broken down by incessant

Death of Dr. Winslow.

[1] For a history of this Dictionary, and for testimonials as to its merits, see *Missionary Herald* for 1863, p. 130.

labors, Dr. Winslow embarked with his wife on the 20th of August, 1864, for the United States, and reached Cape Town on the 20th of October, but in an exhausted condition. He died on the 22d of that month, two days after his arrival, at the age of seventy-five. A frequent expression of his during his last days was, "Great is my peace." And well might it be great. He was closing a long life of devoted service to his Lord and Master, and could not but feel assured that he was near his eternal home.

His character.

In early life he had published a "History of Missions," which interested and benefited the churches of his native land, and must have done much to strengthen his own faith in the work. He entered India in 1819, and his subsequent missionary life wanted only five years of half a century. He could look on his closing career in much the same manner as did the Apostle to the Gentiles.

Dr. Winslow was below the medium stature, but had a comely person, a dignified and courteous bearing, and was eminently a practical man; and a leading influence was cheerfully accorded to him among his brethren. For many years he was Secretary of the Revision and Publication Committee of the Madras Bible Society; and was remarkable for the patient, persevering, unremitted thought he gave to the translation and revision of the Scriptures. And his untiring labors on the Tamil and English Dictionary did not less really subserve the cause of his Lord and Saviour.[1]

Mrs. Winslow returned to her native land; and the declining health of Mr. Hunt, in the climate of India, brought him and Mrs. Hunt home also. As they were the only remaining missionaries of this field, the question was necessarily raised whether the object of the mission had not been attained.

This, as the reader will remember, was to become a printing and publishing establishment for the benefit of the Tamil race; and Mr. Hunt had managed it very successfully for twenty-six years, with that end constantly in view. From July, 1838, to December, 1864, the printing amounted to 228,417,018 pages of Scripture; 105,993,026 pages of tracts; and 110,206,376 of other works; making a grand total of 444,617,020 pages. Mr. Hunt believed it was no longer advisable for the Board to own a large printing establishment at Madras, and that its appropriate work had been so far accomplished, as to warrant the sale of the establishment. The English department had been disposed of some years before. The remaining portion was now purchased by the Society for Promoting Christian Knowledge.

Sale of the establishment.

The Chintadrepettah station was transferred to the

[1] See a brief Memoir of Dr. Winslow in the *Missionary Herald* for March, 1865, pp. 65–69.

Church Missionary Society, and the church building at Royapûram to the Medical Missionary Society of Edinburgh. The dwelling-house at Royapûram was reserved for the convenience of brethren of the Tamil missions when they might have occasion to be at Madras, and was placed in charge of the Madura mission.

Discontinuance of the mission.

The number of persons received into the church at Madras had been about one hundred and fifty; and hundreds upon hundreds of children and youth, of both sexes, had been taught to read the Scriptures. It was no backward movement, no retreat, and no pecuniary sacrifice to transfer the property now into the hands of other faithful men, who could labor to better advantage in that field.

Summary view.

Mr. Hunt having been requested to take charge of the mission press at Peking, the metropolis of China, his response was, after thirty years of similar labors in India; "Without hesitation, and with pure delight, I accept the proposed appointment to the North China Mission, as a missionary printer."

Mr. Hunt's change of designation.

CHAPTER XII.

THE TAMIL PEOPLE.

THE ARCOT MISSION.

1851–1857.

THE commencement of a station at Arcot by Dr. Henry Martyn Scudder, has been already mentioned. It was in 1851, after he had been seven years connected with the Madras mission. He found his newly acquired medical skill a good introduction to him as a minister of the Gospel. His command of the language, moreover, with a natural facility of expression, attracted crowds about him when preaching in the streets of Arcot. Mr. William W. Scudder, a brother, after a connection of five years with the Ceylon mission, was transferred to Arcot in 1853. Joseph, another brother, arrived at the close of that year, and Ezekiel C. and Jared W., two other brothers, and also a sister, joined the company in March, 1856. Mr. W. W. Scudder was bereaved at Madras on the 20th of September, 1854, as he had been in the year 1848 while connected with the Ceylon mission. He had but recently returned from

America with his wife, and her death was a great affliction to the mission, where she was much loved as a friend and fellow-laborer.

The mission occupied the North Arcot District, which had a population of more than a million of souls. The Gospel Propagation Society having withdrawn from Vellore and Chittûr, committed their congregations to the care of the new mission, it being the only missionary body in the district. The stations were at Vellore, Chittûr, and Arnee. The communicants at Vellore were twenty-seven, at Chittûr forty-two, and six at Arnee, making seventy-five in all; of whom forty had been communicants in the congregations of the English Society. The brethren of the mission having all been born in India, of eminently missionary parents, and having been judiciously permitted to learn the spoken language at an early age, had as a mission preëminently the power of using the spoken language in preaching the Gospel, and the bias of their minds was in that direction. "We make it our chief duty," they say, "to go into the streets of the towns and villages of our District, holding up Christ and him crucified as the only hope of the sinner. This work has been extensively carried on by the missionaries and catechists. The Gospel has been fully preached in almost every street of our stations. We have also been on several extended tours, declaring to all that there is none other name under heaven given among men whereby we must be saved, except that of Jesus Christ. A great number of adults, varying from five to thirty a day, have visited the station for books and tracts. To all these the Gospel has been preached and portions of God's Word distributed." There were also six schools for children of professed and nominal Christians, containing one hundred and five pupils. "The chief object of our mission," add the brethren, "being the preaching of the Gospel, we cannot establish schools for heathen children. We have not the time nor the means to enter upon this work, which more properly belongs to those who have the charge of the secular interests of the Hindûs. It is otherwise with Christian children. They belong to us. Many of them are the baptized offspring of our church. We are under special obligations to them. We must see that they are thoroughly educated in the Scriptures, that they are elevated above the ignorance of the mass of the people, that they are kept as much as possible from the influence of heathenism, and that all means are used to secure their purity and intelligence. Our object is not to bestow upon them the elegancies of a foreign education. We therefore instruct them only through the vernacular languages. We strive to impart to them that education, which shall under God's blessing make them useful men and useful Christians."

A railway was running from Madras to Arcot, and

was in progress towards Cûnûr. A congregation had been gathered at this place by Rev. P. P. Schaffter during a temporary residence on the Neilgherry Hills, and was transferred, with a schoolhouse, by W. H. Stanes, Esq., to Mr. Joseph Scudder, whose health obliged him to resort to the Hills in 1856.

There was a Preparandi Class in the mission of baptized lads, of whom two were communicants, to be trained with a special reference to becoming helpers and preachers. In December, 1856, these accompanied the missionaries on a tour of about three hundred miles. "We might have a thousand scholars," say the mission, "but numbers are not our object. Government is making ample provision for the mental training of heathen youth. Our one hundred and twenty-seven pupils, with a very few exceptions, have been dedicated to the Lord in baptism. We regard with interest this little band educated chiefly in the doctrines of the Bible. To it we look for our future schoolmasters, catechists, and even ministers of the Gospel. Our system of education is such as to give no cause of fear that, as soon as fitted for usefulness in the mission, they will hasten to accept higher salaries in secular employments. The English language is not taught, and yet we find no difficulty in communicating truth in its various departments to these youths in their own tongue."

Two new churches were organized this year at Arcot and Cûnûr, making the whole number five, and a commodious church edifice was completed at Vellore. The contributions from residents in India during that year, not including two hundred dollars for the Poor Fund, exceeded a thousand dollars.

The perfectly amicable connection which had subsisted between the American Board and the General Synod of the Reformed Dutch Church since the year 1832, was terminated by mutual agreement in 1857,[1] and the members of the Arcot mission were soon after released, at their own request, from their connection with the Board. The mission has continued to be successfully prosecuted under the direction of the Board of Missions of the Reformed Church.

[1] See *Report of the Board for* 1857, pp. 20–25.

CHAPTER XIII.

THE MAHRATTA AND TAMIL MISSIONS.

MISSIONARY CONFERENCES.

1854 AND 1855.

FOR the first forty years, no executive officer of the American Board had opportunity for personal conference with the missionaries in India. A more varied and perfect knowledge than was attainable either through letters or the visits of missionaries to their native land, at length became necessary. The Prudential Committee of the Board appointed the author, then Foreign Secretary, and the Rev. Augustus C. Thompson, D.D., a member of the Committee, to go as their representatives on a visit specially to the missions in India and Ceylon. E. B. Underhill, Esq., Secretary and representative of the English Baptist Missionary Society, on a similar errand, was a fellow-passenger with them from England.

Necessity of a more varied knowledge of the India missions.

Hence the Deputation.

Those whose posts of duty are at the centres of missionary operations must be better situated, in some respects, than the members

Advantages in central positions.

of any one mission, for obtaining comprehensive practical views of missionary principles and testing their value. They see those principles tried in perhaps a score of missions, and under a variety of circumstances; and the same is true with respect to plans and measures. Generally, they can gain all needful information through written correspondence and personal intercourse with missionaries visiting their native land. But complications sometimes arise in older missions, making it needful that some member or members of the Executive Committee should go upon the ground, and confer with their brethren face to face. Written correspondence across ten thousand miles, is a slow process; and there are sometimes misunderstandings, which greatly retard desirable results, and even prevent them, when a few days or weeks of familiar personal conference would suffice to bring them about, to the gratification of all concerned.

When visits are desirable.

The Deputation landed at Bombay on the 2d of November, 1854; and spent seventy-two days in the Mahratta mission, fifty in the Madura mission, sixty-five in Ceylon, twenty-one at Madras, and twelve at Arcot. Dr. Thompson's pastoral relations making it necessary for him to return, he embarked at Madras on the 10th of July, and reached home, by way of Syria, October 27, 1855, after an absence from his people of one year and a quarter. The other member of the Deputa-

Intercourse with the missions.

tion subsequently spent twenty-four days in Calcutta, fourteen in the Syria mission, forty-six in the Armenian, visiting Kessab, Antioch, Aleppo, Aintab, and Constantinople, and reached home on the 15th of January, 1856, after an absence of nearly one year and a half.

Proceedings of the Conference.

The course pursued was, to hold a Conference with each mission, continued from day to day so long as seemed needful for the full discussion of matters demanding attention. At the opening of each Conference, after prayer and the choice of officers, committees were appointed on business and devotional exercises, and the Deputation read a list of the topics which they desired should receive special attention. These were referred to the business committee, who reported the names of those persons to whom each topic should be assigned. In no case, however, was a report to be presented until the subject had been fully considered in the general meeting.

Printing of the proceedings.

The proceedings of these conferences, and the letters of the Deputation to the several missions, were printed in India, for the use of the missions and of the Prudential Committee at home. They make a volume of about four hundred octavo pages. To these were afterwards added proceedings of the conferences at Beirût and Constantinople, the Report of the Deputation to the Board, and the Report of the Committee of Thirteen, appointed by the Board, at its Special Meeting in Albany to investigate and report on the proceedings of the Deputation, making two hundred pages more. Of this volume Dr. Mullens, then a missionary at Calcutta, and now Foreign Secretary of the London Missionary Society, says, in the published Report of the Liverpool Conference: "It is not too much to say, that no volume of equal size, published during the era of our modern missions, contains so much valuable information, in all the details of missionary experience on several most important fields of missionary labor, as that collection of missionary papers."

The object of these conferences was better secured by means of reports, than by resolutions. The Deputation had liberty to suggest and discuss with all freedom, but neither served on committees, nor had the responsibility of voting. There is space for only some of the more important results of these Conferences; others can be inferred from the subsequent history of the missions.

THE MAHRATTA CONFERENCE.

The Mahratta Mission assembled at Ahmednuggur on the 3d of December, 1854, and remained together till the 25th. There were present Messrs. Munger, Ballantine, Fairbank, Wilder, Hazen, Wood, Bowen, Bissell, and Barker, and the ladies of the mission.

Members of the Conference.

The brethren of the Ahmednuggur branch had previously licensed two of their native converts as preachers of the Gospel, both of whom had been brahmins. It was their purpose to have these preachers ordained as evangelists, on the arrival of the Deputation; but when the matter came up for consideration in the Conference it was arranged, that the Ahmednuggur church be divided and form two churches, and that the candidates be ordained, not as evangelists, but as pastors of those churches. These were the first native pastors ordained by the missions of the Board in India. The reason assigned by the Mahratta brethren for having delayed such ordinations was, that they had not fully understood the importance of having self governing churches in different localities. The missionary himself acted as pastor, feeling that he could better perform the duties of that office. The native preachers shrunk, moreover, from pastoral responsibilities, and at last assumed them with evident reluctance.

Ordination of the first native pastors.

Reason for the delay of such ordinations.

Connected with these ordinations was the expression of an opinion by the Conference adverse to ordaining native preachers as evangelists. The institution of a native pastorate naturally led to efforts for the development of village churches. Coming, as all the missionaries had, from a country where

Against ordaining native evangelists.

Development of village churches.

Edwards, Hopkins, Bellamy, and Dwight were master-spirits in theology, they perhaps had too much distrusted the native experience, where love, consolation, and joy were out of proportion to conviction of sin. But a more careful perusal of the history of the primitive churches and the Epistles of John, in connection with the living manifestations of God's grace in oriental converts, had produced the conviction, that true piety, in some of its beautiful developments, may exist among them with either form of experience. Thus were they led to repose more confidence in the ability of native churches, preachers, and pastors to sustain responsibility, and became more ready to devolve responsibility upon them.

Why distrust of native piety.

A special difficulty presented itself in arranging for village stations. The native roads were nearly impracticable during the rains from bridgeless torrents and deep mud, and there was danger of contracting acute diseases, so that families scrupled to settle where friendly and medical succor would be so difficult of access. But the progress of macadamized roads and railways was rapidly removing this hindrance, and a plan was devised, at this time, by which two rural stations were very soon established.

Difficulty in forming village stations.

The boarding-school for boys at Ahmednuggur had been discontinued two years before, as already stated, and replaced by other

Change in the high school at Ahmednuggur.

schools suited to the times. The action of the Conference was in substantial agreement with those proceedings.

A report on Native Churches and Pastors was drawn up by one of the more experienced missionaries, the following abstract of which will not be thought too extended: —

On native piety.

1. Such deep contrition for sin is rarely seen among the Mahrattas, as is often exhibited among those who have known the Bible from their childhood. But when there is an evident love for the truth in a native, a constant desire to know it, and a continuous effort to do what is right, and especially resistance to strong temptation, or steadfastness under trial, then we may believe him to be a true child of God. His knowledge of the Christian doctrines may be very limited, and yet he be a true Christian. If there be evidence of a change of heart, his ignorance ought not to debar him from the church. Much responsibility should be thrown upon the native church members, who generally form a very correct opinion as to the character of those with whom they are daily conversant. A native pastor will often judge more correctly of the character of a candidate for church membership, than the missionary.

Substitute for a native pastor.

2. When a native pastor is not available for a particular church, a catechist should be put in charge of it, whose business it

should be to give religious instruction to the church, to watch over the conduct of its members, and to give information of irregularities to the missionary under whose care he is placed.

Self-sustaining churches.

3. The aim is to render the churches self-sustaining as soon as possible. Consequently the missionary will perform the duties of pastor no longer than is necessary, and he will be careful to throw as much responsibility upon the church members as he finds they are able to bear without injury to the cause. It would be far better that a native pastor should make some mistakes in the management of his church, than that the missionary should relieve him too largely of responsibility.

Education of native pastors.

4. The education of native pastors should vary according to their talents and their field of labor. In many instances, pastors of churches in the cities or in important places should have a sufficient knowledge of English to consult English commentaries. They should have some knowledge of English science. In large cities many intelligent natives are acquainted with English science, and familiar with English works on various subjects, and native pastors in these places should be prepared to meet this portion of the community, and also those who are deists or infidels. It is even desirable, that some should have such a knowledge of the Sanskrit language, as to be able to show the learned brahmin who opposes Christianity, from his

own sacred books, the absurdities of Hindûism. Pastors of churches in country places do not so much need a knowledge of English science, or of the English language, but should have a good knowledge of their vernacular, and be prepared to explain the Word of God in a satisfactory manner. Persons who are well acquainted with the Scriptures, who understand the great doctrines of the Bible, and are apt to teach without any other literary qualifications, may be ordained as pastors of native churches in the villages, and may be expected to prove good soldiers of Jesus Christ. Between these two extremes there will be various grades of qualification, and each pastor should be placed over the church for which he is especially adapted by his talents and character.

Salaries of native pastors.

5. In general the native pastors placed over churches in cities and important places should not have more than thirty or thirty-five rupees per month, including house rent, and those placed over churches in the villages, from ten to fifteen rupees per month. There may be situations where a salary of from twenty to twenty-five rupees should be given. This will suffice, it is believed, to support the pastors comfortably, and enable them to exercise the duties of benevolence and hospitality, being somewhat above the income of men in the same position in the native community. Our native pastors should not live after

the manner of the heathen, but exhibit the fruits of their religion in cleanliness of person, decency of apparel, and order in their households, setting an example which their flocks may be recommended to follow. And these salaries will not be above the ability of the native churches to give.

Ecclesiastical relations.

6. Missionaries should not belong to ecclesiastical bodies composed of the native pastors. They may attend their meetings, and advise them, but in general it will be found expedient to leave the native pastors to manage their ecclesiastical affairs for themselves. In this way they will become more speedily prepared to maintain the institutions of religion independently of foreign assistance, and their churches to become self-governing and self-sustaining. The departure of the missionary, when that shall finally take place, will then be no sudden disruption of ecclesiastical relations, nor will it weaken the ecclesiastical body which the native pastors have formed.

Native preaching talent.

7. The native brethren are well adapted to the work of preaching the Gospel. They are generally fluent in their own language, and command attention by their free allusions to native customs and ideas. In this respect no foreign missionary can ever compete with them. The preaching of the natives is very valuable. That of the educated among them is not behind the preaching of the missionary. Divine truth is exhibited in

its relations, and applied to the conscience, as well as by the missionaries; and they may be expected to become better preachers than persons from other lands. The members of the Conference declared their joy in this prospect, and their readiness to stand out of the way, and let them take the place which God had evidently assigned them.

The Conference was dissolved after twenty days; the brethren declaring their gratitude for stations occupied, for so many hopeful congregations, and for churches embracing forty-three members from the highest castes (fifteen of them converted brahmins), out of a total of two hundred and twenty-five, with two competent native pastors.

Results in the mission.

"The Mahratta people as a whole," say the brethren, writing in the year 1854, have acquired a large amount of speculative knowledge of Christian truth. As the result of missionary efforts, in which the missions of other societies have also shared, specially by means of schools, extended preaching tours, and the distribution of tracts, we find that a pretty general and correct knowledge of Christianity prevails among the thinking community in both the Concan and the Deccan. There are many, now scattered all over this land, who have committed our catechisms and epitomes of Scripture truth to memory, and who have received much religious instruction. Such persons tell others what Christianity is, and decide correctly when appealed to for information respecting fundamental doctrines. Vast numbers of tracts and Christian books are in circulation, and are read by the people. Of our "First Book for Children," which consists, besides a few lessons on letters and spelling, of the Lord's Prayer and the Ten Commandments, and a simple epitome of the doctrines of grace, more than thirty thousand have been sold within the past five years. Thus, by means which are accessible to the people in the absence of the missionary, the great truths of the Gospel are made known. The twelve millions, who use the Mahratta language, are thus being taught, that Christianity regards them all as guilty for having sinned against the Heavenly Father, and as liable to endless punishment, but also offers them all a Saviour, a Sanctifier, and Eternal Life.

THE CEYLON CONFERENCE.

The Ceylon Conference was held in Jaffna, between April 25 and May 22, 1855; and there were present Messrs. Meigs, Spaulding, Smith, Howland, Hastings, Green, Burnell, Sanders, and Lord, and the ladies of the mission.

Members of the Conference.

The reader may be pleased to know the subjects which occupied the attention of the Conference. They were, in brief, as follows: The Governing Object in Missions; Preaching; Native Churches and Pastors; Caste and Polygamy; Native Schools; Oodooville Female Board-

Subjects discussed by the Conference.

ing-school; Batticotta Seminary; Native Assistants; Modification in the Stations; Restrictions on Correspondence; Printing Establishment; Provision for Widows, Children, and Invalid Missionaries; Grants from Bible and Tract Societies; Visits to the United States; Sanitaria; Salaries; Medical Establishment; Mission Property; Government Grants; Estimates, Appropriations, and Expenditures; Mission Buildings; and Temporal Aid from Mission Funds.

While all the topics above named received careful consideration, a few only can be noticed here.

For nearly forty years the five older stations had enjoyed the labors of some of the ablest and most faithful of missionaries, and there had been every facility which popular schools of every form could give. Yet, separating from the congregations the pupils in the mission schools and those deriving their support from mission employment, only one hundred and twenty-four adults were found in the congregations of those five stations, who were not members of the church. And in respect to the three hundred and seventy-six members of those churches, two hundred and forty-nine derived their support, in some form, from the mission. Mr. Meigs, the oldest member of the mission, stated that both of these results were owing to the hard and barren nature of the soil, and not to the schools, which were at that time generally

Native congregations and churches.

under Christian masters, who taught the lessons the mission required them to teach. They were, in fact, Christian schools.

Usefulness of the higher schools.

It appeared that the boarding-schools had done much for the cause of education and general improvement, much to array the facts of science against the Hindû mythology, and that well educated men were residing in all parts of the community. Hundreds and even thousands were heads of families, whom the common schools had more or less instructed in the fundamental truths of the Gospel. But the higher education had acquired at length a marketable value outside of the mission, and was setting strongly towards the world, through the English language. There was then operating in the native mind, as the result of past educational efforts, an intensely avaricious and ambitious mental activity, which the missionaries could no longer hope to correct, or even control, except by giving themselves more exclusively to prayer and the ministry of the Word.

Tendency of the high schools.

Ordination of the first native pastor.

A village pastor was ordained by the Conference at Karadive, on the 24th of May, — the first native pastor in the mission, — over a church recently gathered, and composed of men and women from castes opposed to each other; and the first of two deacons chosen by the church members, was of pariah origin. It is interesting that Mr. Meigs, of the first company of missionaries which arrived thirty-nine years before, and Mr. Spaulding, of the first reinforcement in 1820, took leading parts in the service. Cornelius the pastor was not born in the province, nor accomplished in English studies, but he had been long laboring in the place, was of good report among the people, and desired by them to be their pastor.

Churches thus furnished for action the Conference proposed to organize wherever the Lord should be pleased to renew by his grace a sufficient number of the inhabitants, and pastors were to be ordained wherever there was a suitable man to fill so responsible an office, and a church that should desire him for its shepherd.

Proposed multiplication of churches.

The ground taken by the Conference in respect to preaching places for village use is worthy of special notice. They would have them native houses, with mud or matted sides, a thatched roof, and a smooth floor of earth covered with mats of palmyra leaf, costing only from twenty-five to seventy-five dollars. The heathen, it was said, would come most readily to places of worship of that description.

Native preaching houses.

The modifications desirable in the higher schools received very careful attention. The Seminary at Batticotta contained, at the close of 1854, six teachers and one hundred pupils. The English studies had been gaining on

Modifications in Batticotta Seminary.

the Tamil until, as stated by the Principal of the institution, they stood related to each other as follows: —

	Tamil.	English and Tamil.	English.
Senior class, during six years . .	5	5	19
Junior class, during four years .	5	5	12
First class, during two years . .	2	4	4
Totals	12	14	35

The Conference agreed that the Seminary should in future be for preparing young men, in a four years' course, to become Christian teachers, catechists, and pastors, and that the studies should be mainly restricted to the vernacular, and be made eminently Biblical. None were to be admitted under the age of fourteen, and all were to be Christians, or from Christian families. A missionary was to have charge of the Seminary, aided by two native teachers.

Oodooville boarding-school.

The studies in the Oodooville Female Boarding-school were to be restricted to the Tamil language, the number of pupils was to be reduced from seventy-three to thirty-five, none were to be admitted under twelve years of age, and the term of residence was not to exceed five years. Those admitted were generally to be Christians, or from the families of church members, or nominal Christians.

It was a significant fact, that the oldest members of the mission were the ones most impressed with the favorable religious changes wrought in the province, and were the ones most confident of future success.

Evidence of piety and progress.

The proceedings of this Conference became the subject of discussion at the Annual Meeting of the Board in Utica, N. Y., in 1855, before the Deputation had returned home, founded on changes reported to have been made in the organization and working of the mission in Ceylon. It was suggested that a special meeting of the Board be called whenever the matters connected with the visit of the Deputation to India should be ready for its consideration.

Proceedings of the Conference misapprehended at home.

Such a meeting was held in the city of Albany, N. Y., on the 4th, 5th, and 6th days of March, 1856; and the great interest taken in the welfare of the Board and its missions was manifest in the attendance during that inclement month of thirty-nine Corporate members, and at least two hundred Honorary members. The Deputation, with the consent of the Prudential Committee, made their Report direct to the Board in a printed form; but did not go into any formal defense of the Conference or of their own proceedings, believing it would result better for the cause of truth, that there be a direct correspondence with the mis-

Special meeting of the Board.

sionaries, individually, in India and Turkey. A committee of thirteen was accordingly appointed, to whom the Report of the Deputation was referred; with full power to investigate all questions pertaining thereto, and to make their report at the next annual meeting of the Board. The members of the committee were Dr. N. S. S. Beman, Dr. Mark Hopkins, Dr. Leonard Bacon, Dr. D. H. Riddle, Governor E. Fairbanks, Hon. Linus Child, Dr. B. C. Taylor, Horace Holden, Esq., Dr. Asa D. Smith, Hon. W. Jessup, R. T. Haynes, Esq., Dr. Ray Palmer, and Dr. P. H. Fowler.

A committee of thirteen.

This committee held five meetings, at which most of the members were present, and spent fourteen days in laborious sessions from eight to eleven hours each day. Their first act was to address a letter of inquiry to each member in the missions visited by the Deputation, and also of the missions in Syria and Turkey visited by Dr. Anderson, and a similar circular was addressed to returned missionaries in this country. At the same time, the Prudential Committee was requested to furnish the Committee with their opinions on the various subjects contained in the Report of the Deputation, indicating generally the principles upon which the India missions should hereafter be conducted, especially in regard to schools and seminaries, the press, the preaching of the Gospel, and the relation of missionaries to the native churches and pastors.

Their investigations.

The Report which the Committee of Thirteen made to the Board at its Annual Meeting in Newark in 1856, may be found in the Report of the Board for that year, pp. 29–67.[1] The following declaration is the only part of it that needs to be here quoted, namely: —

The result.

"In regard to the late visit of the Deputation to the Eastern missions, the Special Committee believe they have performed a great and needful work; that they have discharged their high trust as faithful, devoted men; that they ought to receive the cordial thanks of this Board, and that we may confidently hope that a new spirit may pervade and animate our missions abroad, and a strong missionary impulse be given to our churches by this labor of love."

This resolution was embodied in one adopted also by the Board.

THE MADURA CONFERENCE.

The Madura Conference assembled at the East Madura station on the 26th of February. There were present Messrs. Muzzy, Tracy, Herrick, Rendall, Webb, Taylor, Chandler, Little, Noyes, and Sheldon, with the wives of the missionaries.

Persons present.

The village system of Christian congregations in the Madura mission, already described, came under review in the Conference.

The Christian congregations.

[1] The *Report* was also published in a separate form, 8vo, pp. 61, in two editions.

There were then one hundred and twenty congregations, gathered from one hundred and forty-six villages, and numbering four thousand eight hundred and forty-six members, old and young. Of these, five hundred and sixty-nine, or about one fifth part of the adults, were church members. The existence of these congregations in that heathen land, in which the church members were so far outnumbered by the merely nominal Christians, was deemed an extraordinary fact. The Deputation saw the greater part of the church members, and not a few of the men and women of the congregations, and could not but feel that only the ordinary divine blessing was needed on appropriate and persevering labors, to secure permanent congregations throughout the Collectorate.

The village schools.

It appeared that the system of village schools in this mission had been expensive, and wanting in vigor. The Christian pupils in the seventy schools averaged only about eight to a school. Their annual cost, supposing all equally well provided with instruction, would have exceeded ten thousand rupees, and this for the village schools alone.

Modifications in the Seminary.

Important modifications were made in the Seminary at Pasumalai, adapting it to the existing demands of the field. It was to have a diversity of studies, adapted to different classes of persons: 1st. For young men of promise and piety, between the ages of fifteen and twenty-five, a course purely Tamil, of from two to four years, to prepare them for schoolmasters, catechists, and eventually, in some cases, for pastors. 2d. For the better improvement of some not employed as catechists, who had developed a talent for preaching and pastoral duties, and who would be greatly benefited by a longer or shorter connection with the Seminary. 3d. For those whose talents, piety, and circumstances indicated the propriety of a more extended education. The study of the English language was to be for only a part of this class; and for them not as a medium of instruction in cases where proper text-books in Tamil could be obtained.

English school at Madura.

The English School at Madura, after being in operation twenty years, was discontinued. Not far from five hundred boys had enjoyed its advantages. It had been useful to society, but no member of the school had been known to receive a saving impression from the truths of the Gospel.

Ordination of the first native pastor.

The first native pastor in this mission, Mr. S. Winfred, was ordained at Mallankinarû on the 20th of March. The church was organized and the pastor ordained by a committee of the Madura Mission. The Deputation was invited to assist, and tender the fellowship of the churches at home to the newly formed church, and the fellowship of the pastors at home to the newly ordained pastor. In the charge to the pastor he was informed, that while continuing to receive a part of his support from the Board, he would be expected to make stated reports to the mission, as pastors do in America to Societies from which they receive aid. For the sake of order, his channel of communicating with the mission would be the missionary of the station district, within the bounds of which his church and parish were situated; and he was recommended, when needing advice and encouragement in his new office, to go for them to that missionary.

AT MADRAS.

Why no extended discussions at Madras.

There were no extended discussions at Madras, Messrs. Winslow and Hurd being the only residents there. It was understood that the time had come for restricting the Printing Establishment to the demands of the native language. Mr. Hunt, the printer, returned from the United States when the senior member of the Deputation was about leaving India, and gave that as his decided opinion.

AT ARCOT.

Who were at Arcot.

The Deputation visited the Arcot Mission in June. It was composed, at that time, of Messrs. Henry, William W., and Joseph Scudder, sons of Dr. Scudder. Their three stations were all of recent date; and it was not deemed necessary, nor was there time, to renew the consideration of general principles, which had already been discussed once and again, and some of them for the third time.

OTHER MISSIONARY CONFERENCES.

Dr. Mullens states, in his "Brief Review of Ten Years' Missionary Labor in India, between 1852 and 1861," that "the idea of gathering a General Conference of Missionaries of all Societies for consultation respecting their work and the value of their plans, sprang from the private gatherings of the American Missionaries, who had been called together by the Deputation from Boston." This grew out of the fact, that the American Secretary, on visiting Calcutta in the summer of 1855, took with him the printed Minutes of the Conferences, and left copies with Messrs. Mullens and Ewart, two of the leading missionaries in that city.

BAPTIST MISSIONARY CONFERENCES.

More than a year before the Deputation from the American Board proceeded to India, the Executive Committee of the American Baptist Missionary Union had deputed the Rev. Solomon Peck, D. D., and Rev. J. N. Granger to visit their Mission in Burmah, and had invited the missionaries to meet and consult with them. The missionaries accordingly assembled in convention at Maulmain, in Burmah, on the 4th of April, 1853, and were together till the 17th of May. The proceedings of the Conference were printed for the use of the Executive Committee, and fill one hundred and sixteen pages.

Mr. Underhill held four conferences with the missionaries of the Baptist Missionary Society, between June 26, 1855, and February 18, 1856. The proceedings of these conferences were printed for private use, and fill two hundred and sixty-seven octavo pages. The conferences were held at Calcutta, by the Bengal missionaries; at Agra, by the missionaries of the Northwest Provinces; at Monghir, by missionaries in Behar; and at Colombo by missionaries and native pastors in Ceylon.

GENERAL MISSIONARY CONFERENCES.

There have been six General Missionary Conferences since the summer of 1855. (1.) At Calcutta, for Bengal Protestant missionaries, from the 4th to the 7th of September, 1855. There were present fifty missionaries, and the published proceedings occupy one hundred and eighty-three octavo pages. (2.) At Benares, in January, 1857, for the Northwest Provinces. Fifty missionaries were present, from seven Missionary Societies. The papers of this conference were destroyed in the burning of the Allahabad Missionary Press, during the Mutiny. (3.) At Ootacamund, on the Neilgherry Hills, for South India, from April 19th to May 5th, 1858. Thirty-two missionaries were present, from eight missions. The published proceedings occupy a volume of three hundred and sixty-five large octavo pages. (4.) At Liverpool (England), from the 19th to the 23d of March, 1860, composed of missionaries and others, twenty-five of whom were officers of Missionary Societies. The proceedings were published in a volume of four hundred and twenty-eight octavo pages. (5.) At Lahore, for the Punjab, in December and January, 1862–63. The proceedings make an octavo volume of three hundred and ninety-eight pages. (6.) At Allahabad, in Northern India, 1872–73. One hundred and thirty-six members were present.[1] The proceedings fill six hundred octavo pages.

[1] Of these one hundred and five were ordained missionaries, two were chaplains, seventeen laymen connected with missions, and twelve not connected with missions. The Missionary societies represented were nineteen. The number of members connected with each was as follows: American Board, four; American Presbyterian Board, twenty-one; American Methodist Mission, eighteen; American Reformed Church, one; American United Presbyterian Church, two; Anglo-Indian Church Union, one; Baptist Missionary Society, ten; Christian Vernacular Education Society, two; Chamba Mission, one; Church Missionary Society, twenty-five; Church of Scotland, including two chaplains, three; Free Church of Scotland, twelve; Gossner's Evangelical Lutheran Mission, two; Indian Home Mission to the Santhals, one; Irish Presbyterian Mission, three; London Missionary Society, thirteen; Madras Bible Society, one; United Presbyterian Church, three; Wesleyan Missionary Society, one. The number of foreign members connected with missions was ninety-six; of native members, twenty-eight. Americans numbered thirty-eight, Englishmen thirty-two, Scotchmen nineteen, Irishmen three, Germans three, and one was a Norwegian. Of the native members, Bengalis, nine; Hindûstanis, nine; Mahrattas, four; Tamils, three; Punjabi, one; Parsee convert, one; Travancore Syrian, one. From the Bengal Presidency, eighteen; Northwest Provinces and Oudh, sixty-two; the Punjab, thirteen; Bombay Presidency and Central Provinces, eighteen; Madras Presidency, twelve.

CHAPTER XIV.

MISSION TO THE MAHRATTAS.

1854–1862.

Tour in the Godavari Valley.

EARLY in the autumn of 1854 the members of the Deputation accompanied Messrs. Ballantine and Barker on a tour up the valley of the Godavari. It was over ground that had been more or less cultivated by the mission for a dozen years. The rains were past, the roads were settled, the heat had greatly moderated, and the air was salubrious. We travelled in neat, covered carts, each drawn by a pair of small bullocks, who trotted gently along where the road was smooth. The body of the cart rested on springs, with two seats across and a shelter from the sun, leaving an opening at the sides. The vehicle was respectable and comfortable, being adapted to rough roads. In the vicinity of Bombay and Ahmednuggur there are well made and frequently macadamized roads. It was necessary to carry tents, beds, the means of cooking, and nearly all the provisions. The luggage was conveyed at little cost. The established daily rates, at which native men deemed it a privilege to be employed, were nine cents for a man, fifteen for a horse and man, thirty cents for bullocks and a man to drive them, and the same for cattle and luggage cart; all including the cost of their living.

The villages were generally surrounded by walls of sun-dried bricks, with a gateway of stone, and large towers of the same material. Before the extension of British power over these fair lands, such defenses were needful for the robber-chieftain himself, or against his predatory incursions. But now walls and towers were left to melt away under the periodical rains.

The villages.

At Khokar, the centre of a cluster of villages, Yesûba, one of the most efficient catechists, had assembled his mahar friends to welcome the brethren from a distant land. They had all renounced idolatry, and the visitors found themselves in a Christian assembly forty miles from the seat of the mission. The Sabbath was spent at Wadále, a village near by, where our tents were pitched by the side of a small stream, under the shade of a large banyan tree. The mission had erected a small chapel here several years before, in which Haripunt formerly preached, the well known converted brahmin, who was soon after ordained pastor of the first church in Ahmednuggur. Mr. Ballantine on the Sabbath addressed more than forty adults, collected from Wadále and eight neighboring villages. Eighteen were

Reception by Christian villagers.

Preaching.

church members, and most of the twenty-four others were inquirers. Twelve church members were necessarily absent. The morning sermon did not fully arouse the laboring men, but in the afternoon, while the preacher was expatiating with great fervor on the consequences of a general outpouring of the Holy Spirit in this land, every eye was fixed, and there was great apparent solemnity. The homeward route led through Pimpalgaum, where we made the acquaintance of a second Yesûba and his Christian family.

Location of missionaries.

At the close of the Conference at Ahmednuggur, Messrs. Hazen and Bowen were stationed at Bombay, Messrs. Ballantine and Barker at Ahmednuggur, with Miss Farrar and two native pastors, and Mr. Bissell at Seroor. Mr. Munger was at Satara, Mrs. Graves at Malcolm Peth, and Mr. Wilder at Kolapûr. Mr. Fairbank left soon after for the United States, from whence he returned early in 1857, and took up his residence at Wadále, a village twenty-five miles northeast from Ahmednuggur, on the macadamized road to Aurungabad. He had married a daughter of Mr. Ballantine. Mr. Bowen having adopted sentiments adverse to the baptism of infant children, resigned his connection with the Board, but continued his acceptable aid as a preacher, which he has done to the present time.[1] Messrs. Charles Harding and

Case of Mr. Bowen.

[1] Since the above was written, my attention has been called to *The*

Samuel C. Dean and their wives arrived early in 1857. Mr. and Mrs. Abbott returned to India in June, after an absence of ten years.

Accession to the mission.

The government had now taken up the work of establishing vernacular schools in the villages, and English schools in the large towns, so that the missionaries began to see their way clear to leave the drudgery of secular education to government institutions. Tours for preaching became interesting. Such was one performed by Messrs. Ballantine and Fairbank in the northeastern part of their field. In Dedgaum they admitted six persons to the church, four of whom were from as many different villages, "men of influence among their people, who gave good evidence of a change of character." This part of the valley of the Godavari seemed quite promising. Indeed they spoke of the valley as the "promised land" of Western India. Not less than eighty villages were within ten miles of Wadále, and meetings held in those where Christians resided Mr. Fairbank compares to well remembered school-house meetings in New England parishes, or more aptly, perhaps, to

Government schools.

Itinerant preaching.

Bombay Guardian, edited by Mr. Bowen, of November 1, 1873, in which he announces his return to his former views on this subject. This he does in the following language: "Lately we have come to look at the matter under another light, and believe now that we have been in error in denying the Scriptural warrant for the baptism of the infant children of believers."

the meetings of Methodist riders in the West, sometimes in school-houses, sometimes in private houses, and sometimes under trees.

Interesting events.

Mr. Barker spent fifteen days among the villages of his field, with two native assistants. Reaching Gahû on horseback, at nine in the morning, while waiting for his luggage, the people gathered around him under the shade of a tree, and did all in their power for his comfort. In the evening the tent was filled with interested hearers. Retiring at half-past nine for their evening meal, they afterwards gathered in the *chawadi*[1] to receive instruction, and nothing occurred to call off the attention of the people from the customary exercises of reading, singing, preaching, and prayer.

Five or six of the most prominent mahars had ceased to worship idols, and met daily for reading the Scriptures and prayer, and there could be no reasonable doubt that some of them had passed from death unto life. There was at least one evidence in their favor, they had begun to suffer persecution from their own caste; though chiefly from a wealthy and very wicked man of the cultivator caste, who was the *pateel*[2] of the village. They were importunate for some one to instruct them and their children. A teacher was accordingly sent. The missionary company next pitched their tent at Kolhar, six miles from Gahû, a large village situated

[1] Or Rest-house.

[2] Headman.

on the river Pera, where was the great annual pilgrimage in honor of the goddess Bhawánie. Here they were received very cordially, and importuned for a catechist and teacher. And the same was repeated at Ambee, six miles below Kolhar. The Sabbath was spent at Khokar preaching to an audience of forty-five persons, morning and evening, and there was a similar experience at Pimpalgaum, where they spent an evening in the house of Yesûba, and nearly all the mahars in the village came to see them.

A converted "gosávi."

Intending to commence a station at Khokar, Mr. Barker visited sixty villages at several different times. At Panchegaum he met Harkûdas, a recently converted "gosávi," or religious teacher, who was well known in all that region, and during the many years that he had been exercising his vocation had made about four hundred disciples, many of them men high in authority. He had visited numerous holy places in India, and expended more than two hundred rupees for idols and relics from sacred shrines. A part of these he had disposed of, but the remainder he brought to Mr. Barker, to be sent to America as evidence that the labors of the "Pádre Sáhibs" had not been in vain.

In answer to inquiries, he said that he made disciples by sprinkling water on the head and thighs, and giving the candidates milk to drink. They were also required to make a feast for himself, his attendants, and the people of the village, at an expense of from fifty to one hundred rupees. Wherever he went his disciples and many others had treated him with almost divine honor. "In many ways," said he, "I have deceived my countrymen, by inducing them to trust in false gods, and even in myself, for protection from evil. I have led many of them in an evil way, but now, having as I trust found the right path, I wish to devote all my powers and the remainder of my life to the work of telling them of the Saviour." He was now persecuted, of course, especially by his old disciples, but he bore their reproaches with meekness. Harkûdas accompanied the missionary for several days, and rendered important aid.

Encouraging facts.

Mr. Ballantine, about this time, called attention to certain encouraging facts. One was the great progress of deistical principles among the Hindûs, the effect of education and European ideas. The system adopted professed to be the religion of nature, admitting the existence of one God, but denying a revelation from Him. The number holding these sentiments was so large as perceptibly to weaken the power of caste, and the bondage to Hindûism. Generally it had not the malignant spirit of infidelity in Christian lands, and to a certain extent was auxiliary to the Gospel, for with many it was a stepping-stone from Hindûism to Christianity. Another cheering fact was the influence of the truth on the higher castes beyond the limits of mission schools. Interesting cases of conversion occurred of persons not in missionary employment, nor educated in mission schools. Still another, was the increasing value of the native agency throughout the whole field. An assistant teacher in the government school at Ahmednuggur, when he became a Christian, was in the receipt of fifteen rupees, or seven dollars and a half, a month. Another place was offered him at fifty rupees a month, with a prospect of advancement and still higher pay. He turned away from both for the service of the mission, at a monthly salary of twelve rupees. Another young man declined a salary of forty rupees for the same purpose. The development of Christian character in some of the converts was full of promise.

Mr. Wilder at Kolapûr.

Mr. Wilder's labors at Kolapûr promised well, but ill health obliged him and Mrs. Wilder to visit the United States. Of two brahmin teachers who had been baptized at Kolapûr, one had been an inquirer four years, and his wife and son were candidates for baptism. More than two hundred thousand pages of Scripture were put in circulation. It should be thankfully recorded, that the only loss of life in connection with the great mutiny of 1857 in the Bombay Presidency, was in Kolapûr, and that this did not occur until after the departure of Mr. and Mrs. Wilder. Had they been on the ground, there is much reason to suppose that their lives could not have been saved.

Influence of the mutiny.

The mutiny exerted an unhappy influence, for a time, on the people of Ahmednuggur, where many Mohammedans reside. The missionaries often heard predictions, that their day would soon come, and that the first persons to be attacked would be the missionaries and their converts. Yet they remained, and kept up all the regular religious services, except street-preaching. But the number of hopeful conversions was less than usual.

Mr. Ballantine wrote thus, in 1858, concerning the mutiny in general: "A few native Christians and missionaries were murdered in Northern India, though even there, the great mass of converts were preserved. Those who were called to die for the name of Christ, and many who survived, exhibited the greatest constancy in extreme danger; showing that they preferred giving up their life to abandoning their faith. Facts of this kind have recently come to light in great abundance, proving to the whole world, that the native Christians, whom it has been the fashion in high places to deride as unworthy of any confidence, are really possessed of strong Christian principle, able to sustain them in the hour of greatest temptation. Thus the value of that religion which we are endeavoring to propagate here, has been shown to all; while, on the other hand, such atrocities have been perpetrated by the wild Hindû, and such outrages committed upon innocent and helpless women and children, by natives who had received a good education, that no one can hereafter maintain, as has heretofore been maintained by many, that Hindûism is as good for Hindûs as Christianity for Christians."

Successful efforts at Ahmednuggur.

The school for catechists at Ahmednuggur contained twenty scholars under the special care of Mr. Ballantine; and there was a preparatory school of children of Christian parents, under the care of Miss Farrar; who also had a large school of heathen girls, supported by English ladies and gentlemen at that station. A school for Christian girls, under the charge of Mrs. Ballantine, contained forty pupils. Mr. Ballantine gave lectures on theology, and on portions of the Old Testament, which were well attended. He had also a small class in the Sanskrit language. At the close of 1857, four young men went forth from the school for catechists; and four others from the same school, and two from the girls' school were received into the church. The number of churches in the Ahmednuggur district was now eight, containing two hundred and forty members, of whom fifty-six were received by profession during the year. Nine joined in the darkest period of the rebellion, though assured by their neighbors that speedy martyrdom would be the consequence. One of these was Harkûdas, the "gosávi" already mentioned, who became a zealous preacher.

Yesûba Powar died in December, 1857, at the age of fifty. He was a mahar, born in a small village west of Ahmednuggur. An older brother, previously converted, was a deacon in the first church of Ahmednuggur, and one younger belonged to the church in Satara. Yesûba had been very religious as a pagan. Going to Benares on the Ganges in the service of an English gentleman, he was punctilious in observing all the rites prescribed by the brahmins of that holy place; and brought on his shoulder a load of the Ganges water eight hundred miles to his home, wearing the yellow garb of a pilgrim. This no mahar had ever done before, and the use he made of the water, on his return, procured him great consideration. The people of the villages would fall down at his feet in token of reverence. About twelve years after this he came to Ahmednuggur, where his elder Christian brother resided, and the light of the Gospel soon entered his darkened understanding. He no longer trusted in the waters of the Ganges, but in the blood of Christ. Casting aside the pilgrim's dress, he sought to be clothed with the righteousness of Christ. On the 6th of October, 1844, he was baptized, and joined the Christian Church.

Yesûba Powar as a devotee.

For the remainder of his life, Yesûba was a preacher of the Gospel. During several years he accompanied different missionaries in their itinerant labors; and then he was five years associated with Mr. Munger in his long tours into portions of the country where the Gospel had not been proclaimed. In 1856, being no longer able to endure the fatigues of travel, and a church having been formed at Loni, in his native region, he was appointed to take charge of it, which he did until his death, performing the duties with great faithfulness. He left a wife and four sons, and his eldest son succeeded him for a time in the care of the Loni church.

As a preacher.

Yesûba Salave, of Pimpalgaum, died in the same year with the preceding, on the anniversary of the day in which he and seven others had been formed into the Chánde church. This church of eight members afterwards increased to eighty. He held the office of deacon, and was exemplary in all things. He was a mahar, but from childhood felt above the condition and employments of his race. He chose the business of buying and selling cattle, prospered in it, and was esteemed a man of substance and ability. He was baptized by Mr. Wilder in 1850. A storm of persecution then burst upon him. His cattle and horses were poisoned one after another, until all were gone. But he said, "Though my sorrows become as great as Job's, I will not deny my Lord." His persecutors despairing of success, ceased to

Yesûba Salave.

His persecutions.

annoy him, and he resumed his business. His partners in trade deemed his judgment almost infallible.

As a Christian, he was earnest and decided. In his conversation he dwelt much on religious subjects, and he strove to set a good example. To show that he had no caste feelings, he sought often to drink water from the hands of the despised mangs. He was hospitable and generous. The writer remembers with pleasure the visit to him with Mr. Ballantine. He was untiring in efforts to promote the welfare of his church, and had the joy of seeing his wife and all his children included among the members. Yesûba, though valuable as a fellow-laborer, was never in the service of the mission; and so far from gaining money by a profession of Christianity, he suffered reproach and loss. He loved the Sabbath, and the assembly of the saints; and attended the Sabbath morning service at Wadále, and the afternoon service at Chánde, places two miles from his residence and in opposite directions. In the evening, he had a special service at his own house. That he was a sincere, earnest Christian, was acknowledged even by his enemies.

His character delineated.

As his end drew nigh, he appeared to ripen fast for heaven; and when admonished of approaching death, he set his house in order, and charged his son, who was to have the homestead, "never to forget to put the rupee into the missionary box on the first Monday of the month." At length he asked to be carried to the room where he had been accustomed to have family prayers, and there he gently breathed out his spirit.

Pastor Ramkrishnapunt's removal to Bombay.

Mr. Harding was now able to commence preaching at Bombay in the native language; and in view of the great importance of the station, Ramkrishnapunt exchanged the pastorate of the second church in Ahmednuggur for that of the church in Bombay.

The great problem of the practicability of village stations, was now regarded as settled, and the Ahmednuggur field was divided into districts, with a view to its more perfect cultivation.

Pastor Haripunt at Satara.

Haripunt, one of the native pastors at Ahmednuggur, spent a part of 1857 in very acceptable service as preacher at Satara. Messrs. Munger and Wood had found that people difficult of access. The distance from Ahmednuggur was one hundred and forty miles, and the numerous native helpers were exceedingly averse to residing so far from home. The station at Kolapûr was discontinued in October, 1858.

Kolapûr station discontinued.

Death of Mrs. Wood.

In October, 1859, Mrs. Wood of Satara was attacked by cholera on her return from a meeting of the missionaries at Ahmednuggur, a day's journey from her home. On reaching Satara she had every possible attention, but after three days of extreme suffering, on the 18th of November she entered into rest. Thus was Satara left for the fourth time without the presence of a Christian woman. Mrs. Wood had endeared herself to her missionary associates and to the natives.

Death of a Moslem convert.

Shaik Daood, a converted Mohammedan and member of the church in Ahmednuggur, came to Bombay for the benefit of his health in 1857. As this improved he was much occupied in efforts among the Mohammedans. His health gradually failed, and on the 1st of June he died. For eight years he had been an exemplary Christian. He was baptized in 1847, but soon after renounced his faith, not being able to endure the trial which had come upon him, and struggled against his convictions of truth for five years, when he wished to rejoin the church. His profession of penitence was most satisfactory, and he was received again to church membership in January, 1853. His end was peace. His face beaming with joy, he said to the missionary, "I cannot tell you how precious Christ seems to me, how unspeakably lovely. How wonderful that he should have compassion on one like *me!* His love is infinite, it is divine love." While connected with the church, he prepared several books and tracts which are exerting a good influence. Among these is an adaptation of Leslie's "Short Method with Deists" to the circumstances of the people of India.

A licentiate named Vishnû Karmarkar, who had acted as pastor of the second church in Ahmednuggur in the absence of Ramkrishnapunt, was ordained pastor in June, 1860. Two other native pastors assisted at the ordination, and several native gentlemen were present in token of their respect and esteem for the candidate. The church at Seroor had also a native pastor ordained in June, 1859.

A pastor ordained for Ahmednuggur.

Early in this year, C. E. Frazer Tytler, Esq., Collector in the Ahmednuggur District, while encamped between the Pera and Godavari rivers, near the village of Pimplas, was deprived of a daughter by death. The gentleman and his wife were warm friends of the missionary cause, and on the spot where the child died they erected a neat stone church, and near it a convenient house for the residence of a missionary, which were presented to the mission. The cost was $2,000, and thus originated the rural station of Pimplas.

Generous aid from an English friend.

In August of this year Lord Elphinstone, Governor of Bombay, spending a few weeks with the excellent Collector at Ahmednuggur, signified a wish to see the mission schools. They were accordingly brought together in the mission chapel, and the Governor and his suite came in. The girls of Mrs. Ballantine's school, the boys from the school for catechists, and the members of the theological class, were examined in various branches of study. The audience were much interested, especially when they were told that all those young men, and the

Visit from the Governor of Bombay.

boys and girls of the schools, were either converts or children of converts. A large number of native Christians assembled in the chapel, at the request of Mr. and Mrs. Tytler, and the Governor was pleased to see, that a change of dress was not required of the converts, as it would diminish their influence among their own people.

The exercises were commenced by singing the Mahratta Hymn, "God save the Queen," and closed by singing in Mahratta Bishop Heber's Missionary Hymn, and the whole company stood while these hymns were sung. Lord Elphinstone expressed himself much pleased with the examination, not only to the missionaries personally, but afterwards to Mr. and Mrs. Tytler. On Friday Mrs. Tytler invited the girls of Mrs. Ballantine's and Miss Farrar's schools, and the Christian women, to an entertainment in her garden. The Governor afterwards made a donation of five hundred rupees.

Theological class.

In November, Mr. Ballantine formed a class for a course of study preparatory to becoming preachers and eventually pastors, to be instructed only in the vernacular. Eight were selected, all having been members of the church for two or three years, and some of them assistants of the mission for several years. The course was for three years, seven months in each year being devoted to study, and the pupils were to spend at least every alternate Sabbath in preaching at some neighboring village.

A step was taken by the Government, about this time, of vital importance to the native Christians. The brahmins taught that the public tanks would be defiled by a Christian's drawing water therefrom. The Christians very properly insisted on their rights, and the heathen petitioned the government to order converts not to take water from the public fountains. The decision of Mr. Tytler deserves a grateful notice. "The main statement in this petition," he said, "is untrue. Vishnûpunt's wife is not a mahar, or woman of low caste. Vishnûpunt is a brahmin converted to Christianity. His wife is a Kunabee, also converted. Before conversion he and his wife had full right to draw water from the tank in question. He has not forfeited this right, nor any other, by his conversion to Christianity. On the contrary the law insures him every right which he possessed before his conversion to Christianity. This law will be enforced, and those acting contrary thereto punished. In Bombay and in many other places all classes of the community, Christian converts, Hindûs, and Mohammedans, have free access to all the public tanks and wells. Petitioners seek to debar Vishnûpunt and his family from the use of the public tanks solely because he is a Christian. But it is well known that if a mang or mahar woman marries a Mussulman, she is allowed to use the tanks in virtue of this change in her relations. Cattle,

Important step in religious toleration.

horses, donkeys, prostitutes, all have access to the public tanks, and yet this common and obvious right petitioners seek to deny to a man, whose high respectability they themselves dare not and cannot gainsay."

A petition was then sent to Lord Elphinstone, the Governor in Council at Bombay, and the reply was, if possible, still more decisive, and the decision, upon a renewal of the petition next year, was declared to be final. A similar order was also issued by the government in reference to the admission of native Christian children into the public schools. The ground thus taken was new, and its great importance is manifest.

Jubilee meeting.

At the annual meeting of the Mahratta mission in October, 1860, in connection with the Jubilee meeting of the Board, a very large number of native Christians were in attendance, and there was much enthusiasm. More than four hundred communicants sat down at the table of the Lord, being the largest assembly of native Christians ever gathered together on that side of India.

Erection of chapels.

There was now such demand for houses of worship that Mr. Tytler contributed six hundred dollars toward the erection of chapels in five villages, the Christians engaging to pay the balance; he also paid half the expense of a chapel at Rahûri, costing four hundred dollars.

Recent converts at Rahûri were subjected to persecution. The spread of Christianity had acquired importance in the community by the decisions of Government on the water question. Low caste persons had thus acquired new and important privileges by becoming Christians. They could use water from the public wells, send their children to the public schools, and occupy the public rest-houses. The leaders in the Rahûri persecution were mostly men of wealth and position. The case was tried, and five of them were sentenced each to a month's imprisonment and a fine of fifty rupees; two were fined fifty rupees, and the head-man of the village one hundred rupees.

Persecution and government protection.

The Missionary Herald for 1861 contains a valuable letter from Mr. Ballantine, written early in that year, giving a retrospect of the Ahmednuggur branch of the Mission. When he arrived, in 1835, it had been established only four years. There were then twelve persons in the native church, and three resident missionaries. Seroor was occupied in 1846, Khokar in 1856, Wadále in 1857, and Rahûri in 1860. In 1861, there were five stations in the Ahmednuggur branch, with five married missionaries and one unmarried female; and sixteen native churches contained four hundred and seventy-three members.

Encouraging retrospect.

The following table shows the gradual increase in membership since 1831. The period is divided into terms of five years, that the

Increase in church membership.

progress may be more apparent. Mr. Ballantine thus states the case: —

"Members received from 1831 to 1835, inclusive . .	9
Members received from 1836 to 1840, inclusive . .	7
Members received from 1841 to 1845, inclusive . .	75
Members received from 1846 to 1850, inclusive . .	63
Members received from 1851 to 1855, inclusive . .	78
Members received from 1856 to 1860, inclusive . .	363
"Total	595

"The members received during the last five years are as follows: in 1856, 30; 1857, 56; 1858, 86; 1859, 64; 1860, 127. Total, 363.

"From this it will be seen, that the average for each term of five years, from 1840 to 1855, was just seventy-two, exactly nine times the average of the first two terms of five years; while the number received during the last term of five years, was five times as great as the average for five years from 1840 to 1855, and forty-five times as great as the average for ten years from 1831 to 1840. Again, it appears, that the number received during each year of the last five years was, on an average, seventy-two, the same as the average number received during each period of five years from 1841 to 1855.

Cause of the sudden increase of converts.

"Should it be asked, how the sudden increase in the number of converts in the last term of five years can be accounted for, I would say: there is no doubt that the new policy inaugurated in the mission in 1854, putting missionaries out in the districts to labor among the people, has been the means, in the hands of God, of greatly extending the knowledge of the truth, and of bringing many more converts into our churches. Some members of the mission desired to see this policy pursued ten years before it was adopted; but the discussions of 1854 decided the matter, and the plan was at once put in execution.

Character of the members.

"Of the whole number of converts mentioned above, sixty-two have died, some of them having given striking proofs of love to their Saviour during life, and of joy in the prospect of meeting Him as death approached. The names of Babajee, blind Gopal and his wife Malabain, of Lakhiram, Yesûba Powar, Yesûba Salve, and others, are very dear to the hearts of Christians in this country. No one has exhibited more strikingly the power of Gospel truth, and the sustaining influence of the promises of God, than Shaik Daood, once an apostate from the truth, but brought back by the power of the Spirit. Some have died, who were never numbered among the people of God on earth, but who gave evidence that they had put their trust in Jesus for salvation, and looked forward to meeting Him in heaven.

Whence the converts.

"The converts received to the mission churches have come from every class of the community, Mussulman and Hindû. One of the first conversions here, after I took charge of the church at the close of 1838, was that of Haripunt. Belonging to a high brahmin family, his conversion made a deep impression on the brahmins here as to the power of the Gospel. His baptism was soon followed by that of his brother Narayan, and from that time repeated conversions occurred among the higher castes in Ahmednuggur. In 1856, we had four such conversions. Shahû Dajee, assistant teacher of the government English school, was a brahmin; his friend, Cassimbhaee, the brother of Shaik Daood, was a Mussulman, and two other young men belonged to the weaver caste. A deep conviction, at that time, seemed to pervade all classes, that nothing could resist the power of the truth. Last year, another young man of the weaver caste joined the church, and a spirit of inquiry extended to others of that class. Some are carefully studying the Scriptures, anxious apparently, to ascertain what is truth. How different all this from the state of things in 1835. How very different from what it was from 1831 to 1834."

Interesting facts.

He adds: "In some directions, you can find Christians wherever you go, who are rejoiced to see you, and to meet you in divine worship; and in villages here and there, you find also small chapels or school-houses, where the people are accustomed to come together to hear the Scriptures read and to unite in prayer."

The following additional extracts from Mr. Ballantine are too suggestive to be omitted: —

"We have always been protected by the authorities, and our converts have also received that protection of life and person, which they had a right to claim from their rulers. But when I came here, Christian converts could not inherit any of their parents' property; it must all be given up to the heathen heirs. Children could not claim their own father's estate, even though they were his only children, for his brothers, or other relatives who remained heathens, could claim it for themselves. Such was the law, and the courts of justice could furnish no relief. Now all this is changed.

Protection from government.

"Whether, therefore, we consider the march of events in the political world; the enactment of just laws and regulations, giving equal rights to Christians, and the efforts of Government to promote education and facilities of intercourse; or whether we look at the operations of our own and other missions and benevolent societies in India, we feel that there is abundant cause for thanksgiving to God for past favors, and encouragement to labor for the coming of his kingdom. What has been done is in itself not much, but it is of great importance when considered as a preparation for the future."

This eminent missionary having seen it stated, that the change of policy in 1854 had alienated the good will of the higher castes, and that there had since been no convert from among them, declared that to be a great mistake. Writing in 1861, he said: "We are having more intercourse with the higher castes than we ever had before. And this intercourse is very friendly and pleasant. Some of them are regular attendants on our Sabbath services, apart from inquirers and those desirous of being admitted to the church. We have never had so many persons of high caste brought into our churches in any period of five years before, as since 1856. Our inquirers, too, at the present time, from the higher castes, are more than usual."

Increasing hopefulness from the higher castes.

The railway from Bombay to Madras goes by way of Poona and Solapûr; and in 1861, when the station was commenced at Solapûr, it had been completed to that place, a distance of two hundred and seventy-five miles; excepting six miles on the Ghâts that required immense labor. The population of the city was estimated at 70,000. It is slightly elevated above the surrounding country, and encircled by a high wall. As many as fifty villages lie within ten miles. The distance from thence to Satara is one hundred and twenty miles west, and to Ahmednuggur about the same distance northwest. Mr. Harding regarded this field as very interesting. In respect to the character of the people, and the facilities for reaching them, he thought it second to no other on that side of India.

Solapûr as a station.

Unexpected development of benevolence.

Among the occurrences in the year 1861, was an unexpected development of the benevolent spirit among native church members. The principal means of stirring up the Christians of Ahmednuggur was an account of extraordinary benevolent contributions by Nestorians at Oroomiah, read to them by pastor Vishnûpunt. This was in a letter from a deacon in the Nestorian church. He also read a letter from a member of the Madura mission mentioning similar scenes there, resulting from the same cause, and he felt that he and his brethren should do likewise. After many struggles with his own heart, he said he had determined to give one month's salary to the missionary cause, and so saying he placed twenty-five rupees on the table. This moved the brethren, who immediately began to make their offerings. Many affecting scenes occurred, and most of the congregation were moved to tears. The meeting was adjourned to the next day, when it was yet more evident that the Spirit was shedding the love of Christ into the hearts of Christians. The missionaries were strongly reminded by what they then saw of precious revival seasons in their native land.

At the next monthly concert in Bombay letters were read describing the meeting at Ahmednuggur, and a native who had just come from there made a stirring address. The meeting, though prolonged, was adjourned to the next evening, and the native pledges were three hundred and thirty-five rupees. At Ahmednuggur they were five hundred.

Generous pecuniary aid to the mission.

It was natural, on the breaking out of civil war in America, that the missionaries should apprehend a serious diminution in the funds of the Board, and these apprehensions they made known to their friends, both native and English. Four hundred rupees were received from natives not Christian, six hundred and seventy-three from Christian natives (in part payment of pledges), 11,637 from European friends in India, and 1,497 from friends in England and Scotland, formerly resident in India. They were agreeably surprised, soon after, to find that the war had not seriously affected the benevolent contributions of the American churches.

CHAPTER XV.

MISSION TO THE MAHRATTAS.

1862–1868.

TWENTY-THREE churches were now connected with the Mahratta mission, which had in 1862 about six hundred members, living in nearly a hundred villages and towns. But in half of these villages the mission had not yet been able to place native catechists to conduct religious services on the Sabbath. The raising up of such men was necessarily a slow process.

The native churches.

In the year 1863 a younger brother of Shaik Daood was ordained pastor of the church at Khokar, in the presence of representatives from ten different churches. He had been baptized by Pastor Modak three years before.

Native pastor ordained.

The introduction of sacred hymns into the native churches, sung in the tunes which cheer the hearts of the people of God in Christian lands, was mentioned in the preceding chapter. In addition to this the church pressed into the service of Christ, with good effect, the *Kirttan*, in which a "gosavi" or religious teacher celebrated

The Kirttan

the praises of some god with singing and instrumental music. The experiment of applying the Kirttan to Christian use appears to have been first made at Ahmednuggur, one evening during the anniversary of 1862, and the Man of Calvary was the grand subject. The poetry was chiefly composed by Krishnarow, a young native brother possessed of much poetic feeling. Three or four persons stood back of him on the platform, and at the close of every verse joined in a chorus. After singing a few verses in this manner, an exposition of the song was given by the leader. There was much artistic skill exhibited in the music, and in its adaptation to the poetry.

Death of Miss Farrar.

In 1862, the mission was called to mourn the death of Miss Cynthia Farrar, its oldest member save one, she having been connected with it for almost thirty-five years, first at Bombay, and since 1839 at Ahmednuggur. Her life had been faithfully devoted to the education of her own sex, and her end was peace.

New missionaries.

Messrs. Henry W. Ballantine, a nephew of the veteran missionary, and Henry J. Bruce, joined the mission, with their wives, early in 1863.

Official kindness.

In the summer of that year Sir Bartle Frere, Governor of Bombay, visited Ahmednuggur, and on the morning after his arrival invited the missionaries to call on him. He manifested much interest in their work and in the progress of true knowledge. The schools were examined in his presence, and he expressed much satisfaction with the thoroughness of the religious instruction given. The singing of the children, who had learned many English and native tunes, was also gratifying, and he expressed his opinion that the missions in India had not paid sufficient attention to this accomplishment. At the close, the children sang "God save the Queen" in Mahratta, all rising. The Governor had already made a generous donation to the schools in Satara, in the name of Lady Frere, and a gentleman of his suite made a similar donation for the schools at Ahmednuggur. The same week, William F. Stearns, Esq., an American gentleman, came up from Bombay to judge for himself as to the claims of the mission, and gave five thousand rupees.

Death of Mrs. Barker.

On the 27th of January, 1864, Mrs. Barker, after having been ten years in the field, closed her useful life at Pimplas. "There was noticeable in her," writes some one in India who evidently knew her, "the unusual combination of an elevated poetical habit of mind with excellent common sense and practical benevolence, a love of the beautiful, with a hearty devotedness to the welfare of her fellow men." Her refinement and delicacy of feeling, her cheerfulness, her powers of conversation, and her unaffected piety, made her a valued member of the mission circle, and gave assurance of a strong hold on the native female community.

Death of Mr. Chapin.

Mr. and Mrs. Hazen returned to their missionary labors in 1864, after a temporary visit to their native land, and were accompanied by Rev. William W. Chapin and wife. Mr. and Mrs. Chapin were stationed at Pimplas, but in less than three months, after having awakened hopes of great usefulness, he was cut down by an attack of diphtheria.

Death and character of Haripunt.

The Rev. Hari Ramchander, better known as Haripunt, pastor of the first church in Ahmednuggur, died January 11th of the same year, at the age of about forty-six. He was from a high brahmin family, and the story of his conversion and ordination has been already told. In the year 1860, in view of the wants of the Satara station, he removed thither with his family. Next year Ramkrishnapunt, who had been installed pastor of the church in Bombay, found it necessary to remove his family back into the Deccan on account of the fatal influence of the climate on his children. This led to a temporary exchange of places. Haripunt's health failed in 1863, and he returned to Ahmednuggur, leaving his family at Bombay. At the annual meeting of the mission in October, he spoke of God's great goodness, of his own readiness to die, and of his joy in the prospect of meeting his Saviour in heaven. He officiated with Ramkrishnapunt at the communion, and this was his last opportunity of uniting with his brethren in commemorating the dying love of the Redeemer. He was now urged to return to his family at Bombay, but before doing this he made a tour among some villages south of Ahmednuggur, where the mission wished him to labor. The exposure to cold had such an effect upon him, that he was persuaded to return immediately to the milder climate of Bombay. During the first night after his arrival, he continued talking with his family till three o'clock in the morning, when, feeling drowsy and seeking rest, "he fell asleep, and never waked."

An Ecclesiastical Union formed.

In the year 1865, when there were more than a score of native churches, the mission deemed it expedient that they should form an Ecclesiastical Union. Fourteen of the twenty-three churches were accordingly so united, the Union consisting of the native pastor and a delegate from each church. Missionaries might take part in the discussions, but had no vote, not being members of the Union. The fourth and fifth Articles describe the nature of the organization.

"Art. 4. It belongs to the assembly to give its opinion on questions brought before it by the churches, and references made to it in regard to general principles, whether of doctrines or morals; also, to examine and license candidates for the holy ministry, and to withdraw license when advisable; to ordain, install, remove, and judge ministers connected with the churches belonging to the Union; to condemn erroneous opinions which injure the piety and peace of the church; to unite or divide churches at the request of the people, and to form and receive new churches, and in general to order whatever pertains to the common interests of the churches connected with the Union."

"Art. 5. It does not belong to the assembly to hear and decide appeals from the churches in regard to the discipline of private members. At the same time it may be proper for a church to apply to the assembly for its opinion as to the general principles on which they may proceed in a case of discipline."

Death and character of Mr. Ballantine.

Mr. Ballantine, after thirty years of service in India, died on the 19th of November, 1865, while on his way to the United States with his family for the benefit of his health, and his body was consigned to the ocean off the coast of Portugal. An intimate personal acquaintance and a prolonged correspondence, have led me to assign him a high place among missionaries of the cross. He was an earnest, faithful laborer. To an accurate knowledge of the Mahratta language he added an acquaintance with the Sanskrit, and has left his impress on the version of the Scriptures in the Mahratta. Two hymn-books in the Mahratta were prepared by him, one for use in the churches, the other for the children, containing together four hundred hymns. They are generally translations of hymns and sacred songs found in the English language, and besides being faithfully rendered, both as to spirit and thought, are said often to possess the full force and beauty of the originals. In other ways he enriched the Christian literature of the Mahratta people.

He was an earnest preacher, and a strong advocate of the principle, that preaching the Gospel is the first among the means to be employed for the conversion of the heathen. This was in accordance with his main employment during the last five years of his life in connection with theological classes of young men preparing for the ministry. In the year 1854, I heard him preach to a native congregation at Khokar, forty miles from Ahmednuggur, and was much impressed by the visible effect of his easy, fluent, powerful utterances. Mrs. Ballantine was a help every way meet for him, and their necessary withdrawal from the field, with their well-trained family, seemed an irreparable loss.[1]

[1] Since the above was written, and indeed since the close of this history, Mrs. Ballantine has been called to her heavenly rest. Her death occurred, somewhat suddenly, at Amherst, Mass., on the 8th of May, 1874, in the sixty-third year of her age. In her appropriate sphere of labor she was every way the equal of her eminent husband. The author, when in India, had much opportunity for observing her in her relations to her family and to the native community. It was her custom to have her children up and dressed with the rising sun to accompany her, for air and exercise, to the open fields beyond the city walls, and this was repeated at the close of day. The fine health en-

Seven natives had been licensed by the Evangelical Union, in the year 1866, as preachers of the Gospel. But the churches had been backward to settle them, preferring to have the missionaries for their acting pastors, and to receive the ordinances at their hands. This was mainly owing to unwillingness to assume the native pastors' support. The mission set itself to remedy the evil. Of course the question of support came up for consideration, and the Union discussed the question, whether every church member ought not to set aside a tenth of his income (as the *minimum*) for religious uses. Among the addresses on that occasion was one by the Rev. Ramkrishnapunt, or Pastor Modak, extracts from a translation of which are well deserving of a place in this history.

Movement for a native pastorate.

"How does it happen," said this intelligent native pastor, "that such a question arises in regard to our churches? Do not our Christians provide for their own temporal support; and why do they not then provide also in religious matters? Their souls are certainly as much their own as their bodies. People of other religions, and Christians of other

joyed by this family shows what may be possible in favoring circumstances, even in India. Three of her daughters are now wives of missionaries in India, a son is under appointment as a medical missionary to India, and the rest are all in full sympathy with the work to which their honored parents had devoted their lives. Her labors in connection with the department of female education, form a part of the history of the mission.

lands, support their own religious teachers; why should not Christians here do the same? Does Christianity seem to them of so little value that they are unwilling it should cost them anything? Not so — but there is a proverb which says, 'Who will go afoot when he has a horse to ride?' And in like manner, why should we be at any expense in religious matters, when the mission is ready to bear it all for us? This leads to another question: Why did the mission at first assume this expense? And why have they borne it till the present time, instead of calling upon us to take it? . . . . Unfortunately, the result of this course has proved most disastrous for us. . . . . We have grown up from infancy to maturity, increasing from half a dozen to as many hundreds, and from one to twenty-three churches. The cost of supporting our pastors and schools has largely increased, but we seem to ourselves utterly unable to lift the burden a finger's breadth. Our indulgent mother (the mission) must still carry us in her arms, for she and we both think we cannot yet walk alone. Had we been accustomed from the first to give according to our ability, the ability to give would have increased with our growth, and to-day we might have been able to bear the whole burden. . . . . What if this support on which we are leaning were suddenly withdrawn, where would it leave us? We cannot expect it to be always continued. It behooves us then, as wise men, at once to set things in train for self-support. It is our imperative duty.

"Granted, then, that we ought to be self-supporting, what means can we use to become so? This is our question. *The first and chief means is this, that we now begin to do what we ought to have done long ago. From this time we must begin to pay the cost of our religious privileges.* Well would it be for us if we were as wise and discerning in regard to our spiritual welfare as we are in temporal matters."

He goes on to assign reasons why they should support their own Christian institutions, and then adds: —

"I anticipate here an objection, 'What you say is all true, but we are not able at once to take up this work.' And so we have been saying for a long time. But I believe if we consider it well, we shall not think we cannot do it. If we take hold in earnest, and make proper exertions, we can bear all the ordinary expenses of our Christian institutions. . . . . Did we not buy those lifeless, good-for-nothing idols, build temples for them, and pay for their consecration and worship? Did we not provide the turmeric, frankincense, flowers, lamps, and meat-offerings for the ordinary worship, and special gifts for the festal days of our fictitious household gods? And the still heavier expenses of sacrifices, oblations, and feasts for the numerous worshippers, did we not bear these also? The bootless cost of long pilgrimages to Vithoba, Khandoba, Bhowani, and the rest; the fees and ritual expenses incurred at such places, did we not pay them all? And how much did we give for hearing the legends, purans, kirttans, and other recitations? How much went for needless funeral rites, lunar observances, and feasts for the dead? How much to the fortune-tellers, and various orders of religious mendicants? How much to escape the plagues of evil spirits, unlucky stars, and other bad omens? How much for weddings, holy days, and other festive occasions? For these and other objects called religious, we gave freely when we were heathen; if we gave an equal amount now, I believe it would suffice for the support of our own Christian worship, and leave much to be used in giving the Gospel to others. What we then gave was in the interest of sin and hell; what we now give is for our own and others' spiritual good, and for the glory of God. How cheerfully should we give for such objects! . . . .

"Let us then, dear brethren, now, before God, make this strong resolution, and that we may carry it out, let us bind ourselves by some fixed rule of giving. Let us resolve that we will devote one tenth of our income to religious purposes, — not that we should never give more than this, but that we will not give less than this proportion. If any one thinks this is too much, let him remember that God Himself gave this rule to the Israelites. If we consider that we spend *nine* tenths for our bodies, which in a few days will return to dust, and only *one* tenth for the soul, which is immortal, instead of appearing a great deal, it will seem but a little — *very little* indeed."

Ordination of native pastors.

The result was, that all the seven licentiates received calls to settle from as many churches, and some of them received even two or three. The Union, having been requested by the churches to make arrangements for the ordination of their pastors elect, designated churches, which, by their pastors and delegates, should visit the several churches for that purpose. Two or more missionaries were present on each occasion. It was understood, that the ordination would be deferred in cases where the church did not pledge itself to raise a monthly sum equal to a tenth of the income of its members. Some of the churches required considerable time for considering this question; but at length the male members of each promised to give that proportion of their incomes for the support of their pastors.

At the ordinations, the sermon, the charge to the pastor, and the right hand of fellowship, were by native pastors; and the ordaining prayer, and the charge to the people, were by missionaries. The audiences were crowded and attentive. Following the ordinations were protracted meetings, commencing on Tuesday, and closing with the communion service on the Sabbath. One of the older missionaries, in view of these scenes, thus gave utterance to his feelings: "I confess I have received new ideas of the strength of our native Christians. There is a power here, which is being developed and organized for active effort, and which I believe God is about to use for His glory."

On the 11th of February, 1867, Mrs. Harding died suddenly at Solapûr, ten years after her arrival in India, leaving four children. Though she had left a home of many comforts in America, she lived contented and happy in India, and became continually more interested in the good work of the Lord. Mr. William Henry Atkinson and wife, afterwards laborers at this station, arrived near the close of the year.

Death of Mrs. Harding.

Mr. Munger's last residence was at Bombay, and the annual meeting of the mission for 1868 was appointed in that place, to enjoy the benefit of his counsels and prayers. Before the time of the meeting, he was taken ill with fever, and a partial paralysis ensued. When his brethren arrived, he was scarcely able to recognize them, and died on the 23d of July, at the age of sixty-five. He was the oldest member of the mission, having gone to India in the year 1834, and was to have preached the annual sermon. He was somewhat ungainly in appearance, and rough in manner, but with tender Christian sensibilities. His iron constitution was

Death of Mr. Munger.

20

broken by travel and exposure in preaching the Gospel. While at Jalna, his labors were blessed to some of the English army officers stationed there. One of these came to Ahmednuggur while the Deputation was there, on his way to England, and it was affecting to see this officer of rank and culture throw his arms around the neck of the good missionary, and kiss him, in token of love and gratitude for spiritual benefits formerly received. To the end he was a faithful servant of the Lord Jesus.

CHAPTER XVI.

MISSION TO THE MAHRATTAS.

1868–1873.

Persecution.

In 1868, a brahmin of Solapûr had been admitted to the church in that place, and a younger brother had decided to embrace Christianity. An elder brother, learning the fact, came with other influential brahmins to the mission chapel, where the brothers then were, and used every possible means to induce them to leave. Violence was apprehended, as a large mob had gathered about the house, and the Christians sent for Mr. Harding. After saying a few words to the crowd, he wrote to the Collector, asking protection for the young men. Unfortunately the Collector was absent, and there was considerable delay before the letter reached the second magistrate. Meanwhile three native Christians on the outside of the chapel were cruelly beaten by brahmins and others. The doors were broken open and the two young converts carried away. The magistrate lost no time in ordering the arrest of the leaders, and the liberation of the converts. Ramchandra, the older, was set at liberty and came at once to the mission house.

The Christians who had been waiting in anxious suspense came to rejoice with him. The three were present who had been so cruelly beaten, faint from loss of blood, and their clothes crimsoned from head to foot, yet there were no complaints. One suggested that these sufferings were light compared with those which Christ endured. Another remarked: "Yes, and we are ready, if need be, to give up our lives for His sake."

Three prominent brahmin leaders in this outbreak were tried, convicted, and sentenced to six months' imprisonment with hard labor. After that the Christians had peace, and the fact that a man of the highest caste in the community had given up his caste and religion and become a Christian, naturally led to inquiry and discussion among the people.

The conduct of Ramchandra was very satisfactory. The firmness of the younger brother yielded for a time to the pressure, but he soon came again and applied for baptism. It was thought best, however, on his own account, and for the effect on the community, not to baptize him immediately.

New missionaries.

Messrs. Spencer R. Wells, Charles W. Park, and Richard Winsor, and their wives, joined the mission, the first in 1869, the second in 1870, and the third in 1871. Failure of health obliged Mr. and Mrs. Dean to return home in 1867. Miss Harriet S. Ashley from Milan, Ohio, became connected with the mission in December, 1871.

Native laborers.

Mr. Bruce reported twenty-nine native helpers in the year 1867, within the three districts of Rahuri, Khokar, and Pimplas, and that each of these helpers had a number of villages assigned him to visit as often as possible for the purpose of preaching. According to their monthly reports, they preached 7,362 times during the year, to audiences amounting in the aggregate to 96,373 persons, of whom 16,363 were women. The average audience was about twelve.

Bible-women.

The employment of native "Bible-women" to go out wherever they could collect a small company of women and read and talk to them of Bible truth, commenced about this time. They gained easy access to many of their own sex, from whom the catechist was shut out by the customs of oriental society, read portions of the Scriptures, especially the narratives and parables of the New Testament, and always talked about what they read. For some years two Bible-women were supported in and near Ahmednuggur by the Zenana Society of London. For two years an unknown friend in Bombay supported one at Newase. At length the Woman's Board of Missions in Boston arranged for the employment of Bible-women under the care of the mission, and they are doing much to spread Gospel truth among the people. The native Christian women in Bombay were accustomed to hold a weekly meeting by themselves, for prayer and religious instruction, and great interest was often added to these meetings by the accounts of their work given by the Bible-women.

Six of these were employed under Mrs. Bissell in the villages near Ahmednuggur. Only one was young, and she had been educated in mission schools. Three were widows, whose husbands had been pillars in the churches, and were respected even among the heathen. They and other Christian women met for prayer every Thursday, and once a month they reported their labors at these meetings. They generally went two and two, but sometimes all went together to one village, to reach as many as possible of all classes. Each pair was expected to keep a written journal showing the places visited, the number present, the portions of Scripture or tracts read, and the principal subject discussed.

Efforts of Mrs. Bissell.

Mrs. Bissell was accustomed to visit some of the women of the higher castes. By the help of Ramkrishnapunt, the pastor, who was acquainted with the native gentlemen, she went by invitation from the master of the house, and at an appointed time, thus avoiding all complaint of intrusion, and giving opportunity for the women of the house to call in some of their friends and neighbors, which they almost always did. The wife of the pastor or one of the Bible-women accompanied her in these visits. The master of the house generally kept out of sight, but not always. "On calling a second time at one place," writes Mr. Bissell, "the master of the house came forward, and expressing gratitude for the call, said he knew the women of this country were kept in an ignorant, debased condition, but he was willing to have Mrs. B. speak to the women of his house on any subject she chose, and was sure she would say nothing but what was for their good. His wife and the other women (eight in all) showed great pleasure in seeing her again. The wife had explained to a stranger the substance of what had been said on a previous visit, adding, 'They come to talk to us about such things.'

"After that, they conversed about the character of the true God; how sin entered the world, man's moral weakness and need of divine aid, and similar themes. The women admitted the truth of what was told them, but said they were afraid of their gods, and knew not how to get rid of them. This is probably true. Though they have no love for their gods, they think they are real beings, and will torment them in some way if they cease to honor them. When Mrs. Bissell and her companion were leaving, the wife took Mrs. B.'s hand in both hers and said, 'We shall count the Saturdays till you come.'"

An invitation came one day from the wife of a parabhû, a caste next to the brahmin, who had called together ten of her relatives and near friends. She said she had been a pupil of Miss Farrar's school in Bombay, some thirty years before, and that she remembered her name, and looks, and how she used to talk with her. She had kept up her knowledge of reading, and taught her two little daughters-in-law to read also.[1]

Another incident shows the influence of Miss Farrar's teaching, as related by a Christian woman at one of their meetings. A sick Hindû woman sent for her, and said that when a girl she attended Miss Farrar's school, and believed what she had been taught about Christ. She had since been a great sinner, but had given up her evil ways, and sought forgiveness, and she wished her to pray for her. This she did, and afterwards went to her several times for the same purpose. At last the sick woman sent for her one night, told her that her end was near, and said, "Pray with me once more. Do you think I shall be received? I trust in Him alone." After prayer, she passed away, while her Christian friend was sitting beside her.

One of the obstacles to the prevalence of the Gospel in India, is the custom forbidding the marriage of widows. The marriage of a brahmin widow at Bombay, which took place openly in 1869, with quite a flourish of trumpets, created much excitement. Many high caste young men of the so-

[1] Daughters are usually taken from their mothers, at ten or eleven years of age, to the homes of their husbands, while the sons bring their young wives to live with their mothers.

called "Reformers" pledged themselves to stand by the bridegroom, even should he be deprived of caste. They were so many, that they dared the orthodox Hindûs to touch them; and though threatened, they carried their point.

Evidences of progress.

Writing from Khokar, in 1869, Mr. Bruce, of the Rahûri station, contrasts the reception he met at that time, with that extended to a missionary twelve years before, when Khokar was one of the centres of idolatry. The missionary was then met with all manner of opposition, except positive violence, which they dared not inflict. Mr. Bruce thus describes the changed condition: —

"The opposition of the patil (as of others) has gradually worn away, and no one would suppose, from his hearty greeting of me the other night, that he was the same man who, years ago, tried to drive the missionaries away. 'It has been a long time since you came,' said he; and the tone of his voice was intended to indicate a wish that we would come oftener. We were talking about a new *chowdi* (rest-house) and government school-house that had recently been built, when he, of his own accord, said that he was ready to give a piece of land on which to build a chapel. I went with him to see the place, and found it as desirable a site as I could have chosen myself. The *patil* and villagers are not only ready to give this site, but are urging the early erection of the building.

"On Thursday evening, Pastor Kassanbhai, of Khokar, gave his kirttan, by invitation of the villagers. The new *chowdi* was given for the purpose, and was crowded with attentive listeners. A hundred or more were obliged to sit upon the ground outside. The patil afterwards expressed the greatest satisfaction with the kirttan, and said, 'All the people, even the brahmins, were pleased with it.'"

A new responsibility.

In November, Mr. Hazen was employed for a time in the Bombay University, as one of the examiners in the Mahratta language. About three hundred of the young men were seated indiscriminately, in a large hall, and over five hundred more were under a large awning, each with his little table before him. There were brahmins, Hindûs of various classes and languages, Parsees, Sindhees, Belûchees, Jews, Mohammedans, Portuguese, and a few English youth, representing about a dozen different languages. Five missionaries were among the examiners. Mr. Hazen and his native colleague had to examine one hundred and eighty persons, or half of these who were to be examined in Mahratta.

The two churches at Ahmednuggur were united in 1871, under the pastorate of Ramkrishnapunt, who was earnest in leading his people to a high standard of Christian character. His views, ably stated, as to the support of the ministry, have been already placed before the reader.

In 1871, the native pastors and others at Bombay, conceived the idea of forming a native Christian Alliance, embracing representatives from all the missions. Their object was to show the union actually subsisting between Christians, to strengthen that union, and consult together in regard to their Christian duties. As many as one hundred and fifty persons came together, most of them representative men. Of sixteen native pastors present, eleven were from the American mission. Two long business meetings were held each day for four days, and several for social intercourse, in one of which a large number of European gentlemen and ladies participated. One evening was devoted to the musical performance called "kirttan," by some of the brethren from Ahmednuggur, which excited much interest among Hindûs, as well as Christians.

A native Christian alliance.

Mr. Harding, who communicates these facts, says, there were earnest discussions upon a variety of important subjects; such as, The appreciation of Christian privileges, Care of children of native Christians, Giving systematically, and Our duties to our country. The discussions upon this last subject ended in a resolution to establish a new mission by the Alliance; and four hundred and fifty rupees were subscribed for the expenses of the first year. Rûtnagherry, a city on the coast, two hundred miles south of Bombay, was the place chosen for the station. Not finding the proper agent, this plan was not carried out. An address by one of the village pastors from the Ahmednuggur district, who had never before been in Bombay, moved some of the audience to tears. A resolution of thanks to the missionaries and missionary societies was moved by the Rev. Narayan Sheshadri, well known to those who attended the meeting of the Evangelical Alliance at New York in 1873, seconded by Mr. Shahu Daji, and unanimously agreed to.

Labors of an Evangelist.

Special interest was awakened at Ahmednuggur in 1871, by the Rev. William Taylor, an Evangelist from America connected with the Methodist denomination, who had been preaching for a year at various places in Northern India. His manner is represented as clear, forcible, and direct; and though he spoke through an interpreter, his thoughts were so truthfully rendered into the Mahratta by Pastor Modak, that they seemed to lose none of their power. "The Holy Spirit," writes Dr. Bissell," was manifestly present. Missionaries, native Christians, and also Hindûs showed, by their fixed and often tearful attention, the power of God's truth over their hearts." During the last week, two meetings were held each day. Sometimes as many as a dozen remained after the congregation was dismissed, for religious conversation. The converts were chiefly from Christian families, or had been for years acquainted with Christian truth. Eleven new members were added to the church. Mr. Taylor went from thence to Bombay, at the close of the year, and began a series of meetings in the mission chapel. "For more than a month past," writes Mr. Harding in January, "meetings among the Europeans and Indo-Britons have been held, under the direction of Rev. Wm. Taylor, the Evangelist, and we see now indications of a powerful work of the Holy Spirit. We hear every day of new cases of conversion, — seven or eight yesterday, four or five the previous day, and not long ago as many as twelve in one day. The period of conviction is generally short, and nearly all who are awakened are hopefully converted. Probably from sixty to eighty persons have been brought to Christ within the last six weeks, and the interest increases every day. As the work advances we expect the native community will be reached, though to what extent we cannot tell. In connection with our native church, six or seven persons seem to have been converted, though, with one exception, their experience has not been of the clear, decided character that we see among the Europeans; and this exception is in the case of a boy baptized in infancy, the son of native Christians."

The Mussulmans.

Pastor Mahamadji, of Seroor, reported the numerous Mussulmans, in that city as at first determined not to listen to his preaching, because he had left the Mohammedan religion. But he was glad to say, that their opposition had gradually diminished. He had been able, by means of the *kirttan*, to preach the Gospel to all classes of the people, and in large numbers. This he had done about forty times during the year, and on all these occasions there had been attentive audiences of both sexes, varying from one hundred and fifty to one thousand.

Miss Sarah F. Norris, M. D., sailed from New York in the autumn of 1873, to be stationed at Bombay, where she has the promise of a fine opening.

There was much touring in 1872 and 1873. Messrs. Bissell, Fairbank, Harding, Wells, Atkinson, Park, and Winsor each made favorable reports. Seventy-six persons were received into the church in 1872 — a larger number than in any previous year since 1861, — and sixteen more in the first three months of 1873. Pastor Modak, of Ahmednuggur, reports; "The regular preaching services on the Sabbath and other days of the week, have been attended by more outsiders than ever before. Even at the special meetings of the church for prayer, many have been present, and listened attentively."

Accessions to the church

Mr. Park gives an interesting account of the hopeful conversion of a former "gosavi," or religious teacher, about forty miles from Solapûr, his subsequent faithful efforts for the conversion of others, and the baptism of several members of his family, and others who had been his followers. Through his efforts and influence, over fifty persons, in different villages, were said to be inquiring.

The church at Solapûr received its native pastor at the opening of the year 1874, and started as the first self-supporting church in the Bombay Presidency; the native church all agreeing to pay a tithe of their income, which made up the salary. The ordination sermon was preached by Rev. R. V. Modak (Ramkrishnapunt), pastor of the church at Ahmednuggur, with whom and with Dr. Bissell he had studied.

First self-supporting church.

"Last year," says the Ahmednuggur pastor, "I received to my church thirty-seven souls, which was more than I ever received in one year before." "Our Sabbath school," he adds, "includes not only children, as in Christian lands; it is composed of the whole church, — young and old, men and women. We have some fifteen teachers. I hold a meeting for these teachers every Thursday evening, when I explain to them the lesson for the next Sunday. I have a prayer-meeting for the church on every Friday, a preaching service for the heathen every Wednesday night and Sunday night, besides the Sabbath-school, and a service for the Christians. I meet my inquirers' class every Monday afternoon. So I have in all seven exercises

A native pastor.

every week, out of which the resident missionary takes one only when here, and I take the rest. Then, visiting Christian families, receiving visits from heathen friends, and trying to give them hints on religion, and returning their visits, keeping the records of the church, necessary correspondence, and the like, keep my hands always so employed that I have very little time for anything else."[1]

A summary.

The mission reported, in 1873, twenty-four native preachers, of whom fourteen were pastors in the twenty-two churches, supported in part by their people. The church members were seven hundred and seven, of whom three hundred and sixty-nine were men, and three hundred and thirty-eight women. There were thirty-two male and five female teachers. The number of villages in which Christians resided, was one hundred and nineteen. The number of children baptized from the beginning, was six hundred and forty-three, twelve of them in the year 1873. The number of schools was twenty-nine, and of pupils five hundred and eighty-eight, of whom two hundred and twenty-one were baptized children. The native Bible readers were twenty-one, and Bible women thirteen. The amount of contributions for a year was 2,094 rupees, or $1,047.

The years 1872 and 1873 were noted for an inroad upon the central regions of this mission by the So-

[1] *Missionary Herald*, 1874, p. 119.

ciety for the Propagation of the Gospel, acting through the Bishop of Bombay, in utter disregard of the commonly recognized principles of missionary comity. A missionary of that Society was placed in Ahmednuggur, and native agents in adjacent villages, sometimes where the American mission had had a church and teacher for years, and with salaries larger than that mission had deemed it wise to give. On a recent visit to Ahmednuggur, the Bishop received persons to confirmation and communion, who were under excommunication from the mission churches. On a journey of a hundred miles in the Ahmudnuggur districts, he reported seventy-seven persons confirmed by him, some of whom were members of churches planted by the American missions, others were excommunicated persons, and a large part of the rest resided in villages long occupied as out-stations. Native Christians described them as "pulled up and harvested in a green and unripe state." In the district thus invaded the American mission had nine native pastors, fourteen Bible-readers and preachers, five Bible-women, and eighteen school teachers.

Great breach of comity.

Some account should be given of the visit of Rev. J. H. Seelye, D. D., Professor in the Amherst College, to this mission in 1872. It becoming known that he was expecting to visit different mission fields in Japan, China, India, and Turkey, in a journey round the world, the brethren

Visit and labors of Dr. Seelye.

at Bombay sent an earnest invitation to him to spend two or three months in that city and vicinity, addressing educated natives in the English language, and the Prudential Committee seconded the request. After brief visits in Japan and China, Dr. Seelye came to Calcutta, where, at the request of the Scotch missionaries, he lectured to the English-speaking Hindûs. Then, taking the railway, he visited Benares, Allahabad, Agra, and Delhi. His arrival at Bombay near the last of November, 1872, was opportune. A Calcutta Baboo, a Brahmo missionary, had just completed a course of lectures in the English language in favor of Brahmoism, in the last of which he had violently assailed Christianity. This, and his claim that he had not been answered, gave to Dr. Seelye a fair introduction to the English-speaking natives of Bombay.

The lectures were attended by about three hundred Hindûs, and were requested by them for publication. They had not been previously written, but four of them, written out for the press by the author in India, were published at Bombay, and have been republished in Boston. Besides public lectures, Dr. Seelye had many opportunities of meeting companies of natives at private houses for conversation and discussion, some of which were intensely interesting.

While at Ahmednuggur, he delivered two lectures, by request, to large audiences, almost wholly native, and but few of them Christian. On the Sabbath he preached, through an interpreter, to the largest native audience he had seen in any mission church. They were generally Christians, and the preacher felt amply paid for his journey from Bombay.

Dr. Seelye received, while at Ahmednuggur, an invitation to lecture at Poona, the old capital of the Deccan, one of the centres of brahminical power, and his experience there was remarkable. Poona is a large military post, one of the Governor's residences, and has two colleges and a number of prominent schools. The lecture was delivered in the great court of the old palace of the Peshwa, under the open sky. The number of brahmins present was estimated at from six to eight hundred. At the close of the lecture, a brahmin requested Dr. Seelye to remain and give a second lecture, on the next evening, affirming that such was the wish of the audience. The lecturer shall give his own account of his experience on this occasion.

"The crowd last night was, if possible, greater than the night before. They packed the court and filled the balconies, leaving little more than the bare space for my stand, while a number of peering faces gathered about the door. It was an engaging sight, — the bright eyes and inquisitive looks of something like a thousand brahmins, crowded thick before, behind, and on either side of me, in this court of the old 'palace of peace,' as its name implies — but where so many plottings of war have been seen — numberless candles lighting it up, and the stars looking down from the open heavens above. I shall not forget it. I thought at first that such a spot would be a difficult place in which to speak, but it was not at all so. Though open above, it was inclosed on the four sides, and I think I spoke with even more ease than usual. I certainly never had a more attentive audience. These people, perhaps from their Oriental politeness, know how to constitute a very well-behaved assembly. I spoke exactly an hour, as I did the night before. I leave to-day for Bombay. A week ago I had no thought of stopping here, and I dreaded the journey to Ahmednuggur, but both have been exceedingly interesting experiences, for which I am grateful. The Deccan College, and several schools of note located here, I visited yesterday, under the escort of Colonel Johnson."

Other English lecturing.

Mr. Park, writing next year says, that on a recent visit to Ahmeduggur, he was requested by the English-speaking natives to give them a lecture in English, and they assembled to hear it at the mission church, which had lately been enlarged. "I have seldom had a better audience of brahmins," he says, "than assembled on that occasion. I gave a lecture which, before any other audience, would have been called a sermon, and it was well received."

When we consider the high intelligence of the missionaries of different societies — English, Scotch, and American — who have labored among the Mahrattas, and the confident opinions they have so often expressed on the subject, we cannot doubt, that their labors have exerted a great and beneficial influence. They have not been toiling merely for results that loomed up in the future; they see them in the past and the present.

The estimated result.

Mr. Harding thinks that the small apparent success of the mission in Bombay is owing, (1.) To the influence of social life and the intensified form of every evil in such a city. (2.) To influences tending to divert missionaries from direct and persistent evangelical work. (3.) To the short term of missionary service, and the frequent changes. (4.) To the fact that the centre of our missionary operations was long in the interior, so that the work in Bombay failed in the concentration required to intensify it to such a degree as might be expected to produce extensive and permanent results. (5.) To this fact, also, that four other Missionary Societies have pursued a somewhat different policy, especially in their educational establishments.

Yet the Board has very important facilities for laboring in Bombay, having a valuable dwelling-house adapted to two families, centrally situated, and a commodious house of worship in an excellent location. It has also the right granted by government to occupy several lots in different parts of the city, for the residence of mission families, for native free schools, and other missionary purposes. It was the first missionary station in what is now the greatest city of India, and has sowed much good seed there, which needs only appropriate culture and the blessing of God to yield a harvest. Prosecuting the mission with the single object of raising up effective native churches and an appropriate native ministry, there will be no unhealthful competition with other friendly missions. Their attractive schools may indeed draw upon our young men, as the government college does upon theirs, but in a population, now so near a million, there must be ample room for all.

CHAPTER XVII.

TAMIL PEOPLE.

THE CEYLON MISSION.

1855–1867.

Unexpected change in the Seminary.

THE Batticotta Seminary was in operation thirty-one years, and its cost in that time was about $100,000, including the salaries of its missionary teachers. In its later years, the admission of scholars who paid their board, unexpectedly wrought an unfavorable change in the institution, by introducing students from wealthy families, whose main object was to fit themselves for government service. The influence of this class was not good upon the religious character of the school. In the year 1855, only eleven of the ninety-six students were members of the church.

The number of students, who had been church members up to that time, was six hundred and seventy, — somewhat more than half the whole number; and of these four hundred and fifty were then living. About ninety had been excommunicated, most of them, it appears, for marrying heathen wives. Eighty of the graduates were then in the employ of the American mission, and thirty were in the employ of other missions; and one hundred and fifty-eight were in the service of the Ceylon and India governments. Among those engaged in government and other service, were some who honored their Christian profession by a humble and consistent life.

The institution was modified by the mission to meet the exigencies of the times, and was then called "The Theological and Training Institution;" and the prescribed course of study was eminently Biblical. Mr. Sanders was made the Principal, and had the aid of two native teachers. The institution started on its new career with sixteen students, selected from forty candidates, varying in their ages from sixteen to twenty-six.

This movement not retrograde.

In the United States this movement was regarded by some, at the time, as being retrograde. Yet it was not, nor did it involve any serious reflection upon the past. Missions are progressive, under the teachings of experience. What is good policy at one time, may require modification at another. It was so in the Ceylon mission. The only reasonable doubt is, whether the changes were not too long delayed.

The English schools.

The whole number of pupils in the English schools for preparing pupils for the Seminary, from 1830 to 1848, was seventeen hundred. The largest number at any one time, was six hundred and eighteen. Six years later, there were only two hundred and twenty-nine. The chief cause of this reduction was the belief of the mission, that the cost of English studies ought to devolve mainly on the parents, whose sole motive in sending their children was to secure for them secular advancement. Yet these schools had a missionary value. Besides acquiring the English language, the students pursued a thorough course in the vernacular, including catechisms, Scripture history, and other studies; and these studies served to prolong the school education of the boys.

Female education.

Heathen parents generally saw no advantage in giving their daughters an education, and there were strong prejudices against it. There had been no such custom, until it was introduced by the mission. Hence arose the practice of giving the girls cloths, as an inducement to attend school; which was discontinued in 1855, after an experiment of thirty years. But few girls attended the village schools, and these were mostly of low caste and poor. They came more for the cloth than for education, and it was difficult to retain them until they had learned to read the Bible and received religious impressions. Then the schoolmaster often felt disgraced in teaching such girls. Persons of wealth and high caste rarely sent their daughters to the village schools. The case was somewhat different in the select girls' schools at the stations, supported by government grants, in which cloths and jackets were given twice a year, with additional grants for washing, and for instruction in sewing. Christian teachers were employed in these schools, a good common education was given in them to many girls residing near the stations; and candidates were selected from them for the Seminary at Oodooville.

A native English High School.

One of the good results of discontinuing English in the Batticotta Seminary, was the establishment of an English High School in 1857, by the native community, under the superintendence of Mr. Breckenridge, a native member of the church, who had been one of the best teachers in the Batticotta Seminary. Mr. Breckenridge's new school soon had one hundred and thirty scholars, between the ages of twelve and twenty. This was the beginning of self-sustaining educational institutions among the native Christians in Jaffna. The time had evidently come for devolving the expense of an English education, in great part at least, upon those who were to profit by it.

After two years, the Breckenridge English High School adopted a constitution, which declared its object to be imparting "useful knowledge to native youth upon a Protestant Christian basis;" its course of instruction was to be "Biblical, scientific, and literary, both in Tamil and English;" and its Trustees were all to be "Protestant Christians." Within the district occupied by the mission, there were four other English schools in 1859, supported by natives, and the Bible and Christian lessons were taught in all of them. They numbered, together, over four hundred pupils.

In view of these encouraging facts, the Prudential Committee wrote thus to the mission: —

Position of the Prudential Committee.

"We would encourage the natives in efforts they are disposed to make for supporting Christian schools, however strongly they may run at first in the English direction; though not by our becoming a party and co-laborer in such schools. The merit of their enterprise lies in its being *their own*, independent of missionary support. We cannot well exaggerate the importance of guarding our native Christians against the hope, that we shall ever return to the teaching of their children the English language, to be used as a means of procuring lucrative secular employments. The sooner they understand, that there is no ground for such a hope, the better will it be for them, and the better for the cause.

"The Christian schools for English, originated, taught, supported wholly by the natives, are a very different thing, in their practical bearing, from what they would be in the hands of the mission, supported by the Board. The boon is no longer a charity, nor sought as such. The whole operation is under the laws governing demand and supply.

Excessive production, such as was under the old system, is checked. The young natives, who shrink from going far from home in missionary employment, even so far as Chavagacherry is from Batticotta, will shrink from seeking lucrative employments in the far off regions of Madras, or Burmah. Parents will weigh probabilities, before spending their own money for board and tuition. Then we have no longer the entangling alliances of patrons and beneficiaries, and the consequent dependence and implied obligations. Our relations to the whole thing are changed, and for the better.

"What we purpose, therefore, is this: While you reassure our Christian natives, that we shall not return to our old system, you should also assure them that we shall always be glad to see them helping themselves. This we would show by word and deed; by kind pastoral visits occasionally to the schools; by a cordial attendance and aid at their examinations in studies we do not disapprove; by procuring government aid for them, under prudent restrictions; and by recommendations of worthy pupils when seeking employment.

"The Lord has certainly work to be accomplished in Jaffna, for which (mainly through missionary instrumentalities) He has made much preparation. He has converted many of the people, and He will doubtless yet convert many more. And notwithstanding the sordidness of the native character, notwithstanding the temptations afforded by the English language, by the ambitious, worldly influence of parents, and by the offers of government, traders, and planters, there will be pious young men in Jaffna (as in this country) who, after all, will choose the Gospel ministry, and the unambitious life of the school-teacher; and this number, on the present plan of our mission, will be on the increase. True, we are now in a transition state, and of course are somewhat unsettled; but we are making progress, through the blessing of our Lord and Saviour, toward a higher stage of spirituality and efficiency."

Results of a liberal education.

Speaking of former pupils of the Batticotta Seminary found within the parish of Oodooville, Mr. Spaulding makes the following statement: "The native assistants at this station report fifty-five young men within the limits of this field, including Kokkûville, who have been educated more or less in the Batticotta Seminary, exclusive of those employed in our mission. These statistics show that more than two thirds of these men reside in their own villages, or in the District; more than two thirds have been church-members, and only fourteen are faulted on our books. Those in public office are often at home, and their influence is not small in their villages. Intelligence and a desire for education, are on the increase; these very men, even those of the most hopeless class, are much more easily moved than the impervious minds of the besotted heathen; and those who keep aloof from us, or turn a corner to avoid us, are much more vulnerable than their thick-headed and sensual-hearted neighbors. With the worst construction which can be put on those men and measures, heathenism is a great loser, and Christianity gains a thousand-fold by such education."

The "Training and Theological Institution" was on a vernacular basis, with a purely religious object. At the end of its first year, two thirds of its pupils were hopefully pious, and among them were some who, for talent and piety, bid fair to rank high as teachers and preachers. The institution was the chief hope of the mission in respect to its native pastors and helpers.

The Theological Seminary.

The Prudential Committee wrote thus concerning it in 1858: "Our Theological School will accomplish its object, should it collect all in the District, whose piety, talents, and spirit will make them happy in its pursuits, be their number more or less. We have no funds for supporting a school at Batticotta merely for the sake of having one, or because we have so long had one there. Let us begin cautiously, and be content with having only the men we want. On the plan above proposed, there must needs be a respectable number at our command to begin with. And with the present reduced number of missionaries (and not all of these in health, and some just arrived), the not having the school in session during the whole year, will be a convenience. We hope you will all feel that the school exists solely for the mission. Let it be what you and the Prudential Committee agree in believing it ought to be, and you need not fear that the Christian community at home will be dissatisfied. Missions must be worked, if worked successfully, on their true and proper merits."

In the year 1860, a revival brought three fourths of the pupils into the church. The Principal declared the last six months of that year the happiest in his missionary life.

Death of an old native Christian.

A native member of the church, one of the earliest converted, died in 1859. He was of humble origin and condition, but honored the Christian profession for thirty-seven years. His Christian name was Onesimus. He was originally a slave of the covia caste, and was made free by Mr. Poor in 1821, about the time of his uniting with the church. His age at that time was supposed to be thirty-five, consequently he died at the age of seventy-three. Ten years after his conversion, Onesimus was made a deacon in the church. In this office he continued through life, and though not rising to great influence, he never hesitated to do his duty according to his conception of it, even when it was to warn the wealthy and the learned. His visits from house to house were frequent among the Christians, and sometimes he would visit the missionaries, even at unseasonable hours, that he might kneel with them in prayer for some man or woman whom he regarded as in danger of being lost. In his last years he was enfeebled in body and mind, but was always meek, humble, childlike; and the most effectual alleviation of his severe pains, when on his death-bed, was reading the Scriptures to him and prayer.

New missionaries.

Messrs. Milan H. Hitchcock and James Quick and their wives joined the mission in 1858, and Mr. James A. Bates and wife in 1851. Failure of the wife's health obliged Mr. Hitchcock to return in 1860, Mr. Bates in 1863, and Mr. Quick in 1868.

A Native College projected.

Provision for general education devolves properly on the native community, with the aid of government. In the autumn of 1867, a meeting of native Christians connected with the different Protestant missions in Jaffna was held at Batticotta, to consult about creating a Native College. A large committee was appointed to solicit a subscription of $25,000, and the missionaries of the American Board were requested to act as trustees, with power to associate with themselves an equal number of native gentlemen; while the Board was desired to furnish the Principal, through its mission. The movement indicated an advance in the popular sentiment, and that the time had come for measures looking directly to the close of the mission as a possible result. A Christian College was the more obvious of these measures, constituted, governed, instructed, and sustained in the manner proposed. There was supposed to be piety and learning enough in the native community, and enough of organized religious life and of trustworthy self-reliance, to warrant the expectation of success in this institution.

The substantial advance made by the mission will more clearly appear, if we take into view a statement made in a letter from the mission in the year 1847, eight years before the visit of the Deputation. The leading object of the letter was to show why the mission had been so slow, hitherto, in putting forward a native ministry. The Jaffna field has proved one of the hardest for missionary cultivation, — the result, perhaps, of previous Roman Catholic and Dutch culture, — but nowhere else could the various educational appliances have had more ample scope. The statement was, in substance, as follows: —

Advance in the mission.

1. After the lapse of thirty years, there was but one congregation on the Sabbath in connection with each of the stations, and those congregations had so few voluntary attendants as to make it proper almost to leave them out of the account, being composed chiefly of beneficiaries and dependants.

2. This dependence on the native preachers, schoolmasters, and schools, for a congregation at

the station, hindered the gathering of other congregations in the neighboring villages at the time of the station service.

3. As the result of the system of operations, the mission churches were educated bodies, and so demanded the most efficient pastoral care that could be provided, rendering it exceedingly difficult to train up adequate native pastors. Yet, while the mission supposed that none but missionaries could fill the pastoral office, they believed that the natives, in ordinary life, had few sympathies in common with themselves. The churches were anomalous in their origin, which was in charity boarding-schools; in their character, being educated bodies; and in their position, which to a great extent was one of dependence upon the mission for pecuniary aid.

4. As things then were, neither native pastors nor native preachers were thought to be very necessary, — not as *pastors*, because there were no flocks for them to feed; not as *preachers*, because there were no appropriate congregations for them; nor was there, at that time, any native convert deemed competent to feed the flock at either of the stations, except under the supervision of a missionary. Of the eight natives who had been licensed to preach, not more than two had then given reasonable satisfaction as preachers.

5. The labors of the missionaries had become so various, that those newly arrived found it difficult

to master the language so as to preach fluently and idiomatically, and the great variety of cares made it also difficult for any one to give the attention needful for the proper training of a native ministry.

A desirable change.

In view of this it seemed to those, whose post of duty was at the centre of the operations, that a change was desirable in the course pursued. Accordingly the Prudential Committee advised, that the excessive dependence of the congregations and churches upon the schools, should in some way be brought to an end. Believing the churches and pastorate to be divine institutions, and most intimately correlated, they held that if each were properly adapted to the other, there would be no risk in bringing them together, and that missionaries should be evangelists, and not pastors. They believed the native preachers would be less likely to fail under the responsibilities of the pastorate, than when hanging loosely on religious society as mere evangelists.

Ordination of native pastors.

The first ordination at Karadive, described in the preceding chapter, was regarded as a good step in advance. A still more important one was the ordaining, in the same year, of one of the best educated native helpers as pastor of the church at Chavagacherry, at the opposite end of the field, a station that had been vacated by a missionary. A third native pastor was ordained in 1858 over a new village church at Valany. In 1860 another village church was formed at Navaly. The church purchased land, erected a house of worship, and then extended a call to a native preacher who had labored among them, and he was installed as their pastor in 1861. This pastor was supported by the Native Evangelical Society, the others in part by their own churches.

Of the three native assistants who had been licensed to preach, Mr. Howland wrote, a few years later, that he felt great confidence in them as men of sincere piety, superior intelligence, and growing excellence, and he had been much gratified to notice that such men were gradually rising in influence, even above those of superior talent and education, but less marked for Christian earnestness.

Death of Mr. Meigs.

On the 12th of May, 1862, the Rev. Benjamin C. Meigs died in New York city, in the seventy-third year of his age. He was one of the first company of missionaries to Ceylon, where he spent more than forty years. He sent three of his children to the United States in 1834, and came in 1840 with the rest of his large family. In the following year he returned to Ceylon, leaving his family in the United States, where they remained. When advised, after fifteen years, in view of threatening indications as to his health, to rejoin his family, he remarked that he could have done no better in the past, than he had done for his family, or for the mission. He came to America in 1858, and remained there till his death.

Mr. Meigs's sacrifices in the cause of his Master were great, and he made them cheerfully. His original choice of the missionary life is understood to have been with a singularly calm deliberation, and his adherence to it was in the same spirit. He died as he had lived, bearing testimony to the grace of God. At the close of a prayer, on the night of his death, commending him, his family, the cause of missions, and all the precious interests of the Redeemer's kingdom to God, he lifted his hands, and with deep emotion responded, AMEN.

A step fraught with the highest promise to the cause of Christ in Jaffna was taken at Batticotta in 1867, by the oldest church in the mission. The church decided, not only to have a pastor, but to be self-governed, self-supported, and independent of the mission in everything, except Christian counsel. Altogether this was a decisive proof of the hold the Gospel had taken on the life of the people.

Interesting pastorate at Batticotta.

A meeting of the male members of the church was held on the day of the annual thanksgiving, and one of their number having been chosen chairman, remarks were made by different members on the necessity of having a native pastor, and supporting him without foreign aid. Messrs. Howland and Hastings were present, but only as spectators. On the first point all were agreed, but there was doubt as to the possibility of raising the entire salary. An effort already made had secured only half of it, and even the most sanguine expressed apprehension; but then it was said by some, that they ought not to have a pastor until they could support him. At length one pledged himself to pay the salary for a month, another did the same, and a third said, "I have been thinking that, were I a heathen, I should give annually for ceremonies for my deceased parents, and I will give as much for the support of a pastor." The result was a unanimous vote to support him.

When ready for the choice, the chairman read Acts i. 23–26, and xiii. 1–3, and led in prayer for divine direction. Nearly all the votes were for Benjamin H. Rice, principal native teacher of the Theological and Training Institution, and one of the three recently licensed to preach. He was present, and expressed, in a voice tremulous with emotion, his feeling of unworthiness for the office; but said, as the call had been entirely unsought by himself, he would accept it on the condition, that they would sustain him by their sympathy and prayers. The day for the ordination was stormy, yet more than four hundred were present, and some natives who were connected with the English mission. Mr. Howland says of the occasion: "It was one not soon to be forgotten by those present, and certainly not by me. Twenty-one years before, I preached my first sermon on heathen ground in that pulpit, and it has ever since been peculiarly dear to me." To make room for the new pastor, Mr. Howland removed from Batticotta to Tillipally; and it deserves to be recorded, that the change made by the native pastor from the Seminary to the Pastorate, was at considerable pecuniary sacrifice.

A committee of the church soon after wrote thus to their patrons in this country: —

Letter from the church.

"While this church is no longer under the care and the control of the mission, though subject to its counsel, they feel bound to express their filial gratitude to the churches in America. The name Jaffna, and particularly Batticotta, is dear to thousands through the length and breadth of your Christian land. This district has been colonized, not with men from America, but with American feelings, taste, and religion. The standard of the cross is now erected here, and this church feels it to be her duty, with unfeigned gratitude to acknowledge, that she owes all that she is, and all that she has, under God, to the churches in America. We are now an independent church, with a pastor of our own, and hope before long to be able to support our own schools, and catechists, and preachers. We are forming a congregation from those who are willing to renounce heathenism and adapt themselves to Christian forms and practices, who are increasing in number. We ask your prayers, that this church may not fail in its effort to stand alone, but may preserve its faith to the end, and shine to the glory of Christ, as an example to the Hindû world. May Jesus, our common Lord, grant that we all, in one communion, may shine as precious gems upon his crown throughout eternity."[1]

Looking back from this point (1867), we see very marked progress in the work of this mission. The native church at Batticotta, — with its pastor of the same race, self-governed, self-reliant, looking no longer to the mission except for fraternal counsel, gathering a Christian congregation around it, and aiming to shine to the glory of Christ, — is a monument of success.

A pleasing retrospect.

In that year, there were ten churches within the bounds of the mission, containing four hundred and eighty-four members. Twenty-seven regular services were held on the Sabbath, and frequent meetings among the heathen during the week, on moonlight evenings. Of these meetings Mr. Howland says: "There was formerly more or less opposition in them. Now, opposition or dispute is rare. There seems to be a serious attention, and an apparent conviction on the minds of many that we preach the truth. This is encouraging. The seed sown with tears, by those who have gone before us, for so many years, certainly cannot be in vain; and we sometimes think the time of harvest may be near."

[1] *Missionary Herald,* 1867, pp. 283, 302.

CHAPTER XVIII.

THE TAMIL PEOPLE.

CEYLON MISSION.

1867–1873.

The missionary printing.

It has been already stated, that a printer was sent to this mission in the year 1821, and that he was banished from the island by the Governor. The press was then deposited with the Church missionaries at Vellore, and thus at once became available for printing books and tracts. On the removal of restrictions in 1834, it was returned to the mission, and set up at Manepy. The arrival of Mr. Minor led to an enlargement of the establishment, and in 1838 four presses were in operation, and seventy men employed in the printing-office and bindery. Owing to the climate and native habits, they would do only about half the work of the same number of men in America. This scale of operations was continued, with some variations, for twelve years, and a large amount of printing of various kinds was done in Tamil and English; but in 1850 the number of workmen was reduced one half. There were printed, during the thirteen years in which the press was at Vellore, forty-three tracts and 250,000 copies. A large printing establishment, if it must be constantly employed, becomes exacting in its demands on the time and labor of a mission. It was so with this establishment. It had been the means of great good, but the Ceylon missionaries came at length to the conclusion, that if the press were owned and worked by native Christians, with occasional aid from Madras, the requirements of the mission could still be met; and in 1855, the establishment, after some further reduction, was sold, under certain stipulations, to native Christians in Jaffna, who had been trained in the office. Mr. Burnell, who was in charge of the establishment, was soon after transferred to the Madura mission, where he was ordained as a minister of the Gospel.

In twenty years from 1834, the number of pages printed was nearly 172,000,000, the number of distinct publications being two hundred and ninety. Not less than one hundred and forty of the publications were tracts, issued chiefly at the expense of the American Tract Society. In addition, the Jaffna Tract Society had printed 260,000 copies of an almanac, called the Tamil Calendar. Among the Tamil publications, was a dictionary, of about nine hundred octavo pages, and works on geography, anatomy, algebra, and the like, of about two hundred pages each. Among the publications in English and Tamil were a dictionary of nearly a thousand large octavo pages, and the "Morning Star," a semi-monthly periodical commenced in 1841, embracing sixteen quarto volumes. Of English publications, the number of copies was about fifty thousand, and the grand total of copies was three and a half millions. The volumes issued from the bindery numbered 756,000; and nearly one third of this printed matter was the Word of God.

The "Morning Star" was regarded by the mission as an effective instrument of good. Its columns being open to objections against Christianity, its tendency was to develop public sentiment, and secure a perusal of the answers to those objections. As educated natives became widely scattered, this periodical retained an influence over them, and it was invaluable among the Christian families connected with the mission. After 1855, it was enlarged, and issued as a monthly, wholly in the Tamil language. Its subscribers in 1856 numbered six hundred and forty-five, and more than a third of them were heathen.

The medical department.

The medical department of the mission requires a few additional statements. Messrs. Warren and Richards, of the first mission company, had a knowledge of medicine, and commenced its practice among the people. Dr. Scudder entered upon his labors as a missionary physician in 1819, and trained a few native young men to practice on European principles. Dr. Ward took charge of the department in 1833, and Dr. Green in 1847. Seventy-two young men have been instructed in medicine, and a class of eighteen more will probably graduate near the close of 1875. Several of the graduates have become good practitioners. The medical teaching in English was relinquished in 1864 for teaching in Tamil, and a set of vernacular text books is in course of preparation. Several of the volumes, amounting to about three thousand pages octavo, and copiously illustrated, have been completed.

Deaths from cholera.

The prevalence of the cholera in the early part of 1867 was nearly unprecedented. The deaths in the province, as estimated by the Government, were ten thousand. Twenty-five communicants, and many of the baptized children, were numbered with the dead. It was necessary to disband most of the schools. Rachel, a pious widow with a numerous family, attended upon a son, a son-in-law, and seven grandchildren, who died of the pestilence, and upon others who recovered. At length she also passed away, in full hope of going "to Mount Zion above," as she expressed it. Mr. Howland pronounced her "a mother in Israel," whom he had known for twenty-one years, without being able to recollect a word said against her by any one.

Mr. and Mrs. Sanders returned from the United States at the close of 1867, and were accompanied by Miss Harriet E. Townshend, who was to take charge of the new girls' boarding-school at Oodoopitty. In November of the following year the mission was sorely afflicted by the death of Mrs. Sanders, after a brief sickness, — a woman greatly beloved, and eminently useful.

Death of Mrs. Sanders.

Mr. Capron, of the Madura Mission, instead of going to the Sanitarium on the Pulney Hills, visited Jaffna with his family in June, 1868, and gives an animated view of the mission as it appeared to him in his sojourn.

Interesting view of the mission.

"Jaffna," he says, "and especially Batticotta and Oodooville, were pictures so pleasant in the fancy of my boyhood, that I almost hesitated to dispel the dream. But the reality is as much better than the dream. I found the graves of some of those early missionaries — Harriet Winslow, whose memoir I now read with double interest, and Father Poor, whom I revered perhaps as much as any saint in the calendar. I found also one of those noble men still living, who entered the field before I was born, and who, if he lives another year, will celebrate his semi-centennial on missionary ground. It might disturb his gravity to be classed as yet with saints, but he was a worthy companion of those worthy men who have passed away, and while I delighted in his genial hospitality and social converse, I looked upon him with the reverence which is inspired by a long life of usefulness, and by the thought that he must ere long pass the river, into which he has once dipped his feet and returned.

"His wife lives, and is as worthy of him, as he is of the noble company which has gone before him. We found Miss Agnew, also, after a service of twenty-eight years unbroken by a visit to her native country, still at her post, and full of activity.

"When Father Spaulding had shown me the school-room and dormitories, and the magnificent fruit trees of the school-yard, — his own planting, — he pointed to a long, low building, and said, 'There is where the power lies.' It was a row of small rooms for secret prayer.

"Oodooville is not so very much altered from old times, except for the better, by discarding English, but I was glad to learn that female education has become so popular in Jaffna that pupils, who could not otherwise be admitted, pay a large portion of the expense of their board and tuition.

"Batticotta, as it was and as it is, forms an instructive page of missionary experience. It must have cost the mission a severe struggle to give up the prestige of their splendid English school, and it was certainly a step which the natives have never ceased to deplore. But Batticotta is mightier than ever for the work of Christianizing the island, and Mr. Sanders, I believe, appreciates the value of the influences which are committed to his trust. I found there a training institution, not made up of boys, but of young men, either hopefully converted or, at least, fully committed to the truth of Christianity. I found a flourishing English school of some two hundred members, under Christian management, the Principal[1] showing his own disposition by taking an active part as a member of the church committee, and giving, as I was told, one tenth of his income in benevolence. I found a native church, not only entirely supporting its pastor, but supporting also a good school for girls. I found an intelligent and well-to-do Christian community, living in the enjoyment of the blessings of the Gospel, and compelling the respect of their heathen neighbors. One might well envy the power there is in Batticotta, and indeed in the Jaffna Church, in view of the time when God shall pour out his Holy Spirit.

"Oodoopitty is the most northeasterly station of the mission, and considering its salubrity and the character of its people, is one of the most inviting missionary stations in India. The new female boarding-school has commenced its career of usefulness with about twenty pupils, and Miss Townshend, whose mind was turning toward the missionary field at the very time that the missionaries were looking to the United States for some such young lady, is most happy in her work, and has that work well in hand."

The mission must have enjoyed, at this time, more than usual spiritual prosperity. There was more

[1] Mr. Breckenridge.

than the usual religious activity. This was specially true at Manepy, Tillipally, Panditeripo, and Navaly, in which many had begun to give a tenth of their income to Christian objects. The subject of liberal giving had been discussed at the annual convocation of the churches, held in concert with the annual meeting of the American Board. A native pastor presented, as an example, the efforts of the Christians of Kessab in Central Turkey. Mr. Sanders spoke of the self-sacrificing spirit of many Christians in America, and others referred to the self-supporting churches of Burmah and Eastern Turkey. The occasion was one of the deepest interest, and full of hope for the future. Not the least impressive part of it was the communion-service, presided over by the venerable Dr. Spaulding, assisted by Mr. Stickney, a native pastor, at which three hundred professed followers of Christ renewed their covenant vows to Christ and each other.

Not only was there increased liberality, many were active in personal efforts to commend the Gospel to others. At Tillipally, the Sabbath afternoon service was given up, and the male members went out, two by two, into the villages, with portions of Scripture and tracts, to read and talk with the people, and were generally well received. The women met Mrs. Howland at the same time for prayer, Bible-reading, and study. Mr. Sanders believed that more than four thousand families were reached in his field, during the year, by the native helpers, and Mr. Howland reported fifteen hundred houses as visited in his field. Thus thoroughly was the good seed being sown.

The mission was strengthened in 1869 by the arrival of Mr. William E. De Riemer and his wife.

In 1855, and even some years later, it was difficult for the churches to realize, that natives were needed as pastors. The missionary must preach, baptize, marry their children, visit the sick, bury their dead, and administer the ordinances of the Gospel. But in 1868 the principle was generally admitted, and cordially received by the most influential Christians, that natives should be pastors. The duty of the church to support the Gospel to the extent of its ability was accepted, and the duty of the Christian to return at least a tenth of his income to the Lord in benevolent contributions, was admitted by many, who gave accordingly. One church (at Batticotta) had assumed the full support of its pastor, and two others, under the pastoral care of natives, were rising in their contributions; and those without native pastors were taking upon themselves a part of the support of those who statedly preached to them. The care of church edifices, and of the church poor, was generally assumed by the native Christians.

Change of sentiment as to the native pastorate.

The peculiar adaptation of the native pastorate to the native wants was exemplified when Mr. Hunt, long native pastor at Chavagacherry, was called, by the Directors of the Jaffna College, to take the place of head teacher in that institution. Mr. De Riemer says: "At the pastor's farewell meeting, I was struck by the tenderness of the remarks made by one and another of the church. One, a blacksmith, who has not long been a member, and is the only Christian of his family, wept like a child. When I spoke with him at the close of the meeting, he unwittingly gave the best testimony to the superiority of native over missionary pastors. He said, substantially: 'We respect the missionaries, and wish to please them, but they are white men, and do not know *our* trials. Our pastor knew our trials, our family difficulties, our weaknesses, and our ignorance. He came to our houses and our shops, and instructed us how we should act in a way that the white man cannot do. But now we have lost him, we shall have no teacher.'"

The children instead of the fathers.

The future of missions has much to hope from the sons and daughters of missionaries. Mr. Thomas S. Smith, a son of Mr. J. C. Smith, and his wife, a daughter of Mr. Fairbank of the Mahratta mission, joined the Ceylon mission in July, 1871. Two sons and a daughter of Mr. Howland, of the Ceylon mission, also joined the India missions in 1873, — one going to the Madura mission, the other and the daughter to Ceylon. In the same year, also, a daughter of Mr. Minor joined the

Madura mission as the wife of a son of Mr. Chandler. Mr. J. C. Smith, father of the missionary of that name, had been constrained by failing health to come to the United States with his wife, where she died on the 15th of May, 1873. She had been a faithful and earnest worker since 1837.

Death of Mr. Sanders.

Mr. Sanders visited the United States in 1870, to obtain funds for the proposed Jaffna College; and, soon after his return, died suddenly at Batticotta, on the 29th of August, 1871, at the age of forty-eight. He was struck with apoplexy in the midst of apparent health. The loss was severely felt, he having been eighteen years an active and efficient member of the mission, enjoying the confidence and love of all.

A pleasing incident.

As 1874 was the jubilee year of the Oodooville Seminary, a number of its graduates met in the May preceding, to consider what should be done on that occasion. None but women were at the meeting, and some of these had belonged to the very first class. After devotional exercises, five resolutions were unanimously adopted, and they show the "educated women of Jaffna" to be far in advance of their uneducated predecessors. The preamble and first resolution read as follows: —

"We, the educated women of Jaffna, being deeply sensible of the benefits we have derived from the labors of Protestant missionaries, and feeling special gratitude to our much beloved and venerated instructors, Dr. and Mrs. Spaulding, who have with parental love and care spent more than half a century in self-denying labors for our good and the good of our people, and to our highly esteemed teacher, Miss E. Agnew, who for a third of a century has been untiring in her efforts to promote female education, desire to express in some definite and permanent form our respect and affection for them, and our gratitude for their labors, and desire at the same time to perpetuate their memory. With this object in view, we therefore *Resolve*, —

"1. That we will raise a fund, to be called the Spaulding and Agnew Fund, the interest of which shall be placed at their disposal while they live, and afterwards shall be used for the education of girls needing aid in the Oodooville Female Boarding-school."

In the second resolution, they invite all who have been connected with the institution to meet at the Jubilee, and formally present the fund which should be collected.

Death of Dr. Spaulding.

Dr. Spaulding, after having been longer in active foreign labor than any other missionary of the Board, died on the 18th of June, 1873, the month following this interesting expression of respect. Ten days prior to his death, he had celebrated the fifty-fourth anniversary of his embarkation for Ceylon.

In this, the last biographical sketch in this history, I may be allowed to avail myself of one prepared for Dr. Spaulding by Dr. Augustus C. Thompson for the Missionary Herald; thus reviving our common memories of a great and good man, dating back to our visit to Ceylon, almost twenty years ago: —

"The voyage of the brig *Indus* was memorable for a work of grace on board, during which the entire crew, sixteen in number, expressed the hope, and at the time appeared to give evidence, of a saving change. This might be regarded as a prelude to those interesting revivals in Jaffna, which afforded so much delight to Dr. Spaulding and other laborers there, and to which he gratefully referred in his last sickness.

"He arrived at Jaffna in the early part of 1820. From that time onward he continued faithfully, quietly, and most industriously to labor as an ambassador of our Lord Jesus Christ among the Tamulians of Northern Ceylon, — a people by no means so degraded as many of the heathen, and comparatively independent in their bearing, ingenious and thrifty, while yet thoroughly wedded to their idols, and morally callous, as any that can be found.

"In addition to the usual missionary work at his station, and superintendence of the Oodooville Female Boarding-school, established in 1824, Dr. Spaulding performed a large amount of literary labor. For many years, he had the revision of works carried through the press by the local Tract and Bible Societies, and he acted also as proof-reader. More than twenty Tamil tracts were prepared by him, and many of the best hymns in the vernacular hymn-book were from his pen. He furnished an excellent translation of 'Pilgrim's Progress,' much prized by the people, and compiled a Scripture History, which is used in the schools. To him also the mission is indebted for a Tamil Dictionary, as well as an enlarged and improved edition of an English and Tamil Dictionary, each of which is the best in use on the island. Another work, to which he had given no small amount of time, was a revision of the Holy Scriptures in Tamil. His notes he left to the local Bible Society, in the hope that they may furnish aid in a future improved version. These contributions will no doubt prove valuable, for he was one of the most accurate Tamil scholars in Southern India, having so mastered the language as to use it with great facility, and often with power. This must be reckoned among the reasons for the usefulness, contentment, and length of his missionary life.

"Dr. Spaulding rarely spoke of what he was doing, and still more rarely of what he had done; but not unfrequently of the great work yet to be accomplished, and the short period which a missionary has for this blessed employment. Self-complacency and jealousy for his own comfort and reputation, were not his characteristics. During his term of service, protracted to such an unusual length, he made only one visit to the United States. Many will recollect his presence at the annual meeting of the Board in Worcester in 1844, and the aptness, kindliness, and raciness of the replies to questions publicly put to him on that occasion.

"Father Spaulding was a shrewd man, a man of humor, utterly unostentatious, and quietly industrious; a man of prayer, and wholly devoted to the work to which our Lord had called him. He was decided in his views, free in the expression of them, tenacious in adhering to them, and yet a man of peace. Foreigners of all classes in Ceylon respected him. The esteem and affection of natives were also marked. It was often affecting to witness, during his last sickness, the anxiety shown by them to do anything in their power for the good man's comfort. Some of them were in constant attendance, fanning him, or performing other loving ministries. Two of Dr. Green's former medical students alternated day and night in their services, while either Mr. Hastings or Mr. Smith was at hand throughout his decline. Owing to difficulty of breathing, he could recline but very little during the two weeks of confinement to his room, and his body became so swollen as to make it hard to find an easy position; yet he did not seem to suffer severe pain.

"On account of labored respiration Dr. Spaulding was not able to converse much. No sign of complaint escaped his lips; his own interests, and the missionary work, he committed to the hands of the Master, expressing no solicitude and no fear. Alluding to his death about to take place, he said, characteristically, "Let my funeral be conducted with Puritan simplicity; let there be no words of praise or blame." When Mr. Howland asked what he would say to the native Christians, he replied, "Consecrate everything that is yours to Christ, and ask nothing in prayer which you will not devote to him." One restless night, looking at the watchers who stood about him, and then casting his eyes toward the open window, he exclaimed, 'Watchmen! watchmen! what of the night? Souls are perishing.' And so this venerable servant of Christ, aged almost fourscore and two years, ceased from his labors, and has no doubt entered upon renewed fellowship with Richards and Poor, Scudder and Winslow, Meigs and Sanders, in the presence of Him who saith, 'Well done, good and faithful servant, enter thou into the joy of thy Lord.'

"Mrs. Spaulding, the beloved and valued companion of fifty-four years of toils, trials, and joys, survives at Oodooville, but cannot be expected to remain long behind her departed husband."

The forces of a Christian civilization are evidently gathering on this field. The "Jaffna Native Evangelical Society" takes the place,

Native Evangelical Society.

in the Jaffna Christian community, of our large benevolent Societies at home. To Christians in Jaffna its meetings have all the interest which we find in those of the American Board, and they make an effort to attend them. "I wish," writes a missionary, "that you could have been present at the annual meeting held lately at Batticotta. It was an occasion of intense interest. The missionaries were merely spectators, taking part only in the communion service in the afternoon. The Annual Report, the Report of the Treasurer, — stating the prospect of a £40 debt two months before, and the circulation of a 'special appeal' to the churches, as the result of which contributions came in, till finally, on that very morning, the last farthing was paid, leaving one pound in the treasury; then the addresses, of a high tone of spirituality, and urging to a high standard of consecration, were exercises such as we could hardly look for in a land like this. They were equal to those made at similar gatherings in America. This Society is, we believe, the life of the church, and I watch its prosperity as a physician watches the pulse of his patient."

A Board of Education.

A "Board of Education" has also been formed, consisting of ten native members and two missionaries. Half the native members have no connection with the mission, and of the rest, five are ministers, and one a catechist. The Government now grants its assistance in such a way that the mission can accept it, and sixty schools, containing 1,946 boys and 685 girls, were connected in 1872 with this Board of Education. The Government defrays about four sevenths of the cost of the schools, and has its Director with his assistants. The Mission has its Examiner, who makes monthly visits to the schools. The Oodooville Girls' Boarding-school, under charge of Mrs. Spaulding and Miss Agnew, both venerable for age and long service, had fifty-three pupils in 1872, and such spiritual blessings were granted, that sixteen of the pupils united with the church. Nine of the thirty in the Oodoopitty Girls' Boarding-school, under the care of Miss Townshend, were members of the church in that year.

The Jaffna College.

The Native College in Jaffna, projected in 1867, of which the preliminary steps were described in the preceding chapter, was commenced on the first of July, 1872, under the charge of Mr. Hastings. Twenty-one pupils were then admitted to the first class, out of thirty who presented themselves for examination. A fund had been collected amounting to about $20,000, chiefly in the United States. The first term closed in October with a public examination, which was well sustained by the pupils, and well attended by their friends. Some who came to criticize remained to praise, confessing that they had not anticipated such results. All the students, except one, returned at the opening of the second term. Mr. Hastings regarded himself as favored in his two native associate teachers, both being devoted Christians, and in full sympathy with his desire to make the institution a real aid to the work of evangelization. More recently, a special religious interest pervaded the institution, and several expressed a hope that they had become Christians. Three, who had been baptized in infancy, were received to the church. The Theological Training School had been removed to Tillipally, to be under the care of Mr. Howland, who had gone thither to make way for the new pastor of the Batticotta church.

The expectation appears to be entertained, by those most competent to judge, that the work of this mission may, before very long, be left mainly to the superintendence of the men connected with the College and the Theological Training School.

CHAPTER XIX.

TAMIL PEOPLE ON THE CONTINENT.

THE MADURA MISSION.

1855–1862.

Effect of the Conference.

THE discussions of the Conference had given more practical efficiency to the work of this mission. The truth was more distinctly realized that India is to be evangelized, not so much by missionaries from abroad, as by men raised up from among the people, and that the grand effort henceforth should be in that direction.

The Seminary studies.

The Seminary was to have in charge the following grades of students: 1. Those in a regular course of study, from four to five years, with English to be studied only as a classic. 2. A class of older persons for a vernacular course of two years. 3. Men employed already as catechists, whose limited early advantages were to be supplemented by a year's instruction on subjects selected from the other courses. The Seminary was to be recruited from the station village schools. As there had been a steady increase in Tamil Christian literature, and English was taught only as a classic, there would be time enough for the needed vernacular studies. Students, who left the school too young to be made pastors, were sent to gain experience by teaching village schools, and, subsequently to the establishment of the Normal School of the Vernacular Education Society, were sent for a year or two to that institution.

Higher village schools

The village, village school, and village church all needed to be elevated intellectually. To aid in this, the Prudential Committee, in the year 1865, authorized the establishment of a small boarding-school at each station where there was a resident missionary, to be called the Station school. Each school was allowed an appropriation sufficient for the support of a teacher and eight pupils, and as many pupils might be added as the missionary thought best, provided he could secure their support from his personal friends in India and at home. The school might be for boys, or for girls, or for both. The aim was to give something more than an elementary education to lads of promise, sons of Christian parents, who would be likely to remain in their native districts and become influential in the village congregations and churches. It was also desired to do a good deal more than had been done to create intelligence among the Christian women, and so indirectly to aim a blow at one of the main props of Hindûism — the ignorance of the Hindû women. The plan was cordially approved by the mission, and such schools were put in operation without delay. The one at Tirupûvanam was made a select school of twenty pupils, and in its special relations to the theological training school at Pasumalai seemed likely to solve a problem, which had long perplexed the mission; namely, how they might be enabled to devote their highest educational institution exclusively to the training of young men for spiritual work.

The native pastorate.

The experiment of a native pastorate in the mission dates from 1855. A promising graduate from the Seminary was then ordained as pastor at Mallankinaru. In the fifteen years following, twelve more were ordained. Of these, up to 1872, two had died in the ministry, leaving behind a precious memory; two had left the ministry, and three had changed the scene of their labors. Meanwhile the missionaries had come to feel, not only that the native churches should have the choicest men, but that a native pastor was essential to a native church. Additional experience showed, also, that a disposition for self-support was essential to the prosperity of both church and pastorate. A congregation in the western part of Madura called upon the mission, in 1868, for one of its most valuable men, offering to provide one fourth of his support, and holding out the prospect of an increase. The request was granted; and the mission subsequently voted not to ordain a pastor, in any case, unless there should be a guarantee for at least that proportion of his support.

In the year 1870, the mission readjusted its system of education to the new order of things. The Seminary was modified, so as to be no longer a school for secular education, but a theological school for the purely ministerial education of mature and experienced men, with a course of two or three years' study. The students were to be selected from approved catechists, who were to bring their families with them. At the same time the Girls' Boarding-school at Madura was transferred to Pasumalai, and reorganized as a female seminary for the training of a select class of girls, suitable to become wives of native helpers. Their education was to keep in view these probable future relations, and, so far as was practicable, the same advantages of instruction were to be given to the wives of the catechists mentioned above, as to the members of the female seminary. In this the mission acted on the belief, that the country was advancing in general intelligence, and needed a ministry and churches thoroughly imbued with the Gospel spirit. General education was to be left to the local boarding-schools.

Still further advances.

The result has been all that could have been reasonably expected. The number of native pastors, in 1873, was fifteen. Of these nine had taken the full Seminary course, four the shorter course, and two were educated elsewhere. Although half the pastorates are of not more than four years' standing, the efforts toward a native ministry have had encouraging success. The west church in Madura, already mentioned, increased more than one third in five years, their contributions doubled, they paid the larger part of the pastor's salary, their prayer meetings were well attended, and they were erecting a brick church. The church at Malankinaru, whose first pastor — the first in the mission — was ordained in 1855, pays more than half the salary of its present pastor, sustains its school, has built a new house of worship, and is steadily increasing in numbers and in the grace of benevolence. Of one church of twenty-three members, the pastor reports that all the members have daily family worship. The custom of giving *tenths* has been adopted by all the pastors, and by many of their people. The accessions to the congregations being necessarily from among the heathen, the pastors are reported as active in securing them. One was in the habit of taking volunteers from his church on preaching excursions among the villages.

Early in 1873 the churches and pastors formed three associations for a more convenient performance of ecclesiastical and other duties. It is encouraging that the churches in connection with the Native Evangelical Society stand pledged for the entire salaries of the pastors. The chief obstacle in the way of ordaining pastors has been the belief of the people, that a catechist would cost them less than a pastor. But pastors are more and more sought for, and eight were ordained in the space of three years. Men of all grades of education received calls, but chiefly those of the highest character and talent.

Accession of native pastors.

Albert Barnes, after an experience of twenty-five years as a teacher of the Bible and theology in the Seminary, was ordained pastor of the church at Pasumalai in November, 1871, a position for which he was believed to be eminently prepared. In March of the following year, the churches at Battalagûndu, Dindigul, and Pûlney, each received pastors, and it was most encouraging to notice how appropriately and feelingly the native pastors performed their parts in the ordination services.

It seemed desirable to give such a connected view of the advance in the general character of the work. Other important facts will now be mentioned.

Disturbing influences.

The great India Rebellion of 1857 and 1858, did not extend to the Madras Presidency, and consequently the Madura Mission was not materially disturbed. The civil war in the United States, some years later, stimulated the production of cotton, and so increased the desire for gain, the value of labor, and the cost of living.

The number of regularly organized churches in 1857 was twenty-one, having deacons, and meeting statedly for religious worship and ordinances. Only two native pastors had then been ordained. Six churches were formed in 1856, and six in the following year. The additions by profession, in one of these years, were one hundred and seventy-one, and only fifteen had been excommunicated during the previous seven years. Members were received with caution, and their conduct was generally good, though their temptations were many, and the power of resistance weak. The mission had confidence in regard to the members of the church generally, that they would be owned by Christ as lambs of his fold.

Native churches.

The village congregations were regarded with increased interest. It cost much labor to induce them to break away from idolatry, to abstain from heathen ceremonies, to observe the Sabbath, to attend stated religious worship, and to learn, and cause their children to learn, the great truths of Christianity. But they were helpful to the mission, by furnishing stated places for preaching in the villages, and by bringing men into more favorable position for impression, conviction, and conversion, than the prejudiced heathen under brahminical and family influence. The proportion of church members in the congregations, in 1853, was one to thirteen; in 1855 it was one to ten, and two

Village congregations.

years later nearly one to seven. Mr. Burnell, formerly the printer of the Ceylon mission, but transferred to the Madura mission, was this year ordained as a minister of the Gospel.

The Tamil people possess the oriental fondness for poetry and music. While they may listen impatiently to an address in plain prose, however striking and important the matter, they are captivated by the same thoughts in metrical forms. Mr. Webb, of Dindigul, had given much attention to this subject, and compiled a book of lyrics in Tamil measure, of which an edition of two thousand copies was printed, and other editions have followed. Several selections of the most popular of these lyrics have been circulated as tracts. It has been deemed important in this mission, as among the Mahrattas, to give special attention to the subject of Christian poetry, and the result, in the development of poetical talent among the natives, has been exceeding gratifying.[1]

Native fondness for poetry.

[1] A translation is given of a lyric, said to be the composition of one of the native pastors.

CHORUS.

Than honey's sweetness sweeter is the name of Jesus:
Longing, seeking, running, thou wilt come, O holy Church!

SONG.

1. In the world, with love, He bore distress,
Removing guilt, He put away the curse:
Feel, O my soul!

The last edition of the Lyrics, edited by Mr. Washburn, contains three hundred pieces, many of them of great beauty and poetical merit, by more than thirty different authors. But it is noticeable, in this book, that the lyrics were written almost wholly by natives, only two missionaries being represented. A son of Dr. Caldwell, of Tinnevelly, has put into Tamil metre "Rock of Ages," and Mr. Webb, "Just as I am, without one plea." The natives find the English metres at variance with the genius of their language, and unmanageable.

2. The sinner to save, His life He gladly gave,
Full as the sea, His everlasting grace:
Praise, O my soul!

3. Sovereign Lord! Most glorious, gracious king!
For favor, seek Him with a willing mind;
Thou, O my soul!

4. As the dew of morning, earth shall pass away;
To all eternity, at the feet of God,
Trust, O my soul!

5. Why put your trust in relatives and friends?
Behold! for you is boundless grace with Jesus:
Joy, O my soul!

6. Help in trouble, and in sorrow joy, He gives;
If lovingly you go, embracing, He will keep you:
Long, O my soul!

7. The Name, by earth and heaven praised and sung,
Only take hold on that, and heavenly bliss
Gain, O my soul!

Messrs. William B. Capron and Charles B. White and their wives, arrived in 1857; and Mr. and Mrs. Capron took charge of the boarding-school in Madura during Mrs. Rendall's absence in America, while preparing to occupy their appointed station at Mana Madura. An extract from a letter of Mr. Capron concerning the boarding-school, will be read with interest: —

Girls' boarding-school at Madura.

"A class of eight pupils graduated on the 28th of March, an address well adapted to the occasion being delivered by the principal teacher. These girls are all members of the church, and have become very much endeared to us by their correct deportment, and by the pleasing evidence they give that they are truly children of God. They go back to their villages with a heart to do good, and we are now hearing from them (May 11, at the Pulney Hills) by occasional notes, of their attempts to render themselves useful. Seven of the eight are teaching school, and some of them speak of spending their leisure in teaching the women of the village congregations to read, or in reading to them, and holding prayer-meetings with them. One of Mrs. Capron's proposals to them, on their leaving school, was that they should choose some spot at home for secret prayer, and that on every Wednesday afternoon they should retire there, and remember her, and each other, and the school, at the throne of grace. They remind her, in every note, that they have not forgotten and will not forget their pledge. Some of these girls are from very poor families, and one of them could not think of any retired spot at home except behind the door of the only room of the house; and there, no doubt, she daily resorts for her private devotions.

"The girls have shown much interest in everything they have heard of the revival in America. They often pray that the Lord will pour out his Spirit here, as He has in 'the America country;' and they will, we doubt not, enter heartily into the plan we have formed for the coming term, of a brief noon prayer-meeting, to pray for a revival of religion among them, and in the mission generally."

The mission was reinforced by the arrival of Rev. Edward Chester and wife, and Miss Sarah Ashley, in 1859; and by the return, in the same year, of Mrs. Rendall, Mrs. Noyes, and Mrs. Taylor, from their visits home; and by the arrival of Rev. George T. Washburn and wife, in 1860, and of Rev. David C. Scudder and wife, in 1861. Miss Ashley was married to Mr. William York, Master of the Christian and Vernacular Education Society's school at Madura, in 1864, and died March 23, 1872.

Reinforcements.

The following are mentioned as among the favorable indications of the year 1860, namely: an advance in Scriptural knowledge; an

Encouraging indications.

improved morality; a growing regard for the Sabbath, and for the law of marriage; a decrease in the use of intoxicating drinks; less fondness for going to law; greater interest in improving their houses of worship, and in charitable contributions; a greater disposition in women to attend church, and to study Scripture lessons; and an increased desire among the people to learn to read, and to have their children educated.

"Old Samuel," who died this year in Mr. Taylor's district, deserves a passing notice. He was a native of Tinnevelly, and in his youth a priest in the common demon worship of the country. His zeal for Christ was great from the time of his conversion. While unfitted by his eccentricities for the duties of a regular catechist, his unique dramatic power in exhibiting the absurdities of the common superstitions, and his manifest integrity and boldness, fitted him for evangelistic labor among the heathen. He became well known in the greater part of the Madura district, and somewhat in the Tinnevelly and Tanjore districts. Some would say that he was deficient in good sense; but he knew how to gather and hold an interested audience in a heathen village; and while he made them laugh over their own follies, he would mingle, all through his discourse, the truth as it is in Jesus.

An eccentric native helper.

It will readily be seen, that a true revival among a people feeling the influence of the caste-bound social life of India, is an event of special progress.

Extended revival.

Of course, with the limited amount of Scriptural knowledge possessed by the people, such powerful spiritual results, as are often witnessed where the Gospel has long been enjoyed, could not reasonably be expected. But the close of 1860 and the early part of 1861 did witness a spiritual awakening, analagous in form to the one which resulted in evangelizing the Sandwich Islands, though far less powerful. It began in the north-western part of Tinnevelly, occupied by the Church Missionary Society, bordering on the Tirumangalam station district, and resulted from the ordinary course of missionary labors. It soon began to have a marked effect on the heathen. A member of the Church mission wrote, in November, that one hundred and twenty persons had forsaken idolatry in the villages of his own station, and that six hundred had taken the same step in the villages of an adjoining station; also, that twenty persons were travelling in all parts of his field, holding meetings and preaching the Gospel at their own charge.

Its first appearance within the bounds of the American mission was at Mallankinaru, seventeen miles south of Tirumangalam, in January, 1861. Mr. Herrick received intelligence in that month, which led him to visit the place; and he saw what reminded him more of American revivals, than anything previously seen in the fifteen years of his missionary life. Two young men came to speak to him in private of their sins, and asked him to pray for them. Another young man rose, in a prayer-meeting, and with tears requested prayers. A church member, who had been the first fruit of the Gospel in that place, spoke of his great joy on a day recently spent in fasting and prayer. On a subsequent visit, Mr. Herrick saw further evidence of a genuine work of grace. Cases of disagreement between different members of the church and congregation, some of them of long standing, were healed. A series of meetings was held to pray for a blessing on the new year, and to bring the Gospel before those not accustomed to hear it. The meetings were in the open air in front of the church, and under the light of the full moon; and here the first decisive indications of the revival appeared. Seven or eight women, and about the same number of men, were regarded as hopeful converts.

The fact is not unimportant that the revival commenced at Mallankinaru during the absence of the catechist, and among people of a different caste from the subjects of the revival in Tinnevelly. At a meeting of the "Sungkum," or ministerial association, it soon appeared, that there was an increase of interest in nearly all that part of the field.

Mr. Tracy, the Principal of the Seminary at Pasumalai, has given an account of the revival in that institution, under date of May 27, 1861. He thus writes: —

Revival at the Seminary.

"On the Sabbath preceding the close of the term, the Lord's Supper was administered, three of the students were admitted to the church, and several infants were baptized. The season was one of deep interest, but not more so than we had enjoyed at other times. During family worship in the evening I heard some one come on the verandah sobbing bitterly. I supposed that one of the boys had been stung by a scorpion, not an uncommon occurrence. When we rose from our knees, several of the larger boys came forward supporting a smaller one who was trembling and crying as if in great agony. I now felt sure that my first supposition was correct, but on asking the lad, he replied, 'My sins, oh my sins are piercing me through, I cannot, cannot bear it.' I took him to my room, prayed with him, and tried to point him to Christ, but he could not be comforted. I then sent him back to the Seminary and requested Mr. Barnes, our oldest teacher, to go and see if he could lead him where alone he could find true peace. At this time the students were holding their usual Sabbath evening meeting. Shortly afterwards the sound of loud crying and prayer reached us from the Seminary, and in a few moments Mr. Barnes returned, awe-struck, asking me to come quickly, for he knew not what to do. On reaching the school I found the first-class room crowded with the students and catechists. Some were on their knees with outstretched arms, others prostrate on their faces, some beating their breasts, and others still, in their agony, striking their heads against the floor; all, with loud cries and tears, confessing their sins and praying for pardon. The scene was awe-inspiring.

"Fearing the effects of such intense excitement, I had some removed quietly to their rooms, and this I repeated once or twice, striving, with the aid of others, to direct their minds to the blessed Saviour. At last I had them all brought together, and spent an hour in prayer and singing, but it was well toward midnight before I could leave them and return home. There were few of us that slept much that night. Toward morning the wife of one of the catechists, who had been anything but a praying woman, was deeply affected with a sense of her sins, and her cries for mercy were heard in the stillness of the night to a great distance.

"On Monday an attempt was made at study, but it was impossible, and the day was spent in prayer and conversation with those in distress. At this time probably not more than six or eight among all the students were unaffected. Many continued in deep distress, but during the day some found peace through faith in Christ. In the evening Mr. Capron came, and we commenced a prayer-meeting, but the excitement soon became uncontrollable, and we were obliged to stop and address ourselves to individuals.

"Tuesday was spent much like the preceding day.

In the morning I cautioned all, with good effect, against yielding to mere excitement, and urged them to avoid, as far as possible, giving way to their feelings. They tried, but some, unable to restrain themselves, quietly left the room or were removed, that they might not disturb others. The attempt to go on with the regular exercises of the Seminary was also more successful. Mr. Chester was with us in the evening, and our meeting was one of deep feeling, but of less excitement. A considerable number were rejoicing in hope.

"On Wednesday the seminary committee met for the usual examination at the close of the term, but they could not go on with it. The day was spent principally in religious exercises, and the students were dismissed to their homes, with earnest prayer that the divine blessing might go with them, and make them the means of good to the community.

"I had felt some anxiety lest this visit to their homes should lead them away from Christ; but the reports of their conduct, which I heard from various quarters, have been uniformly favorable, and I rejoice in the hope that a truly divine work has been wrought in many hearts. It deserves notice that the pungent distress, rising in some cases to intense agony, did not in one instance appear to proceed from an apprehension of personal danger, but from a deep sense of the evil of sin committed against a holy but gracious God and Saviour."

The girls' boarding-school at Madura was affected in a similar manner. "Last Thursday evening," wrote Mr. Rendall on the 4th of July, "just after our usual weekly prayer meeting, I was told that the girls in the school had been weeping for a long time, and, with Miss Ashley, I hastened over to ascertain the cause. We found them on their knees in the greatest excitement. It was similar to the state of things in the Pasumalai Seminary just before the end of the last term. God prospered our endeavor to quiet them, and we then conversed and prayed with them. Since that time a number have come frequently to one of us for conversation and prayer."

Revival in the Madura school.

Passing to the western side of the Madura District, we find evidences of the Holy Spirit's special presence in the villages of Periaculam, the station of Mr. Noyes. The annual meeting of the North Local Committee was held in that place, when the native assistants of Pulney, Dindigul, Battalagûndu, and Periaculam came together for examination and mutual conference. The attendance was full, and the devotional meetings, morning and evening, at pastor Seymour's church in the village, were particularly interesting. Mr. Taylor was surprised at the earnestness of some of the native brethren, and deeply affected by their fervent prayers and exhortations. There was a readiness to take part in the exercises, and an unc-

Revival in the Western District.

tion in them, such as he had never before witnessed among the native Christians. He felt that the Lord was with them of a truth, and his heart was warmed, and his hopes in relation to the village work were much encouraged. A work of grace had already begun in a small congregation in a remote part of this district, and the presence of a few native brethren from that vicinity added much to the interest of the meetings.

This small congregation consisted of eight families, numbering thirty-two persons, who were of three different castes. The revival was confined chiefly to young women, of whom only one could read. Soon after the opening of the meeting, they began singing of their own accord, in a very earnest manner but harmoniously, hymns in Tamil metre, expressive of penitence for sin and trust in the Redeemer. They continued singing one hymn after another for twenty minutes, and as they sang they rose upon their knees and wept freely. During prayer, also, and while the Scriptures were read and explained, they showed much feeling. The male members of the congregation were present, and seemed deeply interested, while the heathen about the doors and windows looked on with amazement. There was no confusion or disorder, but the scene was intensely affecting.

Other interesting meetings are on record. The mission reported the additions to the churches on profession as seventy-six in 1860, and ninety-four in 1861.

Periaculam, where Mr. Scudder was stationed, is one of the most populous and influential villages of the Madura District. In this village was a church, one of the few which had a native pastor. The congregation, of more than one hundred, had been sadly divided by a protracted litigation between the two deacons. The quarrel spread until every member of the congregation was arrayed on the one side or the other, and Pastor Seymour said he alone was left between. When Mr. Scudder arrived the case had been decided in court, and one of the deacons had been excommunicated and expressed penitence, but the hostile feeling required time to subside. The enterprising young missionary was putting matters in train for a reformation, and was exciting expectations of uncommon usefulness, when, before the expiration of his first year, on the 19th of November, 1862, he was removed by a sudden and unexpected death, at the age of twenty-seven. He had been to Andipatti, one of his more important outstations, eleven miles southeast, to see a sick catechist, and on returning found the Vaigai river, which he was obliged to cross, swollen with recent rains. Being a good swimmer, and having previously swam the stream at the same point, he did not hesitate now. But he had miscalculated both his own strength and the force of the torrent.

Death of Mr. Scudder.

As soon as he approached the middle of the river he was borne away by the current, and, in sight of one of his catechists, was swept down the stream for a long distance, and suddenly overwhelmed by the flood. This was on Wednesday. His body was found on the following Sabbath at Solavanthan, thirty miles below, and thirteen miles above Madura. Mr. Scudder was buried at the Sanitarium on the Pulney Hills, overlooking his field. During the few months of his missionary life he had been most genial in his intercourse with his associates, most diligent in his application to study, and most earnest and zealous in his efforts to promote the cause of Christ at his station.

CHAPTER XX.

TAMIL PEOPLE ON THE CONTINENT.

THE MADURA MISSION.

1862–1873.

THE hold of idolatry had evidently become loosened on many of the people. Numbers confessed their distrust of it, and the missionary felt a perceptible difference when he went to villages where no Christian labor had been performed. The waning power of superstition was seen in the fact, that very few new temples were erected, while many were falling into decay. In some of the districts visited there was increasing difficulty at the festivals in drawing the idol car. Many said it was not their concern, but that the brahmins might draw it themselves if they chose, and this was openly attributed to a diffusion of Christian truth. At a festival not far from Pasumalai, the manager repeatedly requested the students to withdraw from the vicinity of the car, as the distribution of books and conversations with the people diminished their zeal. More than twice the

Evidences of decline in idolatry.

usual time was consumed in bringing the car to its accustomed place, and it was not accomplished without hiring men from the village. The manager had proposed a reduction in the size of the car, that it might be drawn more easily, but the brahmins had refused.

To the same purport was a feud reported by Mr. Tracy in his neighborhood, between a manager and the brahmins of the temples under his superintendence. He had filled many of the responsible offices with persons of another caste, had represented the brahmins as untrustworthy, and on one occasion described them, in the presence of seminary teachers, as interlopers, with no right to perform the religious ceremonies of the temples, which properly belonged to priests chosen from the other high castes.

As another sign of the times, Mr. Tracy speaks of the shanars, from which caste many of the Tinnevelly Christians came, as much excited in regard to their religious privileges, particularly that of going into the temples as far as the higher castes were allowed to go. They had often expended considerable sums in enlarging and beautifying these temples, in some cases also building temples, into which, or sections of which, they were not allowed to enter as worshippers, though open even to the despised pariahs. They claimed the right of going where any person of good caste might go, and the manager seemed inclined to yield to their claim, as a matter of simple justice. But the brahmins decidedly opposed any such innovation. The shanars were bent on carrying their point, and threatened, if they did not, to throw the brahmins overboard and set up for themselves, or go over in a body to Christianity.

"The introduction of railroads and telegraphic wires," writes a missionary in 1864, "the recent general introduction of Government English schools with English science and literature, even though the Bible is not introduced therewith, and the general introduction of English law into all the courts of the country, are bringing new ideas among the people of India unfavorable to the continuance of the old idolatry. The infidelity, which so often marks the transition period in the belief of a people, is increasing."

One of the chief supports of idolatry.

Mr. Washburn, in approaching Puluey, situated in the extreme northwest of the Madura District, describes what he regarded as one of the grand supports of idolatry, and one of the chief obstacles to the reception of Gospel truth. He says: "Here, as elsewhere, the brahmins have secured the choicest lands. All this waving cultivation, as far as the eye can reach over the plain, is the property of that stone image, whose temple is yonder on the rock; or, to speak more plainly, of its priestly attendants. Were I asked, what are now the chief supports of Hindû idolatry, I would reply, the landed wealth of the temple, and the pecuniary interest of certain non-official portions of the community. Pulney is a sacred town in the eyes of all the Hindûs of South India. It abounds in the most costly temples, rest-houses, and edifices for entertaining pilgrims. Many of them are of hewn granite; each capable of accommodating hundreds of the pilgrims, which yearly fill the town. The pious among the residents have learned to augment their gains and their merits at once, by erecting these spacious structures for the purpose of encouraging pilgrimages."

An itinerant ministry.

The mission had become impressed with the value of *itinerant* labors, as a means of helping on this change in the ideas of the people; and at the annual meeting in May, 1863, divided the missionaries and their native helpers into companies, who should each take their turn for three weeks in such labors.

One of the earliest itineracies was performed by Messrs. Noyes and Washburn, with native helpers, in the villages of Periaculam. The missionary tent was accessible to all from ten in the morning to four in the afternoon, and here they conversed with not a few influential persons. They also preached to large numbers on the encampment ground. In one village of nine hundred houses, it was found that three hundred of the houses belonged to brahmins, and that they were generally rich land-owners, and lived by agriculture and not by their priestly office. They were more accessible and open to conviction, than the same class in the cities.

During a vacation in the Pasumalai Seminary, Mr. Tracy itinerated, with Mr. Chester and several catechists and teachers. They went in four companies, ranging mornings and afternoons within five miles of their encampment, and at noon held a meeting in their tent. In the evenings they went together, and held meetings by moonlight in some of the near villages. Heavy rains compelled them to return, after three days, to Dindigul. They had visited forty villages, held about fifty meetings, preached to nearly two thousand persons, sold a considerable number of books and tracts, and were much encouraged by their reception among the people.

Mr. Rendall, writing in April, 1864, says that, in company with Mr. Burnell, he visited sixty-seven villages connected with his Madura station, and addressed more than four thousand people. The catechists took much interest in this kind of work, and rendered cheerful and efficient aid. In the same year, Mr. Burnell spent twenty days with native helpers, in a preaching tour; had seven encampments, visited one hundred and forty-five villages, and addressed over seven thousand persons. Also, in the same year, Messrs. Taylor and Washburn visited fifty-six villages in the Mandapasalai field, the most southern in the Madura District, and were favorably impressed. Afterwards Messrs. Washburn and Noyes visited more than two hundred villages in the Battalagûndu district, designing to make a thorough exploration of all parts not easily reached by the catechists of the village congregations. They addressed more than six thousand persons, carefully mapped out the field, and took notes for future use.

In 1865, Mr. Washburn described a tour made by himself and Mr. Rendall to one hundred and two villages in his own Battalagûndu district, and sixty-two in that of Madura; the audiences amounting to nine thousand people. "It was a time of hard work, but one very much enjoyed by all. In some encampments, the catechists were obliged to walk long distances, with little rest till late at night, but they always did it cheerfully. I was particularly pleased in noticing the skill they had acquired in addressing large and turbulent crowds, in the village streets. I can see a great improvement in this respect within three years. I doubt whether American ministers would evince more skill, either in managing an audience, or exhibiting religious truth. We sold also between four and five hundred tracts, school-books, and Scripture portions."

A letter from Mr. Chester of Dindigul, gives an account of interesting labors in the itineracy, between the 1st of March and the 4th of May. He was assisted by the catechists of his station, a native pastor, a colporter of the Madras Bible Society, teachers in the mission seminary, and others, and says: "We have had eleven encampments, have worked twenty-nine days, visited four hundred and fourteen villages, and held four hundred and ninety meetings, addressing 17,439 adult hearers, and selling sixty-eight rupees' worth of Scripture portions, tracts, and books." They went out in three and four companies from their encampments, with usually three catechists in each company, aiming to visit every village within six miles of the camping ground. They had, in nearly all cases, most attentive and respectful audiences, with nothing like abuse. Mr. Chester speaks very highly of the native helpers, who labored very hard, but were constantly cheerful and earnest, and most happy when they had most to do, and met with most success. The meetings were "precious seasons." During all this time Mr. Chester was often at his dispensary, performing there the work of three or four days in one, prescribing sometimes for as many as ninety persons in a single day. He had had 1,478 patients, nine hundred and six of them new cases, since the first of January. "This medical work," he says, "pays, with all its toil," giving the missionary favor with all classes of people in the many villages of the station.

The report of the mission for 1866, speaks of the itinerating work as prosecuted with more than the usual interest. There were forty-five encampments, with preaching in 1,209 villages. The number of adult hearers exceeded fifty-nine thousand; and the impression was deepened by the tracts distributed, and the books sold. The visitation in the following year, was to thirteen hundred villages, and more than 57,000 persons heard the truths of the Gospel.

The itineracy had now become a specific department of missionary labor. A sufficient number of tents had been procured; every missionary was expected to itinerate for a longer or shorter period, with a corps of native helpers; and the work was generally found to be a source of much enjoyment to the native brethren. Mr. Capron, after a satisfactory exploration from Mana Madura eastward to the sea, while he speaks of itinerating as hard work, says the helpers returned inspirited, and the more they were out in the field, the more contented and happy they appeared to be.

Accessions to the mission.

Dr. and Mrs. Lord had been transferred to this mission from Ceylon, in 1863. Messrs. Thornton B. Penfield and Hervey C. Hazen, and their wives, joined the mission in 1867 and 1868. Dr. Henry K. Palmer and wife joined in 1869. The Misses Rosella A. Smith, Martha S. Taylor, Sarah Pollock, Carrie Hartley, Mary E. Rendall, and Elizabeth Sisson, joined during the six years following 1866.

At the close of 1867, there were one hundred and sixty-two village congregations, and there were known to be Christians residing in two hundred and fifty-five villages. Religious services were held in one hundred and seventy-five of these places, with preaching once or twice every Sabbath. During that year, the missionaries visited eight hundred villages, and travelled in their missionary tours nearly ten thousand miles. The catechists visited a much larger number, and the Gospel was preached at least once, during the year, to 150,000 people.

Amount of evangelical influence.

The station day school at Dindigul was reported to contain thirty-four brahmins and a number of Mohammedan boys from respectable families. Of the station boarding-schools for girls at Mana Madura it is said: "There can be no more hopeful field for labor than such a school, and it is Mrs. Capron's privilege to have strength and time to devote to it. Probably there is not a happier company, of the same size, in the Madura District; interested in their studies, cheerful in doing their daily task of work, and entering into play with a good deal more than usual zest. It has been specially gratifying to observe the attention of the pupils to religious instruction." The Madura boarding-school for girls, under the superintendence of Mrs. Chandler, aided by Miss Smith, having been thirty years in operation, more than three hundred

Interesting schools.

girls had enjoyed its privileges, and many had died in the faith, and many were wives or mothers of the mission helpers.

The medical branch of the mission.

Dr. Chester preached the Gospel during the year to nearly seven thousand patients, and half as many more of their friends, who had accompanied them. Dr. Cheeseman, the native medical assistant at Madura, treated nearly three thousand patients.

Death of Mrs. Rendall.

Mrs. Rendall, beloved by all, finished her faithful service for Christ in India, and died, after a very brief illness, September 4, 1867, while on her way home with her husband; and her body found its final resting place in the Mediterranean Sea. A few months later, on the 24th of January, 1868, Dr. Lord, having come to the United States greatly prostrated, died at New York. The reader will remember him in connection with both the Ceylon and Madura missions. He suffered much from illness, but gave the strongest evidence of devotion to the cause. When apprised that death was near, he expressed his willingness to go, and calmly yielded his life in the forty-eighth year of his age.

Death of Dr. Lord.

Death and character of Mr. Taylor.

And here I may record also the death of the Rev. Horace S. Taylor, February 3, 1871, at the age of fifty-six, after twenty-seven years of laborious and most faithful service. Excepting Dr. Tracy, he was the oldest member of the mission, having arrived in October, 1844. No other member had the privilege of collecting so many congregations, and of receiving so many converts to the church. At the Mandapasalai station, he gathered about eighteen hundred from the heathen into Christian congregations, and nearly three hundred of these became members of the church. He organized nine village churches, some of them perhaps prematurely; but he looked forward to the time when they would be supplied with native pastors. His mind was active, vigorous, independent, and fertile in resources, so that he was a suggestive and valued correspondent. "He had a decidedly metaphysical turn of mind," wrote Mr. Capron when announcing his death, "which was conspicuous in his writings. But I take more pleasure in remembering, that he was an humble, patient, prayerful laborer in the vineyard. He was a man who lived near to Christ by prayer and the study of the Scriptures; as all could see, who listened to his prayers, or his discourses, his remarks in social meetings, or his conversations with the heathen. He was particularly happy in his occasional expositions of Scripture, in his addresses at the communion table, and in the expression of sympathy and counsel in time of sorrow. I have never heard addresses, which I would more gladly reproduce, than some of his to our missionary circle, as we sat together at the table of our Lord." Says Mr. Rendall, "His simple faith always made him confident and buoyant, even in dark days. His memory in this respect will be very precious to us all. During my eighteen years in Madura, I presume I received nearly a hundred notes from him every year, and I never received one in which he showed the least depression of spirit, or the slightest indication of discouragement."

Mr. Taylor was beloved by his people. His death occurred at the sanitarium on the Pulney Hills; and Mr. Herrick, as he went to Mandapasalai to give the people notice of the event, saw abundant evidence of their warm attachment to their missionary. Stopping a moment to inform a small Christian congregation, which had been under Mr. Taylor's care, a poor widow exclaimed, weeping, "I have no father left." Four miles from the station, he met a woman, weeping, who had been there, and had heard of the death of her missionary.

Prospective influence of native women.

The social life of India cannot be elevated without the coöperation of native women, and that coöperation cannot be expected, to any great extent, among the middle and higher classes, until husbands, fathers, and brothers become impressed with the value of education to their wives, daughters, and sisters. There is now a considerable and increasing number of women who have been educated in the mission schools, and the reports concerning them augur well for the future.

Mrs. Capron, at Mana Madura, in 1868, had gathered into her school some large girls and women, and had prospered in her efforts to induce them to embrace the truth themselves, and labor for the good of others. Believing that some of them could speak Gospel truth intelligently, she sent them out, two and two, to talk with their heathen sisters, going herself with the least experienced party. Their reports were sometimes of willing listeners, sometimes of scoffers. "I have been much interested," she says, "to see how much more the things said by my native companions seemed to strike the mind, and give hope of a permanent impression, than my own words. In one case, a young girl, after I had spoken at some length of the need of a Saviour's death, and met with only a respectful assent, immediately went over the same ground, and adding here and there an apt illustration from native customs, that I never should have thought of, won the closest attention, and did, I trust, some lasting good. I have also been struck with the keenness of their satire on idol worship; and on one occasion the emphatic declaration, 'And such were we, but we are made clean by Jesus' blood and are going to heaven,' was thrilling." The idea among the native women, that young women had come *to them* from America, for the sole purpose of benefiting them, was of itself a power for good. Miss Pollock, writing from Mandapasalai, says: "Everywhere I have been welcome. Everywhere I have found some willing listeners to the truth. The people have readily fallen in with the idea of my working with the women *alone*. When I visit a place, although the men usually come to see me for a few minutes, and pay their respects, whenever I tell them I am ready to begin my talk with the women they quickly withdraw, and leave us to ourselves. I am treated with perfect respect." Bible women were accustomed to go from Pasumalai to the near villages, and were usually accompanied by two or three women of the catechist families, who were thus initiated into the work. The native festivals offered good opportunities, as at least half who attended them were women. The people manifested some surprise, but no displeasure, at seeing Christian women selling books and talking with women and girls, and remarked, that there must be some earnestness among the Christians to spread their views.

Mr. Washburn was put in charge of the seminary in 1870. Mr. Tracy was then in America for the benefit of his health, and on his return assumed the care of the station and high school at Tirupuvanam.

The semi-nary and high school.

The death of Mrs. Rendall has been mentioned. The only companion of her husband, on his return to India, was his daughter Mary. Speaking of a tour he subsequently made with her,

A missionary daughter.

in the neighborhood of Periakulam, he says: "My daughter was with me, and I never knew women in India more interested in listening to the truth, than some of the audiences she met in that tour. Several women were induced to learn to read, and many, both Christians and heathen, showed great affection for her, and interest in listening to the story of Christ. Once she addressed fifty women, all assembled in one courtyard, and there would have been many more had there been room. An old woman said, at the close of the meeting, that in her heart she often prayed to the true God, though she did not know who or where He was; but hereafter she would pray to Jesus, as He must be the true God, and she had heard of his love to them.

Mr. Rendall's closing paragraph will not fail to interest the reader: "While engaged in this work, one day was given up for the ordination of catechist Isaac over the church at Kambam. The occasion was a memorable one for that church. The church-members, and all the congregation, are united in their pastor, and I was much pleased to notice the progress made by this people in order and knowledge during the seven months Isaac had been with them. Forty-three Christian women were at a meeting conducted by my daughter, and more than half of them were well prepared in advanced Bible lessons. The pastor's wife had been most active in instructing the women, and had proved herself a real helpmeet to her husband in his work. A number of the younger women were anxious to learn to read, and they will without doubt redeem the pledge they gave in this matter, as this faithful woman will be instant in season and out of season in teaching them. The Kambam church has a good plan for promoting benevolence, and for reaching their heathen neighbors. They will give half of their pastor's salary at once, and I hope the time is not far distant when they will give the whole. We returned from our tour greatly encouraged, and with the full assurance that God's name will be glorified throughout that station in the conversion of many souls."

Mr. Taylor gives an impressive view of the field of labor that is opening to women.

The field for women.

"I will give no details of the work of the young ladies, for it is their part to write for themselves, but having the station in charge, and opportunities for knowing, it is proper that I should note some of the results as they are manifest to me, and particularly the *indirect* influence of such labors on the men.

"First, I notice that the ladies have no difficulty in gathering audiences. They gather these audiences of women and children in private houses, or, where we have them, in our little churches and school-houses, and those as large perhaps as I could gather among the men. Nor have I observed any special difficulty in making the object of the mission of young ladies here to be understood, and the simple fact that they leave home and friends to come here, and go from village to village and from house to house to look after the women and children, starts the feeling that there must be a reality in the religion they teach.

"I observe two particulars, in which they seem to have some special advantage. One is, that their presentation of the Gospel can be more immediate, direct, and quiet than ours. There is a class of men who will take the defensive if met by me, and be glad of the chance for a discussion, who will not do this, if the truth comes from a woman. The peculiarly humble character of these agents (in their estimation) does not stir their pride, and the acknowledged benevolence of their work also further disarms opposition.

"The other advantage is, that their work is an attack upon the weak side of the heathenism of this country. The Christian woman comes to her with the announcement that she also has a soul. She is told that there is a Saviour and a heaven for *her*, and the good news of the Gospel is unfolded. The missionary of their own sex approaches no guarded foe, but the unarmed, yet sensitive, women of Hindûism. Unrestricted she enters the heart of the household, and can there touch the most vital springs of life, and, with the Saviour's blessing, awaken desires not easily eradicated.

"When the women are thus moved, the men cannot remain as they were. Women here are indeed uneducated, but they are not uninfluential. They will not, simply because they are women, conceal what they have thus learned from one of their own sex. Their facile tongues tell to eager ears, around and outside, what they have learned within doors. Thus the whole community is influenced by this humble attack upon its idolatry. The effect upon the men of this work among the women, is like that of a strong division in a battle coming unexpectedly upon the enemy's rear. The men are taken unawares, and there is such a subduing of tone as does not always follow when they meet us preaching in their streets."

Death of Mr. Penfield.

The Rev. Thornton B. Penfield died at Pasumalai on the 19th of August, 1871, at the age of thirty-six. He had been a member of the mission less than four years and a half. Mr. Washburn says: "His death was a triumph of faith, cloudless as the sunshine that glowed about him."

Native associations.

Associated power is a characteristic of evangelical religion, both at home and abroad, and its gradual introduction is one of the interesting features of the mission. The "Madura Native Evangelical Society" was formed about twenty years ago. In its first few years it supported catechists, but became at length an auxiliary to the churches in the support of their pastors, and might be more appropriately called the "Madura Home Missionary Society." It is understood that this society, in connection with the churches, will pay the salaries of all the native pastors. Its income in 1859 was one hundred and twenty-five rupees; in 1867 it was five hundred and sixty-five rupees; and in 1872 it was nine hundred and sixty-five rupees. Its importance is felt throughout all the congregations. Money is regularly and cheerfully paid to it; even the poor in remote villages sending in their mites.

Another native institution is the "Madura Widows' Aid Society," designed to extend pecuniary aid to the widows and children of its deceased members. Each member pays an entrance fee and a monthly subscription. Its income in 1869 was nine hundred rupees, its members were one hundred and twenty-five, and the amount of its funds was 4,477 rupees.

Summary view.

Our history closes with 1873, the fortieth year from the commencement of the mission. It then numbered eleven stations, one hundred and forty-two outstations or village congregations, eleven missionaries, one physician, fifteen female assistant missionaries, sixteen native pastors, one hundred and five catechists, twelve readers, six seminary and boarding-school teachers, eighty-five school-masters, and twenty-three school mistresses; total number of pupils in the schools, 2,672.

Of churches there were thirty-one, to which one hundred and twenty-five members were added by profession during the year. The number of members received from the beginning had been 2,479, of whom 1,633 were living and in good standing. Of the 7,393 in the village congregations, 2,150 were men, 2,020 were women, and 3,223 children.

Decline of heathenism.

"There seems to be but one opinion," says the report of the mission for 1872, "as to the decreasing influence of heathenism. With the exception of an expensive building within the temple at Madura, we hear of no erection of any new temple. A respectable native, who has charge of the accounts of the temple in Madura, stated, of his own knowledge, that the prestige and revenues of that temple, the most famous in Southern India, were continually decreasing, while Christianity, he said, was on the increase, and must ultimately prevail throughout the country. Another native gentleman, who has the management of the temple funds in Tirupûvanam, informed us, a short time ago, that the temple officials had to buy the necessaries for their worship in the bazaar, from day to day, on account of the poverty of the temple. In another temple, where formerly two or three hundred sheep were annually sacrificed at the principal festival, now only one or two are offered. In several other places in the same neighborhood, festivals formerly celebrated have been given up. These cases are mentioned as evidence of the gradual decay of heathenism in this District, and the same is probably true of the country at large. Heathenism is not dead, and will not die easily, but it seems evident that the Lord is preparing the way for the redemption of the millions of India. The Brahmist movement, which for a while seemed so hopeful in its tendency towards Christianity, appears now to have reached its climax, and to be receding towards Hindûism."

"Seeing the changes God has wrought in these forty years by his blessing on continued labors," says the mission in its last Report, "we are encouraged to go forward hopefully, trustfully waiting, and expecting the salvation of the whole District."

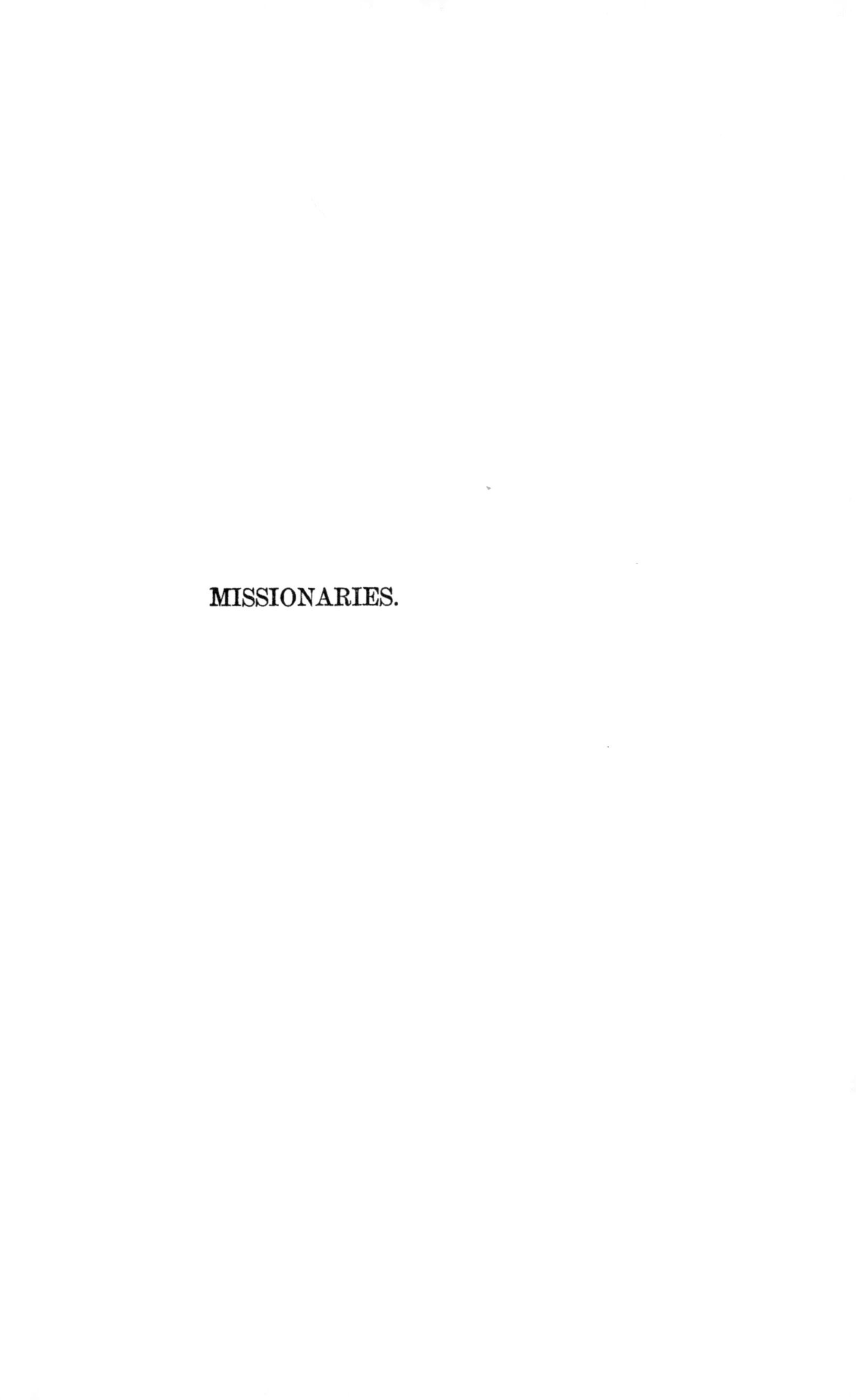

MISSIONARIES.

MISSIONARIES.[1]

WHEN no date occurs on the right hand column, it is because the missionary is still connected with the field.

When the date of the wife's arrival in the field precedes that of the husband, the explanation is, that the wife had been connected with the mission as a teacher previous to marriage.

The asterisk (*) placed before a name, denotes that the person is deceased. When placed before a *date*, in the right hand column, it denotes that the person died *at the time there indicated*, and in the field.

It should be specially noted, that the table is designed to state only the time of a missionary's residence in the field. Absences for health, if of no long duration, are not noted.

I. MISSION TO THE MAHRATTAS.

ORDAINED MISSIONARIES.	WIVES OF MISSIONARIES.	TIME OF ENTERING.	TIME OF LEAVING.
*Gordon Hall . . .	. . . .	Feb. 11, 1813.	*Mar. 20, 1826.
	*Mrs. Margaret Lewis Hall	Dec. 19, 1816.	July 30, 1825.
*Samuel Nott . . .	. . . .	Feb. 11, 1813.	Sept. 7, 1815.
	Mrs. Roxana P. Nott . .	Feb. 11, 1813.	Sept. 7, 1815.
*Samuel Newell . .	. . . .	March 7, 1814.	*May 30, 1821.
	*Mrs. Harriet Newell . .	Died at Sea,	Nov. 30, 1822.
	*Mrs. Philomela Newell . [afterwards Mrs. Garrett]	Feb. 23, 1818.	Oct. 29, 1836.
*Horatio Bardwell, D.D.	. . . .	Nov. 1, 1816.	Jan. 22, 1821.
	Mrs. Rachel Bardwell . .	Nov. 1, 1816.	Jan. 22, 1821.
*John Nichols . . .	. . . .	Feb. 23, 1818.	*Dec. 9, 1824.
	Mrs. Elizabeth Nichols .	Feb. 23, 1818.	Oct. 19, 1826.
*Allen Graves . . .	. . . .	Feb. 23, 1818.	*Dec. 30, 1843.
	Mrs. Mary Graves . . .	Feb. 23, 1818.	*Mar. 23, 1866.
*Edmund Frost . .	[See Ceylon and Madura Missions]	June 28, 1824.	*Oct. 18, 1825.
	Mrs. Clarissa Frost [afterwards, successively, Mrs. Woodward and Mrs. Todd]	June 28, 1824.	*June 1, 1837.

[1] This table was compiled by the Rev. John A. Vinton, of Winchester, Mass.

MISSION TO THE MAHRATTAS. — Continued.

Ordained Missionaries.	Wives of Missionaries.	Time of Entering.	Time of Leaving.
*David Oliver Allen, D.D.	. . . .	Nov. 27, 1827.	1852.
	*Mrs. Myra W. Allen . .	Nov. 27, 1827.	*Feb. 5, 1832.
	*Mrs. Orpah Allen [formerly Miss Graves]	Sept. 10, 1834.	*June 5, 1842.
	*Mrs. Azubah C. Allen [formerly Miss Condit of the Borneo Mission]	Dec. 12, 1843.	*June 11, 1844.
*Cyrus Stone . . .	. . . .	Dec. 29, 1827.	June 20, 1838.
	*Mrs. Atossa Stone . .	Dec. 29, 1827.	*Aug. 7, 1833.
	Mrs. Abigail K. Stone . .	Sept. 10, 1834.	June 20, 1838.
*William Hervey . .	. . . .	March 7, 1831.	*May 13, 1832.
	*Mrs. Elizabeth H. Hervey	March 7, 1831.	*May 3, 1831.
William Ramsey . .	. . . .	March 7, 1831.	July 5, 1834.
	Mrs. Mary Ramsey . . .	March 7, 1831.	*June 11, 1834.
Hollis Read	. . . .	March 7, 1831.	Mar. 18, 1835.
	Mrs. Caroline Read . . .	March 7, 1831.	Mar. 18, 1835.
George W. Boggs . .	. . . .	Sept. 14, 1832.	Dec. 29, 1838.
	Mrs. Isabella W. Boggs .	Sept. 14, 1832.	Dec. 29, 1838.
*Sendol B. Munger .	. . . .	Sept. 10, 1834.	*July 23, 1868.
	*Mrs. Maria L. Munger .	Sept. 10, 1834.	*Mar. 12, 1846.
	*Mrs. Mary E. Munger .	Nov. 17, 1854.	*June 8, 1856.
	Mrs. Sarah S. C. Munger	March 3, 1868.	Sept. 24, 1868.
Amos Abbott . . .	. . . .	Oct. 15, 1834.	July 29, 1847.
	[Second residence] . . .	Sept. 15, 1857.	March, 1869.
	Mrs. Anstress Abbott . .	Oct. 15, 1834.	July 29, 1847.
	[Second residence] . . .	Sept. 18, 1857.	March, 1869.
*Henry Ballantine .	. . . .	Oct. 11, 1835.	Nov. 9, 1865.
	*Mrs. Elizabeth Ballantine	Oct. 11, 1835.	Dec. 1, 1865.
*Ebenezer Burgess .	. . . .	Aug. 10, 1839.	1854.
	*Mrs. Mary Burgess . .	Aug. 10, 1839.	*June 24, 1842.
	*Mrs. Abigail Burgess .	Feb. 27, 1847.	*April 26, 1853.
*Ozro French . . .	. . . .	Aug. 10, 1839.	July 19, 1849.
	Mrs. Jane H. French . .	Aug. 10, 1839.	July 19, 1849.
*Robert W. Hume .	. . . .	Aug. 10, 1839.	*Sept. 20, 1854.
	Mrs. Hannah D. Hume .	Aug. 10, 1839.	Sept. 20, 1854.
Royal G. Wilder . .	. . . .	Sept. 20, 1846.	1857.
	Mrs. Eliza J. Wilder . .	Sept. 20, 1846.	1857.
Samuel B. Fairbank .	. . . .	Sept. 20, 1846.	
	*Mrs. Abbie A. Fairbank	Sept. 20, 1846.	*Aug. 21, 1852.
	Mrs. Mary Fairbank . .	Jan. 12, 1857.	
Allen Hazen, D. D. .	. . . .	Feb. 27, 1847.	
	Mrs. Martha R. Hazen .	Feb. 27, 1847.	
William Wood . . .	. . . .	Jan. 19, 1848.	
	*Mrs. Lucy Maria Wood .	Jan. 19, 1848.	*Aug. 13, 1851.
	*Mrs. Eliza W. Wood . .	Jan. 12, 1857.	*Nov. 18, 1859.
	Mrs. Eliza Maria Wood .	Aug. 3, 1865.	
George Bowen . . .	. . . .	Jan. 19, 1848.	Oct. 30, 1855.
Lemuel Bissell, D. D.	. . . .	Aug. 27, 1851.	
	Mrs. Mary Elizabeth Bissell	Aug. 27, 1851.	
William P. Barker .	. . . .	Dec. 15, 1853.	1869.
	*Mrs. Lucelia U. Barker .	Dec. 15, 1853.	*Jan. 27, 1864.
Samuel C. Dean . .	. . . .	Jan. 12, 1857.	1867.
	Mrs. Elizabeth A. Dean .	Jan. 12, 1857.	1867.
Charles Harding . .	. . . .	Jan. 12, 1857.	
	*Mrs. Julia M. Harding .	Jan. 12, 1857.	*Feb. 11, 1867.
	Mrs. Elizabeth D. Harding	January, 1870.	
Henry James Bruce .	. . . .	March 3, 1863.	
	Mrs. Hephzibah P. Bruce	March 3, 1863.	

MISSION TO THE MAHRATTAS. — CONTINUED.

ORDAINED MISSIONARIES.	WIVES OF MISSIONARIES.	TIME OF ENTERING.	TIME OF LEAVING.
Henry W. Ballantine	. . . .	March 3, 1863.	April 30, 1865.
	Mrs. Mary E. Ballantine .	March 3, 1863.	April 30, 1865.
*William W. Chapin	. . . .	May 19, 1864.	*Mar. 22, 1865.
	Mrs. Catharine I. Chapin	May 19, 1864.	Dec. 1, 1865.
Wm. Henry Atkinson	. . . .	Dec. 18, 1867.	
	Mrs. Calista Atkinson . .	Dec. 18, 1867.	
Spencer R. Wells . .	. . . .	Nov. 13, 1869.	
	Mrs. Mary Wells . . .	Nov. 13, 1869.	
Charles W. Park . .	. . . .	Sept. 16, 1870.	
	Mrs. Anna Maria Park .	Sept. 16, 1870.	
Richard Winsor . .	. . . .	June 22, 1871.	
	Mrs. Mary C. Winsor . .	June 22, 1871.	
ASSISTANT MISSIONARIES.			
*James Garrett . .	. . . .	May 9, 1821.	*July 16, 1831.
	*Mrs. Philomela Garrett . [formerly Mrs. Newell]	Feb. 23, 1818.	Oct. 29, 1831.
*William C. Sampson	. . . .	Nov. 22, 1833.	*Dec. 22, 1835.
	Mrs. Mary L. Sampson .	Nov. 22, 1833.	June, 1836.
George W. Hubbard .	. . . .	Sept. 10, 1834.	June 20, 1837.
	Mrs. Emma Hubbard . .	Sept. 10, 1834.	June 20, 1837.
Elijah A. Webster .	. . . .	Oct. 11, 1835.	1842.
	Mrs. Marietta Webster .	Oct. 11, 1835.	1842.
	*Miss Cynthia Farrar . .	Dec. 29, 1827.	*Jan. 25, 1862.
	Miss Arpah Graves . . .	April 10, 1834.	*June 5, 1842.
	Miss Azubah Condit . .	Dec. 12, 1843.	June 11, 1844.
	Miss Harriet S. Ashley .	Dec. 14, 1871.	

II. MISSION TO CEYLON.

*James Richards . .	. . . .	October, 1816.	*Aug. 3, 1822.
	*Mrs. Sarah Richards . .	October, 1816.	Sept. 17, 1823.
*Edward Warren . .	. . . .	Oct. 15, 1816.	*Aug. 11, 1818.
*Benjamin C. Meigs .	. . . .	Oct. 2, 1816.	October, 1857.
	Mrs. Sarah Maria Meigs .	Oct. 2, 1816.	Jan. 16, 1840.
*Daniel Poor, D. D. .	[See Madura Mission] . .	Oct. 15, 1816.	*Feb. 3, 1855.
	*Mrs. Susan Poor . . .	Oct. 15, 1816.	*May 7, 1821.
	Mrs. Ann K. Poor . . .	Jan. 21, 1823.	October, 1835.
*Miron Winslow, D. D.	[See Madras Mission] . .	Feb. 18, 1820.	*Oct. 22, 1864.
	*Mrs. Harriet L. Winslow	Feb. 18, 1820.	*Jan. 14, 1833.
*Levi Spaulding, D. D.	. . . .	Feb. 18, 1820.	*June 18, 1873.
	Mrs. Mary L. Spaulding .	Feb. 18, 1820.	
*Henry Woodward .	. . . .	Feb. 3, 1820.	*Aug. 3, 1834.
	*Mrs. Lydia Woodward .	Feb. 3, 1820.	*Nov. 24, 1825.
	*Mrs. Clarissa Woodward [formerly Mrs. Frost, afterwards Mrs. Todd]	Oct. 12, 1826.	*June 1, 1837.
*John Scudder, M. D.	[See Madura Mission]		
	*Mrs. Harriet Scudder .	Dec. 17, 1819.	Sept. 21, 1836.
	[See Madras Mission]	Dec. 17, 1819.	Sept. 21, 1836.

MISSION TO CEYLON. — Continued.

Ordained Missionaries.	Wives of Missionaries.	Time of Entering.	Time of Leaving.
*George Henry Apthorp	. . . .	Oct. 28, 1833.	*June 8, 1845.
	*Mrs. Mary Apthorp	Oct. 28, 1833.	*Sept. 3, 1849.
William Todd	[See Madura Mission]	Oct. 28, 1833.	July 21, 1834.
	*Mrs. Lucy Todd	Oct. 28, 1833.	July 21, 1834.
Henry R. Hoisington	[See Madura Mission]	Oct. 28, 1833.	March 5, 1850.
	Mrs. Nancy Hoisington	Oct. 28, 1833.	March 5, 1850.
Samuel Hutchings	[See Madras Mission]	Oct. 28, 1833.	April, 1842.
	Mrs. Elizabeth C. Hutchings	Oct. 28, 1833.	April, 1842.
	[See Madras Mission]		
James Read Eckard	At Madura, 1835–1837	March 5, 1834.	Feb. 9, 1835.
	Returned to Ceylon	1837.	Sept., 1843.
	Mrs. Margaret E. Eckard	March 5, 1834.	Feb., 1835.
	Returned to Ceylon	1837.	Sept., 1843.
*John M. S. Perry	. . . .	Sept. 24, 1835.	*Mar. 13, 1837.
	*Mrs. Harriet J. Perry	Sept. 24, 1835.	*Mar. 13, 1837.
*Samuel G. Whittelsey	. . . .	April 1, 1842.	*Mar. 10, 1847.
	Mrs. Anna C. Whittelsey	April 1, 1842.	1848.
Edward Cope	[See Madura Mission]	January, 1840.	April, 1849.
	Mrs. Emily K. Cope	January, 1840.	April, 1849.
John Curtis Smith	. . . .	April 1, 1842.	May 15, 1873.
	*Mrs. Eunice T. Smith	April 1, 1842.	*May 9, 1842.
	*Mrs. Mary Smith [formerly Mrs. John Steele]	October, 1843.	May 15 1873.
	[See Madura Mission]		
*Robert Wyman	. . . .	April 1, 1842.	*Jan. 13, 1845.
	Mrs. Martha E. Wyman	April 1, 1842.	Dec. 27, 1844.
Adin H. Fletcher	. . . .	June 1, 1846.	1850.
	Mrs. Elizabeth W. Fletcher	June 1, 1846.	1850.
William W. Howland	. . . .	May, 1846.	
	Mrs. Susan R. Howland	May, 1846.	
William W. Scudder	[See Arcot Mission]	April, 1847.	1852.
	*Mrs. Catharine E. Scudder	April, 1847.	*Mar. 11, 1849.
Eurotas P. Hastings	. . . .	April, 1847.	
	Mrs. Anne C. Hastings	Oct. 16, 1853.	
Joseph T. Noyes	[See Madura Mission]	March 6, 1849.	1853.
	Mrs. Elizabeth A. Noyes	March 6, 1849.	1853.
Cyrus T. Mills	. . . .	March 1, 1849.	Sept., 1853.
	Mrs. Susan L. Mills	March 1, 1849.	Sept., 1853.
*Marshall D. Sanders	. . . .	March 12, 1852.	*Aug. 29, 1871.
	*Mrs. Georgiana Sanders	March 12, 1852.	*Nov. 2, 1868.
	Mrs. Caroline Z. Sanders	July 4, 1871.	October, 1871.
*Nathan L. Lord, M.D	[See Madura Mission]	June 9, 1853.	May, 1858.
	Mrs. Laura W. Lord	June 9, 1853.	May, 1858.
Milan H. Hitchcock	[See Mission to Armenians]	April 28, 1858.	Autumn, 1860.
	Mrs. Lucy A. Hitchcock	April 28, 1858.	Autumn, 1860.
James Quick	. . . .	April 30, 1858.	Nov. 27, 1868.
	Mrs. Maria E. Quick	April 30, 1858.	Nov. 27, 1868.
James A. Bates	. . . .	April 21, 1861.	October, 1863.
	Mrs. Sarah A. Bates	April 21, 1861.	October, 1863.
William E. De Riemer	. . . .	March 16, 1869.	
	Mrs. Emily F. De Riemer	March 16, 1869.	
Thomas S. Smith	. . . .	July 4, 1871.	
	Mrs. Emily M. Smith	July 4, 1871.	
Samuel W. Howland	. . . .	1873.	
	Mrs. E. R. Howland	1873.	

MISSION TO CEYLON. — CONTINUED.

Missionary Physicians.		Time of Entering.	Time of Leaving.
*Nathan Ward, M. D.	. . . .	Oct. 28, 1833.	1847.
	Mrs. Hannah W. Ward .	Oct. 28, 1833.	1847.
Samuel F. Green, M. D.	. . . .	October, 1847.	
	Mrs. Margaret P. Green .	October, 1862.	
Assistant Missionaries.			
Eastman S. Minor .	. . . .	March 5, 1834.	Spring, 1851.
	*Mrs. Lucy B. Minor . .	March 5, 1834.	*June 29, 1837.
	Mrs. Judith M. Minor .	Jan. 1, 1840.	Spring, 1851.
Thomas S. Burnell .	[See Madura Mission] . .	Feb. 27, 1849.	Autumn, 1855.
	Mrs. Martha Burnell . .	Feb. 27, 1849.	Autumn, 1855.
	Miss Eliza Agnew . . .	Jan. 27, 1840.	
	Miss Sarah F. Brown . .	Jan. 27, 1840.	August, 1841.
	*Miss Jane E. Lathrop . [afterwards Mrs. Cherry]	Jan. 27, 1840.	June, 1840.
	Mary Ann Capell [afterwards Mrs. Muzzy]	May, 1846.	Feb. 1, 1848.
	Miss Harriet E. Townsend	Dec. 18, 1867.	
	Miss Hester A. Hillis . .	May, 1870.	
	Miss Susan R. Howland .	1873.	

III. MADURA MISSION.

Ordained Missionaries.	Wives of Missionaries.	Time of Entering.	Time of Leaving.
William Todd . . .	. . . .	July 31, 1834.	Feb. 28, 1839.
	*Mrs. Lucy Todd . . .	July 31, 1834.	*Sept. 11, 1835.
	*Mrs. Clarissa Todd . . [formerly Mrs. Frost and Mrs. Woodward]	Dec. 22, 1836.	*June 1, 1837.
Henry R. Hoisington	[See Ceylon Mission] . .	July 31, 1834.	Feb. 1835.
James R. Eckard . .	[See Ceylon Mission] . .	Feb. 9, 1835.	Summer, 1837.
	Mrs. Margaret E. Eckard	Feb. 9, 1835.	Summer, 1837.
Alanson C. Hall . .	. . . .	Oct. 18, 1835.	Sept., 1836.
	*Mrs. Frances A. Hall .	Oct. 18, 1835.	*Jan. 2, 1836.
*John Jay Lawrence	. . . .	Oct. 18, 1835.	*Dec. 20, 1846.
	Mrs. Mary H. Lawrence .	Oct. 18, 1835.	1847.
*Daniel Poor, D. D. .	[See Ceylon Mission] . .	Oct. 18, 1835.	October, 1841.
	Mrs. Ann Poor	Mar. 16, 1836.	October, 1841.
	[See Ceylon Mission] . .		
*Robert O. Dwight .	. . . .	April 22, 1836.	*Jan. 8, 1844.
	*Mrs. Mary B. Dwight . [afterwards Mrs. Winslow]	April 22, 1836.	Mar. 12, 1845.
Henry Cherry . .	. . . .	Mar. 21, 1837.	1850.
	*Mrs. Charlotte K. Cherry	Mar. 21, 1837.	*Nov. 4, 1837.
	*Mrs. Jane E. Cherry . .	January, 1840.	*Jan. 19, 1844.
	Mrs. Henrietta Cherry .	Nov. 9, 1844.	1850.
Edward Cope . . .	[See Ceylon Mission] . .	May 10, 1837.	January, 1840.
	Mrs. Emily K. Cope . .	May 10, 1837.	January, 1840.
Nathaniel M. Crane .	. . . .	May 10, 1837.	May, 1845.
	Mrs. Julia A. J. Crane .	May 10, 1837.	May, 1845.

MADURA MISSION. — Continued.

Ordained Missionaries.	Wives of Missionaries.	Time of Entering.	Time of Leaving.
Clarendon F. Muzzy .	. . . .	May 10, 1837.	May, 1857.
	*Mrs. Semantha B. Muzzy	May 10, 1837.	*Dec. 3, 1846.
	Mrs. Mary Ann Muzzy . [formerly Miss Capell]	Feb. 1, 1848	May, 1857.
William Tracy, D. D.	. . . .	Oct. 9, 1837.	
	Mrs. Emily F. Tracy . .	Oct. 9, 1837.	
Ferdinand D. W. Ward	[See Madras Mission] . .	Oct. 9, 1837.	Early in 1843.
	Mrs Jane Shaw Ward .	Oct. 9, 1837.	Early in 1843.
*Horace S. Taylor .	. . . .	Oct. 10, 1844.	*Feb. 3, 1871.
	Mrs. Martha S. Taylor .	Oct. 10, 1844.	
James Herrick . . .	. . . .	April 29, 1846.	
	Mrs. Elizabeth H. Herrick	April 29, 1846.	
Edward Webb . . .	. . . .	April 29, 1846.	July 12, 1864.
	Mrs. Nancy A. Foote Webb	April 29, 1846.	July 12, 1864.
John Rendall . . .	. . . .	April 29, 1846.	
	*Mrs. Jane B. Rendall .	April 29, 1846.	*Sept. 4, 1867.
George W. McMillan	. . . .	July, 1846.	Nov. 8, 1854.
	Mrs. Rebecca N. McMillan	July, 1846.	Nov. 8, 1854.
John E. Chandler .	. . . .	April, 1847.	
	Mrs. Charlotte M. Chandler	April, 1847.	
George Ford . . .	. . . .	April, 1847.	1853.
	Mrs. Ann Jennet Ford .	April, 1847.	1853.
Charles Little . . .	. . . .	May, 1848.	Feb., 1859.
	*Mrs. Amelia Little . .	May, 1848.	*July 18, 1848.
	Mrs. Susan R. Little . .	1854.	1859.
Joseph T. Noyes . .	[See Ceylon Mission] . .	1853.	
	Mrs. Elizabeth A. Noyes .	1853.	
*Nathan L. Lord, M. D.	[See Ceylon Mission] . .	Dec., 1863.	March, 1867.
	Mrs. Laura W. Lord . .	Dec., 1863.	March, 1867.
Thomas S. Burnell .	[See Ceylon Mission] . .	Sept., 1855.	
	Mrs. Martha S. Burnell .	Sept., 1855.	
William B. Capron .	. . . .	April 6, 1857.	
	Mrs. Sarah B. Capron . .	April 6, 1857.	
Charles T. White . .	. . . .	April 4, 1857.	1869.
	Mrs. Anna Maria White .	April 4, 1857.	1869.
Edward Chester . .	. . . .	May, 1859.	
	Mrs. Sophia Chester . .	May, 1859.	
George T. Washburn	. . . .	May 1, 1860.	
	Mrs. Eliza E. Washburn .	May 1, 1860.	
*David C. Scudder .	. . . .	July, 1861.	*Nov. 19, 1862.
	Mrs. Harriet L. Scudder .	July, 1861.	May, 1863.
*Thornton B. Penfield	. . . .	May, 1867.	*Aug. 19, 1871.
	Mrs. Charlotte E. Penfield	May, 1867.	
Hervey C. Hazen . .	. . . .	January, 1868.	1869.
	Mrs. Ida Julia Hazen . .	January, 1868.	1869.
William S. Howland .	. . . .	1873.	
	Mrs. Mary L. Howland .	1873.	
John E. Chandler . .	. . . .	1873.	
	Mrs. Jennie E. Chandler .	1873.	

MADURA MISSION. — CONTINUED.

MISSIONARY PHYSICIANS.		TIME OF ENTERING.	TIME OF LEAVING.
*John Steele, M. D. .	[See Ceylon Mission] . .	May 10, 1837.	*Oct. 6, 1842.
	Mrs. Mary Steele . . . [afterwards Mrs. Smith]	May 10, 1837.	October, 1843.
Charles S. Shelton, M.D.	. . . .	Mar. 23, 1849.	May 7, 1856.
	Mrs. Henrietta M. Shelton	Mar. 23, 1849.	May 7, 1856.
Henry K. Palmer, M.D.	. . . .	March 5, 1869.	
	Mrs. Flora Day Palmer .	March 5, 1869.	
ASSISTANT MISSIONARIES.			
*Alfred North . . .	Form. of Singapore Mission	Jan. 1, 1844.	1847.
	*Mrs. Minerva North . .	Jan. 1, 1844.	*Jan. 13, 1844.
	*Miss Sarah W. Ashley .	May, 1859.	Mar. 15, 1864.
	Miss Rosella A. Smith .	May, 1867.	1872.
	Miss Martha S. Taylor .	Dec. 29, 1867.	
	Miss Sarah Pollock . . .	January, 1868.	
	Miss Carrie Hartley . .	March 5, 1869.	
	Miss Mary E. Rendall . .	May, 1870.	
	Miss Elizabeth Sisson . .	April, 1872.	

IV. MADRAS MISSION.

ORDAINED MISSIONARIES.	WIVES OF MISSIONARIES.	TIME OF ENTERING.	TIME OF LEAVING.
*Miron Winslow, D. D.	[See Ceylon Mission] . .	Mar. 22, 1836.	*Oct. 22, 1864.
	*Mrs. Catharine W. Winslow	Mar. 22, 1836.	*Sept. 23, 1837.
	*Mrs. Anne S. Winslow .	Sept. 12, 1838.	*June 20, 1843.
	*Mrs. Mary B. Winslow .	Mar. 12, 1845.	*April 20, 1852.
	Mrs. Ellen A. Winslow .	1858.	1864.
*John Scudder, M. D.	[See Ceylon Mission] . .	Sept. 21, 1836.	*Jan. 13, 1855.
	*Mrs. Harriet Scudder .	Sept. 21, 1836.	*Nov. 19, 1849.
Samuel Hutchings .	[See Ceylon Mission] . .	April, 1842.	Dec., 1843.
	Mrs. Elizabeth C. Hutchings	April, 1842.	Dec., 1843.
Ferdinand D. W. Ward	[See Madura Mission] . .	Early in 1843.	1846.
	Mrs. Jane Shaw Ward .	Early in 1843.	1846.
Henry M. Scudder .	[See Arcot Mission] . .	Sept. 5, 1844.	1851.
	Mrs. Fanny L. Scudder .	Sept. 5, 1844.	1851.
John W. Dulles . .	. . . .	Feb. 20, 1849.	1853.
	Mrs. Harriet L. Dulles .	Feb. 20, 1849.	1853.
Isaac Newton Hurd .	. . . .	July 13, 1852.	Aug. 27, 1858.
	*Mrs. Mary C. Hurd . .	July 18, 1852.	*Jan. 30, 1854.
ASSISTANT MISSIONARY.			
Phinehas R. Hunt . [Printer at Madras 27 years]	[Since June, 1868, of the North China Mission]	Mar. 19, 1840.	1866.
	Mrs. Abigail N. Hunt . .	Mar. 19, 1840.	1866.

V. ARCOT MISSIONS.

Ordained Missionaries.	Wives of Missionaries.	Time of Entering.	Time of Leaving.
Henry M. Scudder, M.D.	[See Madras Mission] . .	1851.	1857.
	Mrs. Fanny L. Scudder . [See Madras Mission]	1851.	1857.
William W. Scudder	[See Ceylon Mission] . .	1853.	1857.
	*Mrs. Elizabeth O. Scudder	1853.	*Sept. 14, 1854.
Joseph Scudder . .	. . . .	1853.	1857.
	*Mrs. Sarah A. Scudder .	1853.	1857.
Ezekiel C. Scudder .	. . . .	1856.	1857.
	Mrs. Sarah R. Scudder .	1856.	1857.
Jared W. Scudder .	. . . .	1856.	1857.
	Mrs. Julia C. Scudder . .	1856.	1857.
Assistant Missionary.			
	Miss Louisa Scudder . .	1856.	1857.

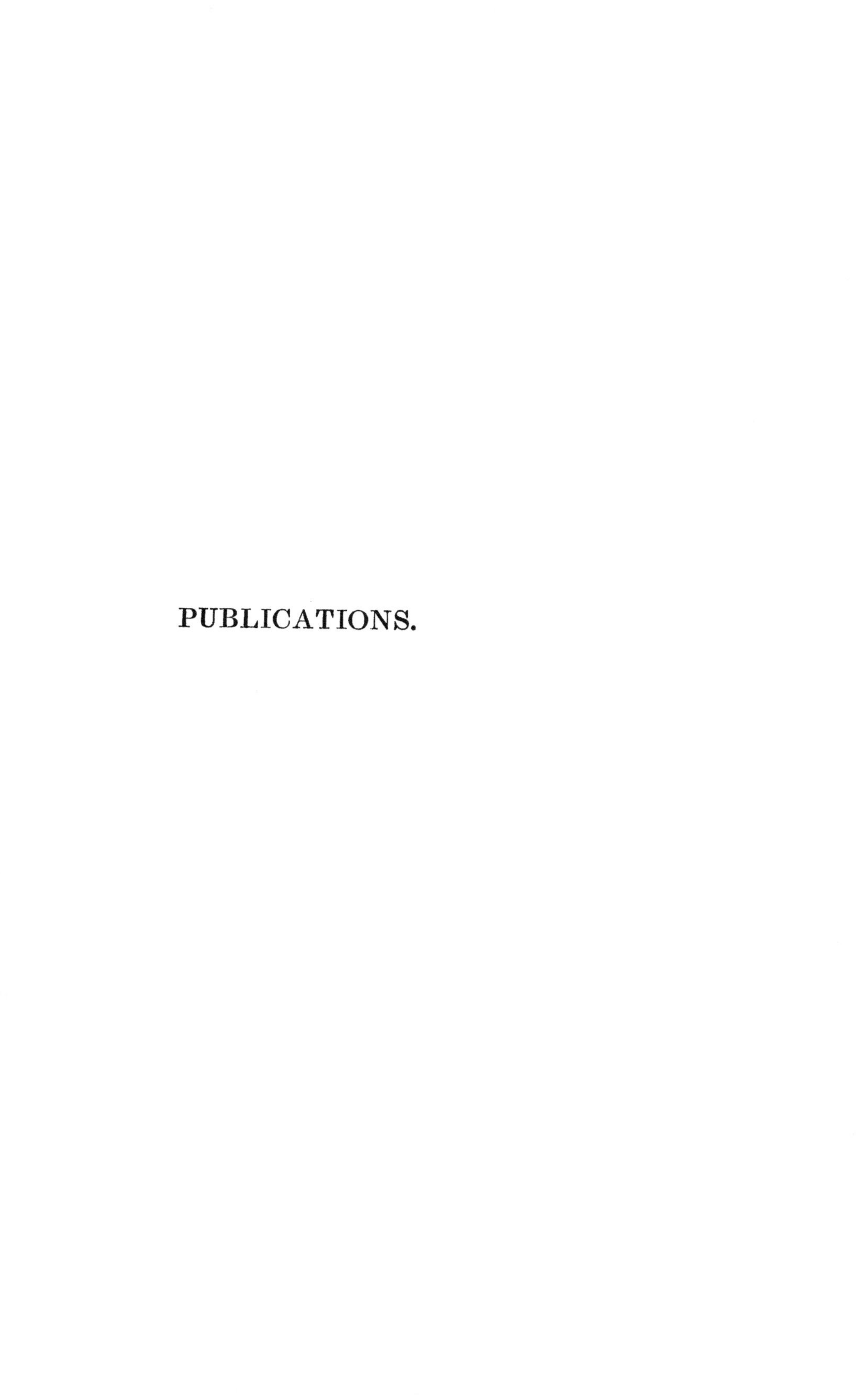

PUBLICATIONS.

CATALOGUE OF PUBLICATIONS

ISSUED BY THE SEVERAL INDIA MISSIONS OF THE BOARD.

[The author acknowledges important aid from the Rev. John A. Vinton, in the construction of this catalogue.]

I. Printing at Bombay, chiefly in the Mahratta Language.

In 1817–1824:

Gospel of Matthew.

Acts of the Apostles, and Select Portions of Scripture.

The Heavenly Way, 72 pp.

A Scripture History.

Reading Book for Schools.

A Catechism.

Easy Method of acquiring the English Language.

The Compassion of Christ towards Sinful Man.

The Book of Genesis.

The Gospels of Mark, Luke, and John, and the Sermon on the Mount.

The Epistles of James, Peter, John, and Jude.

Ten Commandments, with other passages of Scripture.

A Tract containing Prayers, Hymns, etc.

Elements of Geography and Astronomy for Schools, 80 pp., 8vo.

The Three Worlds, 72 pp., 8vo.

Good Tidings, 46 pp., 8vo.

These were repeatedly reprinted, some of them with enlargement.

In 1825 and 1826: Epistles to the Romans, Corinthians, Galatians, Philemon, and Hebrews, and the Revelation.

A Sermon by Mr. Graves, 24 pp., 8vo.

The Miracles of Christ, 36 pp., 12mo.

Elementary Arithmetic, 48 pp., 8vo.

The Discourses of our Saviour, 24 pp., 12mo.

The Parables of Christ, 22 pp., 12mo.

In 1826-1828: The entire New Testament, translated by the Mission.

Previous to the close of 1829: The Unreasonableness of Idolatry, a letter addressed by Bengalee converts to their countrymen, 22 pp.

Relief to the Sin-burdened, 20 pp., 12mo.

In whom shall we trust? 33 pp., 12mo.

The Wrath to Come, 28 pp., 12mo.

Marks of the True Religion, 32 pp., 12mo.

The First Part of Genesis, 56 pp., 12mo.

In 1829: 26,000 copies, containing 1,057,000 pages.

In 1830: A revised edition of the New Testament.

In Güzerattee. — Portions of Scripture and Tracts.

In Portuguese. — Reasons for Separating from the Church of Rome, 11 pp., 12mo.

In 1830: 35,800 copies, containing 1,136,700 pages.

Between 1830 and 1834:

A Spelling Book, 34 pp.

A Catechism, 20 pp.

A Scripture Catechism, 12mo, 3,000 copies.

The True Worship of God, 12mo, 2,500 copies.

Prayers and Hymns, 12mo, 3d edition in 1832, 3,000 copies.

Summary of the Holy Scriptures, 8vo, 2,500 copies.

Nature of Prayer, with Prayers and Hymns for Schools, 12mo, 600 copies.

Glad Tidings, 12mo, 4th edition, 3,000 copies.

First Book for Schools, 12mo, 6th edition, revised, 3,000 copies.

Gospel of Matthew, 4to, 1,000 copies.

In 1834:

Hymns for Public Worship.
Good Instructions.
Concerning Salvation.
Free Remedy for Sinners.
The True Atonement.
The Birth of Christ.
The Sufferings and Death of Christ.
Preparation for Death.
On Regeneration.
Biblical Instruction.
Scripture Doctrines (revised).
Little Henry and His Bearer.
Exodus.

In 1835:

First Book for Children, 16 pp., 2,000 copies.
Catechism, 24 pp., 3,000 copies.
Barakhudya, 26 pp., 2,000 copies.
Hymns, 32 pp., 2,000 copies.
Experience of Babajee, a converted Brahmin, 22 pp., 2,000 copies.
The Way of Salvation, 14 pp., 2,000 copies.
Romans and Corinthians, 108 pp., 2,000 copies.
Gospel of Luke, 88 pp., 2,000 copies.
Gospel of John, 66 pp. 2,000 copies.
Acts of the Apostles, 83 pp., 8,000 copies.
Scripture Narratives, 52 pp., 2,000 copies.

The printing for 1840, was more than 2,000,000 pages; for 1841, about 2,500,000 pages; for 1842, 1,792,000 pages; for 1843, nearly 500,000 pages.

The Mission was printing, in 1844, an English and Mahratta Dictionary, prepared by the Bombay government. Several periodicals were printed, among them the "Dnyanodaya" (Rise of Knowledge), a semi-monthly publication, commenced at Ahmednuggur in 1842, and transferred to Bombay in January, 1845; also the "Bombay Witness," a religious newspaper in English, and the "Bombay Temperance Advocate," conducted on the principle of total abstinence from all that can intoxicate.

On the first day of March, 1847, the Rev. David Oliver Allen, who had the superintendence of the Press at Bombay, had the satisfaction of possessing a complete copy of the Bible in Mahratta, issued from that press, and, at that time, the only complete copy in the world.

In the year 1849 : —

1. In Mahratta.	Size.	Pages.	Copies.	Total pages.
Articles of Faith in the Church at Ahmednuggur	12mo.	8	250	2,000
Gospel of Luke	8vo.	73	2,000	146,000
Mahratta Hymns		14	500	7,000
Good Tidings	32mo.	32	2,000	64,000
Mahratta Primer	18mo.	52	2,000	104,000
Shepherd of Salisbury Plain	16mo.	58	2,000	116,000
The School Boy	16mo.	30	2,000	60,000
Summary of Scripture Doctrines	12mo.	70	2,000	140,000
First Book for Children	18mo.	60	2,500	150,000
Good Tidings	32mo.	32	1,000	32,000
The same in Modh	18mo.	24	2,000	48,000
History of British India (for Board of Education)	8vo.	274	2,000	548,000
Memoir of Columbus (for Board of Education)		178	1,000	178,000
Work on Railways	8vo.	49	600	29,400
Importance of Cleanliness to Health and Character	12mo.	24	1,000	24,000
Works for Bombay Tract and Bible Societies				200,000
The Dnyanodaya				
2. In Gûzerattee.				
Gallaudet's Youth's Book of Natural Theology (for the Board of Education)	12mo.	254	750	190,500
Memoir of Columbus (for the Board of Education)		144	1,000	144,000
Essay against Female Infanticide (for the Bombay Government)		55	1,500	82,500
Idiomatical Exercises, in English and Gûzerattee		370	1,000	370,000
3. In Scindee.				
Scindee and English Dictionary (for Bombay Government)	8vo.	241	500	120,500
Scindee Grammar (for Bombay Government)	8vo.	178	500	89,000

	Copies.	Pages.
In 1850, Books in the native languages .	24,275	4,190,600
Tracts and Pamphlets in the native languages . . .	111,250	4,062,350
Scripture portions in the native languages	8,300	1,041,200
English books and pamphlets .	12,130	967,000
English circulars . . .	322,308	3,463,537
	478,263	13,724,687
In 1851, Books in the native languages .	24,225	4,262,075
Tracts in the native languages	75,340	3,336,850
Scriptural portions in the native languages	10,250	1,314,800
English publications, circulars, etc.	294,920	2,666,693
	404,735	11,580,418
In 1852, Books in the native languages .	12,169	2,208,279
Tracts in the native languages	74,000	3,216,000
Scriptural portions in the native languages	9,000	1,575,000
English publications . .	378,025	3,060,052
	473,194	10,059,331
In 1853, Scripture portions in native languages	. .	1,362,000
Tracts in the native languages	. .	4,215,500
English publications . . .	. .	5,261,294
		10,838,794

The whole number of pages printed from the beginning, was 135,719,747.

The missionaries continued to edit and to issue the "Dnyanodaya," in English and Mahratta, once in two weeks, which had a large circulation among the educated and influential classes, reaching many who could be reached in no other way. They also edited, in part, the "Bombay Temperance Repository," a quarterly magazine of forty pages. Their publications, of all kinds, were mostly sold, the practice of gratuitous distribution having been some time discontinued.

The demand for Christian books and tracts continued in the following years, but not in the same degree as previously. It was thought best, by the missionaries, to give more of their attention to preaching and to schools, and the missionary force had been weakened by the departure of some of the most efficient laborers.

In the progress of events, moreover, there was no longer need of so large an establishment to carry on the work of missions in that part of India, and the pecuniary gain thence arising did not authorize the employment of so large a part of the missionary force in conducting it. That part of the establishment, therefore, which was required for English job-printing, was sold in 1855, while the printing of the Scriptures and of religious books and tracts was continued as before.

The amount of printing in 1856 was as follows: —

For the American Mission, seven distinct works .	598,900 pp.
For the Bombay Auxiliary Bible Society, Old Testament in part	3,476,000 pp.
For the Bombay Tract and Book Society, twenty-two distinct works	1,807,000 pp.
	5,863,900 pp.

The printing of a new and revised edition of the Mahratta Bible was completed in 1857.

In 1867, there were new editions of Old Testament Selections, 230 pp., 12mo; Mahratta Primer, 52 pp., 16mo; Catechism, 40 pp., 32mo; a Geography, illustrated, 168 pp., 12mo; Devotional Songs, in favorite native melodies, 52 pp., 16mo.

The mission still issued the "Dnyánodaya," which had now, 1867, completed its twenty-sixth volume, each volume containing about 400 pages, royal octavo. It was ably edited by Sháhû Dáji Kûhadè, an energetic native convert, and has been continued thirty years in all, to the present time.

The Mahratta New Testament, with references, was issued in 1868.

II. Printing in Ceylon, chiefly in the Tamil Language.

Previous to 1833:

Spiritual Light, 8 pp., 10,000 copies.
The Heavenly Way, 4 pp., 10,000 copies.
The Means of Bliss, 16 pp., 8,000 copies.
Martyrdom of Polycarp, Bishop of Smyrna, 8 pp., 4,000 copies.
Letters to the Brahmins and Priests, exposing the absurdities of their religion, 16 pp., 6,000 copies.
A Doctrinal Catechism, 35 pp., 12mo.
A School Book, 64 pp.
A Hymn Book, 450 pp.
The Blind Girl.

Portions of the Scriptures and some Tracts were printed from year to year, of which we have no particular account. In the year 1830 nine new tracts were printed, and second editions of two others. Four of the new tracts were portions of a series entitled "The Blind Way." They contained an exposure of the absurdities of idolatry, derived from approved writers among the Hindûs themselves. Another of the new tracts contained the Secret Prayer of the Brahmins, taken from the Four Vedas, but not known to the people at large. Other tracts were —

Good Instruction.
The Marriage of Priests.
The Swearer's Prayer.
Francis Newport.
An Abridgment of Scripture History for Schools.
The Articles and Covenant of the Church.

In 1833:

Dr. Sewall's Tract on Temperance.

Honesty is the Best Policy.

The Negro Servant.

Life of Philip P——, of Birmingham.

Krishnû Pal.

The Mountain Miller.

Three Tracts, of 10,000 each.

In 1834 and 1835:

	Pages.	Copies.	Whole number of Pages.
Twenty-five tracts, titles not given	312	242,000	2,560,000
Almanac	68	1,000	68,000
Catechism	24	450	10,800
Notice and Invitation . . .	12	700	8,400
First Lessons, English and Tamil	64	3,000	192,000
Picture Reading Book . . .	56	1,500	84,000
Almanac	50	4,000	200,000
Cards	12	4,000	48,000
Spelling and Reading Book .	12	6,000	72,000
Tamil and English Prayers . .	36	1,500	54,000
Reading Book for Schools . .	16	4,000	64,000
Spelling Book	48	10,000	480,000
Definitions	84	6,000	504,000
Reading Book, 2d edition, enlarged	64	6,000	384,000
Total	858	290,150	4,729,200

The printing during the year 1835 was 3,383,500 pages.

The printing in 1836 was 346,500 copies, and 8,947,800 pages, making 14,785,400 pages from the beginning.

In 1837, it amounted to 65,500 bound volumes, 311,000 tracts, and 12,436,000 pages.

The volumes in 1838 were 39,000; tracts, 493,000; pages, 17,649,200.

During the first half of the year 1839, 96,000 copies, and 13,256,000 pages, as follows:

	Size.	Pages.	Copies.	No. of pages.
Oriental Temperance Advocate	4to.	16	1,000	16,000
Report of Jaffna Bible Society	8vo.	24	300	7,200
List of Church Members	8vo.	24	1,000	24,000
Catechism, two forms .	12mo.	24	3,000	72,000
Appendix to Almanac .	12mo.	28	3,000	84,000
Friendly Epistle (to Catholics)	12mo.	16	20,000	320,000
Spiritual Milk . .	12mo.	8	20,000	160,000
Scripture History, with Questions . . .	18mo.	324	30,000	9,720,000
Deuteronomy. . .	18mo.	230	10,000	2,300,000
First Book for Spelling and Reading . . .	24mo.	60	10,000	600,000

From July 1, 1839, to July 1, 1840, 9,144,400 pages, and 31,465 volumes of various sizes bound. During the last six months of 1840, 13,172,350 pages were printed, of which 9,500,000 pages were portions of the Scriptures.

The printing from the beginning of the mission to the end of 1839, amounted to 519,000 copies, and 30,905,200 pages.

In 1840 the number of pages exceeded 11,300,000.

In 1841 nearly 17,500,000 pages; and a large number of volumes bound.

In 1842, 10,362,600 pages, of which 3,826,000 were of Scripture, and 4,240,000 tracts.

In 1843, the printing was nearly 7,824,540 pages, of which 337,500 were in 4to, 3,310,600 in 8vo, and the remainder in smaller sizes. The number of volumes 15,000, of tracts 139,000; 3,345,000 pages were of the Scriptures, and 2,919,600 pages of tracts; 7,170,440 pages were in Tamil, 220,600 in English, the remainder in Tamil and English.

During 1844, the pages were 5,809,000. Of these 1,546,000 were of Scripture, and 2,844 pages of tracts.

During 1845, about 6,000,000 pages were printed, and numerous volumes bound.

In 1847, 1,108,000 pages of Scripture were printed, and 2,705,800 pages of tracts; of other printing, 2,480,000 pages; total, 6,293,800 pages.

In 1848, pages of Scripture, 680,000; of tracts, 2,659,000.

In 1849, pages of Scripture, 168,000; of tracts, 4,090,000; total, 6,627,400. Whole number from the beginning, 152,104,098 pages.

In 1850, the printing amounted to 6,227,800 pages; of which 2,015,600 were of Scripture, and 3,427,200 were of tracts.

In 1851, the number of pages printed was but 3,023,000; resulting from the fact that the Jaffna Tract Society, which had hitherto supplied, in great measure, the means for printing tracts, was in debt.

In 1852, the amount of printing was 2,082,440 pages. This further diminution was due, in part, to the fact that large supplies of Scripture and tracts remained on hand, and in part to the endeavor to sell books, rather than give them away, as formerly.

In 1853, the number of pages printed was only 1,595,400; less than in any previous year since 1833. Among the works issued were Bunyan's "Pilgrim's Progress," translated by Mrs. Spaulding, 1,500 copies, and a work on Anatomy and Physiology, translated by Dr. Samuel F. Green, 1,000 copies. Several religious tracts, of from two to fifty-two pages each, were printed in editions of from 3,000 to nearly 7,000 copies. More than 15,000 volumes were bound. The "Morning Star," a semi-monthly periodical, in Tamil, but partly in English, had been commenced some years previous.

In 1854, the printing rose to 3,408,600 pages; and 23,494 volumes were bound. Among the works printed were a new Tamil

Hymn Book, a Manual of Private Devotion for the Church Mission, and an Algebra in Tamil. Forty-one persons were employed in the printing and binding departments.

In 1855, the printing establishment was sold, under certain conditions, to the native workmen who had long been employed therein. The first work printed by the new proprietors was a tract in Tamil, entitled "The Poor Widow," giving an account furnished by Dr. Augustus C. Thompson, of a deceased member of his church in Roxbury, Mass. The "Morning Star," now wholly in Tamil and edited by the mission, continued to be issued.

A monthly paper in Tamil, entitled "The Youth's Friend," was issued and circulated by the native printers.

The practice of distributing books, tracts, and papers, *by sale*, became general about 1861.

One thousand copies of a new Mental Arithmetic were printed in 1863, and two tracts, a Pastoral Letter, and the "Week of Prayer." A School Geography, of 40 pages, in 1864. Of the tract, "The Brazen Serpent," 3,000 copies were issued in 1865, and 3,000 of the "Third Tamil Instructor."

The printing done for the mission by the native printers in 1866 amounted to 658,040 pages. In 1867 to 354,400 pages.

In 1868 there were printed for the mission:

The Book of Proverbs	1,000 copies,	102,000 pp.
Questions on Proverbs	1,000 copies,	72,000 pp.
Mental Arithmetic	2,500 copies,	200,000 pp.
Tamil Surgery	250 copies,	126,000 pp.
	4,750 copies,	500,000 pp.

III. Printing at Madras, in the Tamil and other Languages.

In May, 1838, the large printing establishment in Madras, previously belonging to the English Church Missionary Society, was purchased, and in June set to work for the American Mission.

During the last half of the year 1838, 30,000 volumes, large and small, were printed, and 150,000 tracts.

In 1839 the issues, with those of the preceding half year, amounted to about 21,000,000 pages.

In 1840, about 11,660,000 pages were printed of the Tamil language, besides a large amount in English.

During 1841, the printing amounted to 20,966,739 pages, of which 10,820,200 pages were religious tracts in Tamil, English, and Telûgû, and 8,252,817 pages were portions of the Bible in the native languages.

In 1842, more than 19,000,000 pages in Tamil were printed.

In 1843, eighteen volumes were printed — the number of copies not specified, — besides twenty-seven different tracts. Pages of Scripture printed, 3,248,000, and of tracts, 3,914,000. Among the works printed at these presses, was a monthly Tamil newspaper, and a monthly Tamil magazine.

During 1844, there were printed 15,950,951 pages. An edition of the Bible in Tamil, of 6,000 copies, was completed. "The Aurora," a semi-monthly journal in Tamil, and a semi-monthly pamphlet containing reading lessons for each day in the month, were printed; also a volume of 400 pages, containing expositions of the Parables of Christ, prepared by Mr. Ward, one of the missionaries.

In 1845, nearly 27,000,000 pages were printed, and in 1846 about 15,000,000. In 1847, 9,253,800 pages of Scripture, 6,391,000 pages of tracts, and 367,000 pages of other works. Total, 16,011,800 pages.

Seven years from 1838, the American Bible Society appropriated for printing at Madras, $21,000. The American Tract Society, at the end of 1845, had granted for printing Tracts in Madras, $13,800.

The number of pages printed in 1848, was 11,693,252, of which 3,250,874 pages were in English.

The printing in 1849 stood thus: in Tamil, 4,002,500 pages; in Telûgû, 1,892,400 pages; in English, 1,742,988 pages; total, 7,637,888 pages.

The printing from the beginning was 170,007,390 pages.

In 1850 the number of pages printed was 22,400,831. The whole Bible in Tamil, in one volume royal octavo, a new version and in new type, was completed in November.

The amount of printing in 1851 was 14,552,081 pages.

In 1852, 12,958,472 pages, of which 4,440,000 pages were of the Scriptures.

In 1853, the number of pages was 27,813,246, and more than 12,000,000 of these pages were of the Bible. Five thousand copies each of the Gospels in Telûgû were printed, at the charge of the Madras Auxiliary Bible Society.

In 1854, the number of pages was 14,401,846, of which 7,868,000 were of Scripture, and 2,846,000 of Tracts.

The English Department of the Printing Establishment was sold in 1855, and all English printing, except in works requiring both languages, and the private work of the mission, ceased about the middle of 1856.

The following three works are mentioned as issued for the Arcot Mission in 1854 and 1855:

"The Jewel Mine of Salvation," in Tamil; the same in Telûgû. "Spiritual Teaching," in Tamil; the same in Telûgû.

In 1856, a volume entitled "Sweet Savors of Divine Truth," in Tamil. Their connection with the Board ceased in 1857.

At Madras, in 1856, the printing was as follows:

Scriptures in the vernacular languages . .	12,848,000 pp.
Tracts in the same	2,161,000 pp.
Other books in the same, including the Tamil and English Dictionary begun, which had long been in preparation	3,080,517 pp.
Total in the vernacular . . .	18,089,517 pp.

Books in English		472,798 pp.
Total in pages		18,562,315 pp.

In 1857, the printing was as follows:

Tamil Scriptures . . .	9,398,000 pp.	
Telûgû Scriptures . .	4,208,000 pp.	
Hindûstanee Scriptures . .	401,300 pp.	
Total, Scriptures .	14,007,300 pp.—	14,007,300 pp.
Tamil Tracts		19,500 pp.
Tamil Books . . .	3,984,620 pp.	
Telûgû Books	145,000 pp.	
Hindûstanee Books . .	222,000 pp.	
Total, Books . .	4,351,620 pp.—	4,351,620 pp.
Total pages		18,378,420 pp.

The printing done in 1858 was as follows:

In Tamil, Scriptures . .	13,690,200 pp.	
Tracts . . .	954,000 pp.	
School-books . .	2,950,300 pp.	
Pamphlets . .	28,640 pp.—	17,623,140 pp.
In Telûgû, Scriptures . .	900,000 pp.	
School-books .	1,462,000 pp.	
Pamphlets . .	2,300 pp.—	2,364,000 pp.
In Hindûstanee, Scriptures .	732,000 pp.	
Pamphlets .	500 pp.—	732,500 pp.
Tamil — English Dictionary in part, continued		96,000 pp.
English and Tamil School-books		70,000 pp.
English and Telûgû School-books . .		144,000 pp.
English		30,200 pp.
Total		21,060,140 pp.

Printing in 1859:

Scriptures, in Tamil . .	14,029,872 pp.	
in Telûgû . .	2,400,000 pp.—	16,429,872 pp.

Tracts —	Tamil . . .	3,601,500 pp.	
	Telûgû . . .	209,000 pp.	
	Hindûstanee . .	39,800 pp.	
	English . .	15,300 pp.	
	English and Hindûstanee	48,000 pp.—	3,913,600 pp
School-books —	Tamil . .	1,272,000 pp.	
	Telûgû .	929,000 pp.	
	English . .	56,000 pp.	
	Tamil and English	2,400 pp.—	2,259,400 pp.
Reports, English and Telûgû, 4,400; Tamil, 2,100; English, 9,400			15,900 pp.
Circulars, etc., Tamil, 5,464; English, 6,492			11,956 pp.
Dravidian Alphabets			250 pp.
Total pages of all languages . .			22,630,978 pp.

The printing during the year 1860, in all languages, amounted to 18,654,079 pages, of which 14,353,536 were in Tamil, and 3,440,000 Telûgû. Dr. Winslow's Tamil and English Dictionary was issued from the press in 1862. Besides this, there was no report of the printing for 1861 or 1862.

In 1863, there were printed, in all, 14,363,043 pages, of which 9,216,400 were of the Scriptures, and 3,566,300 of Tracts.

The printing for 1864 amounted to 17,670,363 pages, of which more than 9,000,000 pages were of the Scriptures. The English Department of the printing establishment was, as heretofore stated, sold in 1855. The remaining department, that for native printing, was sold in 1865 to the Society for Promoting Christian Knowledge. The total amount of printing from July, 1838, to December, 1864, was as follows:

Scriptures	228,417,018 pp.
Tracts	105,993,626 pp.
Other works	110,206,376 pp.
Making a grand total of . . .	444,617,020 pp.

INDEX.

Abbott, Rev. Amos, 79, 269.
Abbott, Mrs. Anstress, 79, 269.
Agnew, Miss Eliza, 180.
Ahmednuggur, a new station, 84; church at, 114; successful efforts, 275; pastors ordained, 243, 281; change in the high school, 246; union of churches, 314; Dr. Seelye's lectures, 321; Mr. Park's, 324.
Allen, Rev. David O., 75, 87, 90, 92, 94, 97, 110, 119.
Allen, Mrs. Myra W., 87.
Allen, Mrs. Orpah, 101.
American Board of Commissioners for Foreign Missions, formation of, 1; its ecclesiastical connections, 2; events leading to its formation, 2; rise of its first mission, 4; special meeting of, 257; special committee and their report, 258.
Appeal, an eloquent, 19.
Apthorp, Rev. George Henry, 171, 183.
Apthorp, Mrs. Mary, 171, 183, 191.
Arcot Mission, 229, 236–240, 262; its transfer to the Reformed Dutch Church, 240.
Ashley, Miss Sarah (Mrs. York), 374.
Ashley, Miss Harriet S., 308.
Association, a Native, 402.
Atkinson, Rev. William Henry, 305.
Atkinson, Mrs. Calista, 305.

Babajee, a brahmin convert, 76, 84, 88, 89; remarkable character of his wife, 85.
Ballantine, Rev. Henry, 79, 90, 117, 118, 244, 272, 285; his death and character, 298.
Ballantine, Mrs. Elizabeth, 79, 90, 299.
Ballantine, Rev. Henry W., 294.
Ballantine, Mrs. Mary E., 294.
Baptist Missionary Society, English, 28, 29, 38.
Bardwell, Rev. Horatio, 56, 61, 130.
Bardwell, Mrs. Rachel, 56.
Barker, Rev. William P., 121, 244.
Barker, Mrs. Lucilia U., 121, 295.
Bates, Rev. James A., 336.
Bates, Mrs. Sarah A., 336.
Batticotta, interesting pastorate at, 341.
Batticotta Seminary, 150, 172, 176, 182, 185, 255, 327.
Battle of Missions, Great, 38.
Bible, Tamil, pocket edition of, 232.
Bible-women, 309, 310, 395, 400.
Bie, Colonel, Governor of Serampore, 33.
Bissell, Rev. Samuel, 118, 244, 311.
Bissell, Mrs. Mary Elizabeth, 118, 310.
Board of Missions in Boston, Woman's, 309.
Boggs, Rev. George W., 79, 87.
Boggs, Mrs. Isabella W., 79, 87.
Bogue, Rev. Dr., 31.

Bombay, Dr. Seelye's English lectures in, 322.
Bombay, 14–21, 47, 59, 74, 122; why no more success, 325; important facilities there, 325.
Bombay University, a new responsibility, 314.
Bowen, Rev. George, 109, 244, 268, 269.
Brahmins, public discussions with, 86; baptism of, 98, 288, 290; native estimate of, 202.
Brahminic Philosophy, bearing of education on, 165.
British and Foreign Bible Society, 38.
Brown, Rev. David, 8, 18.
Brown, Miss Sarah F., 180.
Brownrigg, Governor of Ceylon, 129.
Bruce, Rev. Henry J., 294, 309, 313.
Bruce, Mrs. Hephzibah P., 294.
Burgess, Rev. Ebenezer, 99, 117, 118, 124.
Burgess, Mrs. Mary, 99, 102, 117.
Burgess, Mrs. Abigail, 120.
Burnell, Rev. Thomas S., 188, 252.
Burnell, Mrs. Martha, 188.

Calcutta, 7.
Capron, Rev. William B., 349, 373.
Capron, Mrs. Sarah B., 373, 397.
Caravan, ship, 7, 9.
Carey, Dr. William, 7, 18, 24, 29, 36, 46.
Cases, interesting, 81.
Castes, 211, 226, 290.
Ceylon Conference, 252.
Ceylon Mission, chapters on, 129, 146, 172, 327, 345.
Ceylon Mission, 130, 132, 137, 146, 172, 191, 251, 337; a pleasing retrospect, 344; an interesting view, 349.
Chandler, Rev. John E., 211, 259.
Chandler, Mrs. Charlotte M., 259.
Chapels, erection of, 284.
Chapin, Rev. William W., 296.
Chapin, Mrs. Catharine I., 296.
Cherry, Rev. Henry, 199.
Cherry, Mrs. Charlotte H., 199.
Cherry, Mrs. Jane E., 200.
Cherry, Mrs. Henrietta, 413.
Chester, Rev. Edward, 374.
Chester, Mrs. Sophia, 374.
Cholera in Ceylon, deaths from, 348.
Christian Alliance, native formed at Bombay, 315.
Christian Congregations, 207, 253.
Church, admissions to, 180, 210, 213, 225, 285, 318, 319.
Churches, self-sustaining, 248.
Church membership, increase of, 285; cause of a sudden increase of converts, 286; character of members, 287; whence the converts, 288.
Church Missionary Society, 38.
Clergy, singular position of the, 26, 28.
College in Jaffna, proposal for, 147; commenced, 336.
Committee of Thirteen, the, 257, 259.
Comparison of Ten Years, 66.
Conference in Ceylon, the, misapprehended, 257.
Conferences, Missionary, 241–262; influence of, 263.
Conferences, Baptist Missionary, 263.
Conferences, General Missionary, 264.
Congregations, Christian, 259.
Continent, labors on the, 86.
Cope, Rev. Edward, 182, 190, 199.
Cope, Mrs. Emily K., 182, 190, 199.
Crane, Rev. Nathaniel M., 199.
Crane, Mrs. Julia A. J., 199.

Dajiba, 85, 89.
Danish missionaries, excellent spirit of, 144.
Daood, Shaik, death of, 286.

Dean, Rev. Samuel C., 269.
Dean, Mrs. Elizabeth A., 269.
Deputation to the India Missions, 241, 242.
De Riemer, Rev. William, 353, 354.
De Riemer, Mrs. Emily F., 353.
Dictionaries, Tamil, 181, 232.
Dixon, Rev. J. B., a translator, 110.
Dnyánodaya (Rise of Knowledge), 109.
Dulles, Rev. John W., 227, 229.
Dulles, Mrs. Harriet L., 227, 229.
Dutch in Jaffna, 133.
Dwight, Rev. Robert O., 199, 202, 203, 220.
Dwight, Mrs. Mary B., 199, 208.

East India Company, when chartered, 22; its early disposition, 22; subsequent hostility, 23; its tolerance and protection, 46.
Ecclesiastical Union formed at Bombay, 297.
Eckard, Rev. James R., 171, 197.
Eckard, Mrs. Margaret E., 171.
Ellora, the excavations at, 94.
Elphinstone, Hon. Mount Stuart, 60, 74.
Embarkation, a missionary, 131.
Encouraging facts, 272.
Encouraging prospect, 285.
English, Jaffna occupied by the, 135.
English Friend, generous aid from, 281.
English language, consequences of teaching the, 176.
Evangelical influence, amount of, 393.
Evangelical policy, results of an, 206.
Evangelist, labors of, 316.
Evangelists, native, against ordaining, 245.
Ewing, Rev. Grenville, 31.

Fairbank, Rev. Samuel B., 109, 117, 244, 268.
Fairbank, Mrs. Abbia A., 109, 120.
Fairbank, Mrs. Mary B., 268.
Farrar, Miss Cynthia, 75, 294, 311.
Fires, destructive, 169, 175.
Fletcher, Rev. Adam H., 187.
Fletcher, Mrs. Elizabeth W., 187.
Ford, Rev. George, 211.
Ford, Mrs. Ann Jennet, 211.
French, Rev. Ozro, 99, 109, 117.
French, Mrs. Jane H., 99, 109.
Frere, Sir Bartle, Governor of Bombay, visit of, 294.
Frost, Rev. Edmund, 64, 69.
Frost, Mrs. Clarissa, 64, 75.
Fuller, Rev. Andrew, 26, 39.
Funds, difficulty in remitting, 141.

Garrett, James, 62, 82.
Garrett, Mrs. Philomela, 62.
Godaveri Valley, tour in the, 266.
Gosávi, a converted, 271, 318.
Gospel benevolence illustrated, 174.
Government, enlightened policy of, 227.
Government connection with idolatry, 201.
Government patronage of education, 123, 179, 200, 209.
Governor of Bombay, visit from, 281.
Governor of Ceylon, testimony of, 191.
Grant, Charles, 23, 31, 44, 46.
Graves, Rev. Allen, 56, 58, 74, 89, 91, 102, 110, 268.
Graves, Mrs. Mary, 58, 89, 124.
Graves, Miss Orphah, 79.
Green, Dr. Samuel F., 187, 192, 252.
Green, Mrs. Margaret P., 413.
Griffin, Rev. Dr., 3.
Gûnga, a native teacher, 65.
Gûrûs, Mahar, 100, 106.

Haldane, Mr., 30.

Hall, Rev. Gordon, 5, 7, 19, 55, 56, 60; his death and character, 70; his place of burial, 79.
Hall, Mrs. Margaret, 56, 70, 73.
Hall, Rev. Alanson C., 197.
Hall, Mrs. Frances A., 197.
Harding, Rev. Charles, 268, 279.
Harding, Mrs. Julia M., 268, 305.
Harding, Mrs. Elizabeth D., 410.
Harington, Hon. John, 18.
Haripunt, 98, 115, 279, 296.
Harmony, ship, 7, 10.
Hartley, Miss Carrie, 392.
Hastings, Marquis of, 44, 49.
Hastings, Rev. Eurotas P., 187, 252.
Hastings, Mrs. Anna C., 187.
Hazen, Rev. Allen, 109, 118, 244, 296.
Hazen, Mrs. Martha R., 109, 118, 296.
Hazen, Rev. Harvey C., 392.
Hazen, Mrs. Ida Julia, 392.
Heathenism, decline of, 404.
Helpers, native, value of, 185.
Herrick, Rev. James, 208, 259.
Herrick, Mrs. Elizabeth K., 208.
Hitchcock, Rev. Milan H., 336.
Hitchcock, Mrs. Lucy A., 336.
Hoisington, Rev. Henry R., 171, 177, 183, 190, 196, 197.
Hoisington, Mrs. Nancy, 171, 190.
Holmes, Rev. Dr., 3.
Horton, Sir Robert William, opens Jaffna to the mission, 171.
Howland, Rev. William W., 187, 252, 340, 342.
Howland, Mrs. Susan R , 187.
Howland, Rev. Samuel W., 354.
Howland, Mrs. Mary E., 354.
Howland, Rev. William S., 354.
Howland, Mrs. E. R., 354.
Hubbard, Mr. George W., 79.
Hubbard, Mrs. Emma, 79.
Hume, Rev. Robert W., 99, 109, 125; his character, 125, 126.
Hume, Mrs. Hannah D., 99, 124, 125.
Hunt, Mr. Phineas R., 234, 235.
Hunt, Mrs. Abigail N., 239.
Hurd, Rev. Isaac N., 229, 230.
Hurd, Mrs. Mary C., 229.
Hutchings, Rev. Samuel, 171, 183, 193, 225.

Idolatry, evidence of decline in, 385; one of its chief supports, 387.
Index to the volume, 435.
India missions, rise of, 4.
India, Southern, delineated, 194.
Innes, Mr., 31.
Interesting facts, 270, 288.
Isle of France, experiences at, 11–13.
Itinerant preaching, 213, 318, 352, 388–391.

Jaffna, by what missions preoccupied, 132; sudden relapse to idolatry, 136; described, 137.
Jalna, a native Christian society at, 92, 97; temporary station at, 97.
Jesuit Mission, the, 214–219.
Johnstone, Sir Alexander, 129.
Judson, Rev. Adoniram, 5, 7, 12, 13,
Judson, Mrs. Nancy, 7, 10, 13, 54.

Kader Yar Khan, the first convert. 59.
Karens, mission to, how it arose, 14.
Kimball, Miss Abigail N., 79, 91.
Kirttan, applied to Christian use, 293, 318.
Knight, Rev. Mr., 75.
Kolapûr discontinued as a station, 279. See *Wilder*.

Large-hearted Bishop, a, 170.
Lathrop, Miss Jane E., 180.
Law Christianized, 116.
Lawrence, Rev. John Jay, 175, 197, 208.
Lawrence, Mrs. Mary H., 175, 197.

Legacy at Bombay, 78.
Leipsic Missionary Society, 206.
Liberality, seasonable, 98.
Little, Rev. Charles, 211, 259.
Little, Mrs. Amelia, 21.
Little, Mrs. Susan R., 414.
Lodge, Jordan, 160.
London Missionary Society, 6, 30, 38.
Lord, Rev. Nathan L., 193, 252, 302, 394.
Lord, Mrs. Laura W., 193, 302.

McMillan, Rev. George W., 208.
McMillan, Mrs. Rebecca N., 208.
Madras Mission, its origin, 220; early proceedings, 221; summary, 229; its relinquishment, 234; its printing establishment, 222, 226, 231, 234.
Madura Collectorate described, 194, 196.
Madura Mission, chapters on the, 194, 259, 364, 385.
Madura Mission, the preliminary measures, 196; Mr. Poor's removal to, 198; Christian congregations instituted, 207; extent of its field, 213; the Conference, 259.
Madura City, 197, 198.
Madura English school, 261.
Madura Seminary, 260, 373.
Madura Home Missionary Society, 403.
Madura Widows' Mite Society, 403.
Mahabuleshwar, visited by Gordon Hall, 69.
Mahars, 99, 101, 105.
Mahratta Mission, chapters on, 47, 74, 97, 118, 244, 266, 293, 307; its plan of polity, 51; method of support, 52; obstacles to be overcome, 52; the Conference, 244; results of Conference, 251; Jubilee meeting, 284; churches in, 293; summary, 320.
Mahrattas, their population and country, 47; their marauding character, 48; their subjugation, 50.
Mahratta Horse, the, 48.
Malcolm, Sir John, 74.
Malleappa, Francis, 159.
Manepy, destructive fire at, 169.
Mang caste, conversion in the, 106; singular intolerance, 107; salutary discipline, 108.
Maps illustrating the Mahratta mission, 47; the Ceylon mission, 129; the Madura mission, 194.
Maps, note explanatory of, v.
Marriage, an influential native, 160.
Marriages, Christian, 210.
Married missionaries, why employed, 53; the popular opinion, 53; that opinion wrong, 54; their comparative value, 55.
Marshman, Dr. Joshua, 32.
Marûtee, 104.
Marshman's Life of Carey referred to, 25, 28, 33, 36, 39.
Marquis of Hastings, favorable agency of, 44.
Medical Department, 192, 212, 214, 347, 394.
Memorial Volume referred to, 2.
Meigs, Rev. Benjamin C., 130, 140, 164; his death, 340.
Meigs, Mrs. Sarah Maria, 140.
Mills, Rev. Samuel J., 5, 6.
Mills, Rev. Cyrus T., 188, 190, 193.
Mills, Mrs. Susan L., 188, 193.
Ministers of the Gospel, strange apathy of, 26, 28.
Minor, Mr. Eastman S., 171, 175, 192.
Minor, Mrs. Lucy B., 171.
Minor, Mrs. Judith M., 192.
Minto, Lord, 45.
Mission Chapel Congregation, 75.

Mission Compound, 114.
Mission policy, a lesson on, 118.
Missionaries, ordination of the first, 6; their experience at Calcutta, 7-10; ecclesiastical relations of, 250; a general list of, 407.
Missionaries, children of, a hopeful prospect, 354.
Missionary, a pagan, 210.
Missionary service, extraordinary length of, 204.
Missionary Societies, English, when formed, 28, 30, 38.
Missionary conferences, 241–265; Baptist, 263; general, 264.
Missionary comity, a great breach of, 320.
Money, William T., 14, 19, 64.
Mooyart, J. N., 130.
Morse, Dr. Jedidiah, 6.
Mullens, Rev. Dr., quoted, 244.
Munger, Rev. Sendol B., 79, 118, 244, 268, 305.
Munger, Mrs. Maria L., 79, 109.
Munger, Mrs. Mary E.
Munger, Mrs. Sarah S. C.
Mutiny, influence of the Vellore, 274.
Muzzy, Rev. Clarendon F., 199, 203, 259.
Muzzy, Mrs. Semantha B., 199, 209.
Muzzy, Mrs. Mary Ann.

Nana Sahib, mention of, 50.
Narayan, 98, 99.
Native Pastorate, movement for a, 300.
Native pastor, first in Madura mission, ordination of, 261.
Native preachers, 201, 213, 214.
Nepean, Sir Evan, 14, 18, 19, 58, 60.
Newell, Rev. Samuel, 5, 7, 11, 58, 62, 129, 130.
Newell, Mrs. Harriet, 12, 54.
Newell, Mrs. Philomela, 58.
Nichols, Rev. John, 56, 58, 64.
Nichols, Mrs. Elizabeth, 56, 75.
Niles, Nathaniel, 160.
Norris, Miss Sarah F., 318.
North, Alfred, 203.
North, Mrs. Minerva, 203.
Nott, Rev. Samuel, 5, 6, 7, 52, 55.
Nott, Mrs. Roxana P., 7, 52.
Noyes, Rev. Joseph T., 188, 193, 259.
Noyes, Mrs. Elizabeth A., 188, 193 374.

Oodooville, seminary at, 150, 186, 256.
Ordination of missionaries, 6.
Ordination of native pastors, the first in Western India, 245; the first in Ceylon, 254; the first in the Madura mission, 261.
Oriental Christian Spectator, 78.
Ottley, Sir Richard, a patron of the Batticotta Seminary, 149.

Palmer, Dr. Henry K., 392.
Palmer, Mrs. Flora D., 392.
Parish, Rev. Dr., 3.
Park, Rev. Charles W., 308, 324.
Park, Mrs. Ann Maria, 308.
Pastors, native, ordination of seven, 304.
Pastors, native, 245, 248, 249, 254, 293, 324, 353, 354.
Pasumalai Seminary, 209, 212, 398.
Penfield, Rev. Thornton B., 392, 402.
Penfield, Mrs. Charlotte E., 392.
Permander, Nicholas, 160.
Perry, Rev. John M. S., 171, 179.
Perry, Mrs. Harriett J., 171, 179.
Persecution and government protection, 285, 307.
Persecution, Roman Catholic, 187.
Philadelphia, generous contribution at, 7.

Pindarees, their plundering excursions, 48; their subjugation, 49.
Piety, on native, 246, 247.
Poetry, Tamil fondness for, 371; specimen of, 372.
Poona, Dr. Seelye's English lectures in, 323.
Pollock, Miss Sarah, 392.
Poor, Rev. Daniel, 130, 140, 163, 164, 177, 182, 187, 188, 197, 198.
Poor, Mrs. Susan, 130, 145.
Poor, Mrs. Ann K., 163.
Portuguese in Jaffna, 132.
Preachers, native, 115, 159; talent of, 250.
Preaching in Tamil, 139.
Preaching tours, 78, 89, 267.
Preaching, itinerant, 213, 222, 269.
Preface, i.
Preparandi, 212.
Press, at Bombay, 56, 111, 112, 123.
Press, in Ceylon, 142, 345, 346.
Press, in Madras, 222, 231, 234.
Printer banished from Ceylon, 143.
Printing, 69, 78, 111, 186, 222, 226, 229, 234, 345.
Progress, evidence of, 80, 257.
Protestant place of worship for native Christians, the first in Western India, 63.
Prudential Committee, the first to missionaries, 7.
Publications, general statement of, 417.
Puthukotai, 211.

Quick, Rev. James, 336.
Quick, Mrs. Maria E., 336.

Railways, a vast system of, 121-123.
Ramkrishnapunt, 103, 115, 279; his appeal for self-supporting churches, 300; his pastoral labors, 319.
Ramsey, Rev. William, 79, 89, 91.
Ramsey, Mrs. Mary, 79, 91.
Read, Rev. Hollis, 79, 87, 89, 90, 92.
Read, Mrs. Caroline, 79, 92.
Religious toleration, important step in, 283.
Rendall, Rev. John, 208, 259, 399.
Rendall, Mrs. Jane B., 208, 374, 394.
Rendall, Miss Mary E., 392, 398.
Revivals of religion in Ceylon, 152-158; in the Madura Mission, 376-383.
Revival of religion at Ahmednuggur, and Bombay, 316, 317.
Revivals of religion in the Madura Mission, 212.
Rice, Rev. Luther, 5, 7, 13.
Richards, Rev. James, 5, 130, 161.
Richards, Mrs. Sarah, 130, 164.
Roman Catholics in Bombay, 77.

Samuel, Old, 375.
Sampson, William C., 79, 88, 91.
Sampson, Mrs. Mary L., 79, 88, 91.
Sanders, Rev. Marshall D., 193, 252, 348, 355.
Sanders, Mrs. Georgiana, 193, 349.
Sanders, Mrs. Catharine Z., 412.
Sanitarium, Madura, 195.
Satara, station at, 116.
Scene, an affecting, 178.
Schools as converting institutions, 152.
Schools in the Mahratta mission, 56, 58, 61, 65, 74, 77, 79, 105, 113, 114, 117, 123, 246, 269.
Schools in Ceylon, 138, 146, 149, 152, 158, 164, 169, 176, 177, 178, 185, 254, 328-335.
Schools in the Madura Mission, 199, 200, 209, 213, 254, 260, 393.
Schools in the Madras Mission, 229.
Schools in the Arcot Mission, 238, 239.
Scott, Dr. Thomas, mention of, 25.
Scriptures, translation of, 56, 75; publication of, 109, 110, 228.

Scudder, Dr. John, 140, 183, 211, 220, 221, 224, 227, 229, 230.
Scudder, Mrs. Harriet, 140, 211, 224, 228.
Scudder, Rev. William W., 187, 236.
Scudder, Mrs. Catharine E., 187, 189.
Scudder, Mrs. Elizabeth O., 233.
Scudder, Rev. Henry Martyn, 225, 228, 236.
Scudder, Mrs. Fanny L., 225.
Scudder, Rev. Joseph, 230, 236.
Scudder, Mrs. Sarah A., 236.
Scudder, Rev. Ezekiel, 236.
Scudder, Mrs. Sarah R., 236.
Scudder, Rev. Jared, 236.
Scudder, Mrs. Julia C., 236.
Scudder, Miss Louisa, 236.
Scudder, Rev. David C., 374; his sudden death, 383.
Scudder, Mrs. Harriet L., 374.
Seelye, Dr. J. H., his visit and labors in India, 221.
Seminary in Madura mission, 209.
Serampore, a missionary refuge, 32.
Sheldon, Dr. Charles S., 211, 269.
Sheldon, Mrs. Henrietta M., 211.
Sisson, Miss Elizabeth, 392.
Slavery in Jaffna, 163.
Smead, Daniel, 160.
Smith, Rev. John C., 182, 252, 355.
Smith, Mrs. Eunice T., 182.
Smith, Mrs. Mary, 182, 202, 355.
Smith, Rev. Thomas S., 354.
Smith, Mrs. Emily M., 354.
Smith, Miss Rosella A., 392.
Society for Propagation of the Gospel, 199.
Solapûr as a station, 290, 307; the church self-supporting, 319.
Song, native service of, improvement in, 89.
Spaulding, Rev. Levi, 140, 183, 187, 196, 252, 352.
Spring, Dr. Samuel, 6.
Steele, Dr. John, 199, 200.
Steele, Mrs. Mary, 199, 202.
Stone, Rev. Cyrus, 75.
Stone, Mrs. Atossa, 75, 89.
Subjects discussed in the Ceylon Conference, 252.
Sympathy, illustration of native, 126.

Taylor, Rev. Horace S., 203, 212, 259, 400; death and character of, 394.
Taylor, Mrs. Martha S., 203, 374
Taylor, Miss Martha S., 392.
Teignmouth, Lord, mention of, 39.
Theological class at Ahmednuggur, 282.
Thomas, Dr. John, 28.
Thomason, Rev. Thomas, 7, 19.
Tissera, Gabriel, 154.
Todd, Rev. William, 171, 175, 196, 200.
Todd, Mrs. Lucy, 171, 197.
Todd, Mrs. Clarissa, 199.
Toleration secured for India, 42; increased, 102.
Townsend, Miss Harriett E., 349, 351.
Turner, Bishop, his catholic spirit, 170.
Tracy, Rev. William, 199, 398.
Tracy, Mrs. Emily F., 199.
Tranquebar Mission, 204, 205.
Translations of Scripture, 221, 228.
Twistleton, Rev. Mr., 129.

Udney, Hon. George, 19, 30.

Vellore, labors at, 223.
Village churches, necessity of, 115; development of, 245.
Village stations, difficulty in forming, 246.
Village schools, 260.
Villagers, Christian reception by, 267.
Vishnû, 104.

Visits to Missions, occasional necessity for, 241.

Wade, Lieutenant, 17.
War with England, effect of, 7.
Ward, Dr. William, 32.
Ward, Dr. Nathan, 171, 203.
Ward, Mrs. Hannah W., 171, 203.
Ward, Rev. F. D. W., 199, 225.
Ward, Mrs. Jane Shaw, 199.
Waring, Major Scott, 38.
Warren, Rev. Edward, 130, 139, 140.
Washburn, Rev. George T., 374, 398.
Washburn, Mrs. Eliza E., 374.
Webb, Rev. Edward, 208, 259.
Webb, Mrs. Nancy Allyn Foote, 208.
Webster, Elijah A., 79, 90.
Webster, Mrs. Marietta, 79, 90.
Welles, Rev. Spencer R., 308.
Welles, Mrs. Mary, 308.
Wellesley, Marquis of, 34, 36.
Wellington, Duke of, 48.
White, Rev. Charles, 373.
White, Mrs. Anna Maria, 373.
Whittelsey, Rev. Samuel G., 182, 183, 186, 187.
Whittelsey, Mrs. Anna C., 182.
Widows, marriage of, 312.
Wilberforce, William, 31, 41, 46.
Wilder, Rev. Royal G., 109, 115, 117 118, 121, 244, 268, 273.
Wilder, Mrs. Eliza J., 109.
Wilderness, perils in the, 223.
Wilson, Rev. Dr., 86.
Winslow, Rev. Miron, 140, 164, 173. 220, 225, 228, 230, 231, 232.
Winslow, Mrs. Harriet L., 140, 172.
Winslow, Mrs. Catharine W., 221.
Winslow, Mrs. Anne S., 225.
Winslow, Mrs. Mary B., 208.
Winslow, Mrs. Ellen A., 231, 234.
Winsor, Rev. Richard, 308.
Winsor, Mrs. Mary C., 308.
Women, native, their prospective influence, 396; field for them, 400.
Wood, Rev. William, 109, 116, 124, 244.
Wood, Mrs. Lucy Maria, 109, 116, 120.
Wood, Mrs. Eliza Maria, 279.
Wood, Mrs. Eliza W., 410.
Woodward, Rev. Henry, 75, 140, 173.
Woodward, Mrs. Lydia, 140, 164, 174.
Worcester, Dr. Samuel, 4, 6.
Wyman, Rev. Robert, 182, 186.
Wyman, Mrs. Martha E., 182, 186.

Yesûba, 115, 276, 277, 278.
York, Mr. William, 374.

END OF THE VOLUME.